Analysing Everyday Experience

Analysing Everyday Experience

Social Research and Political Change

Niamh Stephenson and Dimitris Papadopoulos

First published 2006 by
PALGRAVE MACMILLAN
Houndmills, Basingstoke, Hampshire RG21 6XS and
175 Fifth Avenue, New York, N.Y. 10010
Companies and representatives throughout the world

PALGRAVE MACMILLAN is the global academic imprint of the Palgrave Macmillan division of St. Martin's Press, LLC and of Palgrave Macmillan Ltd. Macmillan® is a registered trademark in the United States, United Kingdom and other countries. Palgrave is a registered trademark in the European Union and other countries.

ISBN 13: 978–1–4039–3558–8   hardback
ISBN 10: 1–4039–3558–0   hardback

This book is printed on paper suitable for recycling and made from fully managed and sustained forest sources.

A catalogue record for this book is available from the British Library.

Library of Congress Cataloging-in-Publication Data

Stephenson, Niamh.
    Analysing everyday experience : social research and political change / Niamh Stephenson and Dimitris Papadopoulos.
        p. cm.
    Includes bibliographical references and index.
    ISBN 1–4039–3558–0
        1. Social sciences–Research. 2. Experience. I. Papadopoulos, Dimitris.
    II. Title.

H62.S75424 2006
300.72–dc22   2006040117

10   9   8   7   6   5   4   3   2   1
15 14 13 12 11 10 09 08 07 06

Printed and bound in Great Britain by
Antony Rowe Ltd, Chippenham and Eastbourne

To our parents

Contents

Acknowledgements

This book began at the Centre for Cultural Studies at the University of California in Santa Cruz. We are indebted to James Clifford, Chris Connery and Gail Hershatter for their generosity with ideas and emotions. Many thanks also to the Department of Community Studies at UCSC, particularly Nancy Stoler, and to the Office for History of Science and Technology at the University of California, Berkeley, especially to Cathryn Carson, whose support proved crucial in the realization of this project.

The work was sustained by the collegiality of staff in the School of Public Health & Community Medicine, University of New South Wales and in the School of Social Sciences at Cardiff University – in particular Anthony Zwi, Deborah Black, Deborah Debono, Alan Hodgkinson, Huw Beynon and Valerie Walkerdine. The support of Colleagues from the Centre for Critical Psychology at the University of Western Sydney and the Department of Psychology and Education at the Free University of Berlin was vital. At the Free University, Martin Hildebrand-Nilshon's continuous and invaluable input and interest made this book possible. The editorial support of Daniel Bunyard and Jill Lake at Palgrave has been critical and indispensable throughout the writing of the book. Much of the work we present here hinges on the insights about ongoing shifts in everyday experiences of HIV and gay community, insights which participants in research projects shared with us. If we believed in intellectual property we would want to see it returned to them.

Through their long, provocative and inspiring engagement with thoughts-in-the-making, several people have contributed to this book more than they themselves realize: Susan Kippax, Kane Race, Ernst Schraube, Vassilis Tsianos.

Much of the work in this book had its genesis in sometimes virtual, sometimes real-time, always warm conversations with Thomas Atzert, Ciaran Benson, Ben Bradley, Steven Brown, Erica Burman, Jayne Bye, Amanda Ehrenstein, Eugenie Georgaca, Irina Giles, Ros Gill, Angel Gordo-Lopez, Frigga Haug, Douglas Henderson, Ian Hodges, Arnd Hofmeister, Rick Iedema, Vassilis Karavezyris, Chung-Woon Kim, Hannah Landecker, Brent Mackie, Helen Malson, Athanasios Marvakis, Catherine Mills, Jill Morawski, Leo Mos, Paul O'Beirne, Mary Orgel, Ute Osterkamp, Efthimia Panagiotidis, Ian Parker, Marianne Pieper, Marsha Rosengarten, Vicki

Ryan, Jane Selby, Hank Stam, Paul Stenner, Charles Tolman, the participants of the colloquium on culture at the Free University of Berlin, the students in our seminars, and friends in the theory and border activist network Frassanito and the EuroMayDay mobilizations.

Opportunities to present and discuss these ideas with staff at the Australian National Centre for HIV Social Research and the Centre for Contemporary Art & Politics at the University of New South Wales and with participants at the Crossroads Conferences for Cultural Studies, the Annual Meetings of the Society for the Social Studies of Science and the conferences of the International Society for Theoretical Psychology have all been significant as the book developed.

The projects on which we draw here could not have been undertaken without the assistance of the Alexander von Humboldt Foundation, the German Research Foundation, the New South Wales Department of Health, the Australian Federation of AIDS Organizations and the Commonwealth Department of Health and Aging. Martin Holt's research skills have been invaluable to the HIV project, and the assistance of Carlos Calero from the UNSW library made all the difference to writing the final chapter.

A deep thanks to Ioannis Savvidis for providing us with the cover art and for 'lending us his eyes' so many times during all these years.

Throughout the writing we have been really grateful to our families, new members and old, for their consistent interest in and advice about the project.

Some of the ideas presented here arose in the writing of journal papers: Chapter 1 began life as a paper published in *Continuum: Journal of Media and Cultural Studies* (http://www.tandf.co.uk); and earlier versions of Chapters 3 and 4 were published in the *International Journal for Critical Psychology*.

University of New South Wales & Cardiff University,
December 2005

Prologue

Desiring metamorphosis

Werner Herzog's film *Grizzly Man* (Nelson & Herzog, 2005) relates the events leading up to the deaths of Timothy Treadwell and Amie Huguenard. Treadwell had amassed hundreds of hours of survivalist genre video with his camera, documenting himself alone amongst the bears, recording the bears with whom he was familiar and probably even the strange bear that killed them, as well as the sounds of his and Huguenard's deaths. Herzog edits the footage of Treadwell and the bears, together with interviews he undertook with people close to Treadwell, people who know about bears and know how to navigate the wilderness they inhabit and people who became involved in the aftermath of the two deaths. A misanthropic lover of bears and self-proclaimed, lone grizzly activist, what is so noteworthy about Treadwell's death is its apparent predictability. Being devoured by a bear was an end he seemed to be waiting for – more than this, the film invites us to consider the possibility that Treadwell was courting, moving towards this death.

Treadwell wanted to become a bear. Many of those interviewed, like the filmmaker, are critical of Treadwell's project to save the bears, and see the deaths as unnecessary or irresponsible. That is, the specific difficulties and deadly course of Treadwell's desire are all held up, turned around, examined from numerous angles and questioned by others in the film. But the desire for metamorphosis is implicitly present in all the different voices included in the film, even voices critical of Treadwell's life. For most of those close to the events, locals, scientists, park rangers, close friends, family, medics – people who inhabit the world in which Treadwell and Huguenard died – the desire to move beyond oneself seems relatively unproblematic, or even more, it seems to be the common ground of experience. Strangely enough, what connects all these disparate experiences is a sense of a way past, that is, a possible move towards something which is not immediately accessible and present in the lives of the people involved in the Treadwell case. Herzog's viewers repeatedly hear, in rounded, slow, non-judgemental tones: 'well, he wanted to become a bear, and then ...' (there is a notable exception: 'he wanted to *become* a bear!'). In working with Treadwell's desire for metamorphosis as it turns towards death, Herzog avoids amplifying the extraordinary elements of this desire and, instead, sews it back into the ordinary details of other people's shared experiences of transformation. Moreover, this common thread is never declared or announced in the film. It is simply there as a familiar and close element of people's own everyday experience, their own living. It allows those close to Treadwell to follow his negative trajectory towards death without turning towards death themselves. The film's rendering of this experience as something familiar, travelling, indeterminate and present enables viewers to navigate the incommensurability of our experience and that of Treadwell and Huguenard.

Experience and the everyday: An indeterminate relation

The everyday is the site in which experience circulates and transforms. And these transformations are not necessarily intelligible to the actors involved in their realization. *Grizzly Man* presents the everyday as an amorphous plane which holds all the innumerable experiences of those involved together, without unifying them or without assigning an overall meaning to the sequence of events. Moreover, Herzog's reading of events returns Treadwell's death to the realm of the everyday. This death affects others, not because it is a failed instance of self-overcoming, but because, even as a failure, it evokes people's own ordinary desires for metamorphosis. Herzog presents the everyday as a force which keeps events and experiences together, letting them interact without determining their meaning and without demanding that all elements of the story be compatible with each other.

Despite the unintelligibility of Treadwell's becoming bear, despite the failure of his move towards becoming other, his experience affects others, connects with their experiences, even reaching us the film viewers – displaced in space and time. For example, as compared with Treadwell's trajectory, Huguenard's life remains elusive. She was almost completely absent from Treadwell's own film-making. Her presence did not fit with the narrative he was constructing of himself as a solitary figure taking on the world. None of the interviewees claim to know her, but a few offer an explanation: Huguenard was a woman supporting her man without fully ascribing to his project herself. That she was suppressed by the unfolding of a heteronormative relationship seems highly possible. Yet, this explanation is unconvincing. It does not bring us any closer to *Huguenard's* experience of events; hence it only serves to make her even more indiscernible. The absence of Huguenard's experience in *Grizzly Man* is palpable.

The everyday is the medium through which experience gets under the skin and materializes, affecting selves, others and situations. There is nothing exceptional to this functioning of the everyday. As Lefebvre (1991) says, it is the realm where all extraordinary, specialized activity has been eliminated. And it is here, where the everyday is not yet over-determined by a specific interpretation or a specific action, that different experiences thrive and change each other. Treadwell's experience of becoming bear through death arises out of the everyday and returns back to it, without ever being compatible with the other experiences circulating in the world that he inhabits. Experiences which remain incommensurable and which cannot be assimilated are still integrally involved in altering the social conditions of our everyday existence.

This last point is the crux of every theory on experience: How to grasp something which is incommensurable? Experience and the everyday world belong together; they are intimately connected – but how to conceptualize a relation which is essentially indeterminate? Their connection, which seems to be in a constant state of flux, has troubled every attempt to define and understand what experience is. Does the realm of the everyday structure our experience? Or is experience a tool which produces representations of the everyday?

Responding to indeterminacy: Three explanations of experience

One possible approach to these questions is to understand experience as lived experience: neither the everyday constitutes experience, nor is experience the instrument which lets the everyday emerge. The notion of lived experience asserts that we are always in the flux of life, and experience occurs as individuals embody the incessant changes of the everyday. Such an approach appeals to everyday experience simply as it is lived and refuses to assign any other characteristics to it. William James' (1996) radical idea that experience is the absolute basis of everyday existence – and that consciousness is this ceaseless stream of connections, disjunctions, substitutions and deceptions of experience – illustrates how lived experience can be thought. The concept of lived experience represents the only explanation of experience which tries to do justice to the indeterminacy of the relation between experience and the everyday. However, it is characterized by a serious problem: lived experience is a conservative understanding of experience, it fails to embrace creation. It cannot take account of the emergence of experience as a productive, forceful, passionate process; it cannot take account of the moment when experience turns against the everyday, trying to attack it and change it, the moment when experience becomes its own radical critique (Debord, 1981). The concept of lived experience lends no purchase on experience as a process which carries the seeds of innumerate possibilities for increasing the capacity to act – some of which take hold, some never do (as Herzog conveys in *Grizzly Man*). Thus, lived experience does not explain the relation between experience and the everyday world; lived experience is what must be explained.

The quest, to explain what lived experience is, has shaped all major attempts to understand experience. Almost all of the theories which have arisen attempt to eliminate the indeterminacy of the relation between experience and the everyday. To date, we have three possible answers to this relation, each offering a distinctive approach to explicating experience. The first one invokes magic: there is something mysterious which transforms lived experience into legitimate knowledge of the everyday world. From Kant to Chomsky, the magicians' stick has had many names and one function, to expose universal structures which are hidden but constitutive of our lived experience. There is an innate force in each individual's mind which solidifies the flux of lived experience and produces a structured and coherent representation of the everyday. This account grants primacy to universal structures which enable experiencing in the world to evolve into representable experiences of the world.

Then there is the humanist answer: what matters about lived experience is that it is lived by a person. From Hume to Stuart Hall, humanist approaches to experience place the person at the centre of the world. Here experience is not the product of innate mental operations or ideas but the result of how the external world impinges on each individual person. Contrary to magical understandings of experience, there is no universal subject prior to the immediate relation between person and the everyday world. Experience exists by virtue of the fact that it makes sense for each one of us. Hence, from this perspective, understanding lived experience necessitates understanding the innumerable meanings it can have.

As is usually the case when we have to choose between two possibilities, there is a third position which questions either of these possibilities. In this case, the third approach to experience is blasphemy: there is no such thing as lived experience and our efforts to construct it – even if they are entertaining – will illuminate nothing. From Nietzsche to Foucault, many have tried to discount experience as the false consciousness of the underdogs of our society. Experience is a total fallacy.

The everyday is neither represented in experience nor does it affect or structure experience. Will, force and action are what make the everyday.

The impossibility of representing experience …

But things strike back in unexpected ways. Now it is increasingly clear that experience exceeds each of these attempts to explain it and none of them any longer hold. The structures through which experience was supposedly constituted have been exposed by feminist and post-colonial critics. These structures are neither universal nor transcendent, rather they are the products of a highly particular social and geopolitical position which presents itself as objective. Similarly, the promise of humanist attempts to place the person at the centre of the universe has been undermined. Technoscientific imagination unleashes the future of a post-humanist world and post-Fordism embraces the liberation of the person as one of its central productive forces. Now humanism promises, not the liberation of subjects, but the production of efficient subjects well suited to do the work required of them. And finally, the blasphemous attempt to eradicate experience, replacing it with action, has been completely unsuccessful. In our 'tell-your-own-story' culture, experience proliferates now as it never has before: experience permeates through identity politics, the psychologization of life, therapeutic culture, fundamentalisms. Museums are becoming feel-it, touch-it experiential theme parks, the appeal of biographies, reality TV, talk shows, trauma, travel experiences continues to increase. Only under the reign of 'the experience' can visitor information centres reasonably assure tourists that they can have their experience of this new place without having to leave the car.

Representing experience is not only a contested project without guarantees, it has become virtually impossible, an almost futile enterprise. This impossibility is our point of departure. *Analysing Everyday Experience* explores, not what experience is, but what different understandings and conceptualizations of experience do. The book tracks the massacre of the representation of experience which occurs as experience is taken up as an object of social research, examined, affirmed and discarded many times over. In addition, we investigate how these different concepts of experience shape social and political action. We propose that experience is a vital element of socio-political change, and that the peculiarities and contingencies of the present cannot be usefully explicated without differentiating between various approaches to experience and diverse notions of the relation between experience and the everyday.

... becomes harder to contest: Humanism, stucturalism, governmentality and cultural studies

In Part I, we locate the idea of experience in the broader context of recent cultural and political debates about *The Problem of Experience*. Initially, we consider how social and cultural researchers have approached experience with humanism and blasphemy, developing corresponding theories of culturalism and structuralism (Chapter 1). Debates over the tensions arising between these two approaches continue and have given rise to an important criticism of research which takes experience as its object. From the perspective of this critique, that is governmentality studies, the intensification of research on experience is a mere effect of current social and political regulation, an effect which facilitates the deployment of current neoliberal rationalities. We consider this position through an analysis of a complex and conflict-ridden experience of taking HIV medication. The argument we present here is that governmentality studies are mesmerized by that which they attempt to explain. However, we contend that politically useful analyses of experience can counter the seduction of contemporary political rationalities and can exceed neoliberal forms of government.

Any claim that analysing experience can be one means of contesting regulation creates its own questions: How does experience contribute to devising viable ways of structuring political action? Which experiences can contest hegemonic politics? And what of experiences that are overlooked or excluded in the process of making these attempts? Here we turn to the concept of articulation (Chapter 2) as formulated in the 'studies-discourse' of cultural studies, gender studies and science studies. Through a reading of Luis Buñuel's film *Tristana*, we consider how the 'studies discourse' attempts to oppose the fundamental exclusions (from both symbolic and material realms) lived by many. The concept of articulation is a tool of this political project, and as such it has been immensely productive in shaping everyday life in post-colonial societies and amongst diasporas. However, we argue that much still remains unvoiced in the understanding of the relation between experience and the everyday entailed in articulation. What remains unvoiced is a whole world, World 2 as we call it, which resides inside the social space of liberal integration but deploys different forms of experience. The rest of the book is dedicated to the exploration of this excess of experience, all these different forms of experience which cannot be grasped by culturalism, structuralism, governmentality studies, and the political project of articulation.

Social research responds: Revalidating experience as a collective enterprise

In Part II – *Working With A Moving Target In Social Research* – we investigate theories that approach this excess of experience as a genuinely collective and social affair. Here experience is valued as a transformative move beyond the self. If we accept that social research is not simply a matter of representation, but involves actively intervening in and constructing our current social and political conditions, we are then presented with a set of problems about how this happens in the process of researching experience. Memory-work is introduced in Chapter 3: this methodology has been specifically developed for the purposes of undertaking politically engaged social research on experience. We discuss how memory-work offers techniques for undoing the subject of linear, causal, biographical narratives and how it involves a notion of the subject as collectively constituted. But, this concept of collectivity risks reintroducing a foundationalist idea of a structured, collective political subject. Nevertheless, memory-work involves the analysis of how we actively appropriate power relations, weaving ourselves into social structures in ways which may or may not modify them. Hence, it foregrounds the question of agency, the topic of the next chapter.

In contrast to social research which invokes agency as a capacity of the individual, we work with agency as it emerges in social relations (Chapter 4). Through an analysis of HIV positive gay men's accounts of 'feeling infectious', we argue that change is not an individual affair but a matter of sociability. Reworking the social order, becoming-other to oneself, occurs in social relations. Although exclusion is enacted in social relations they are not completely constrained by liberal political rationalities or practices. They carry an excess which can open possibilities for contesting hegemonic forms of exclusion. This argument begs questions as to the specific forms of experience and political action involved in these kinds of transformations, and these are further discussed in Parts III and IV.

Working with the excess of experience: From the aesthetics of the self to individuation

The first two Parts of *Analysing Everyday Experience* focus on the perils and the socio-political implications of representing experience: contemporary approaches to experience, even if they contest current forms of exclusion and discrimination, perpetuate neoliberal integration. However, this book contests insidious laments over the difficulties of acting outside of or against the terms of the contemporary political situation, it disputes any idea that our present was inevitable and that the future will be more of the same, and it suggests that the present is always, already different from the familiar, hegemonic terms in which we represent it. *Analysing Everyday Experience* is an agenda for ordinary political action. This agenda is developed in the final two Parts of the book. In Part III – *Experience And Socio-Political Transformation* – we turn to recent attempts to consider the massacre of the representation of experience together with its implications for our everyday political engagement. Part IV – *Continuous Experience* – is devoted to describing the coordinates of a new concept of experience and how it relates to specific modes of political action.

Foucault answered the problem of experience with blasphemy; he was devoted to exposing the groundlessness of experience. Yet, in his later work he was interested in how people work on their experiences. Chapter 5 draws on his ideas about the aesthetics of existence to explore people's active participation in and reworking of existing modes of HIV subjectification. Foucault's account of subjectification provides fertile ground for thinking and working with the politics of everyday experience. However, the aesthetics of existence is easily harnessed by the entrepreneurial structure of post-Fordist production, and historically this has been the case. Refiguring the terms of subjectification, moving beyond the self, is more than an individual act; its political promise neither stems from nor returns to a particular individual. We develop our discussion of the political potential of transformative moves beyond the self by considering the collective dimension of the aesthetics of existence. To break with neoliberal and post-Fordist rationalities requires more than new modes of subjectification, it involves the externalization of relations with the self and others and their materialization in 'the field of historical practice' (Améry, 1964/1980, p. 69). And this, by necessity, is a collective affair.

In Chapter 6, we provide a fuller account of the assemblages through which subjectification is challenged: they are held together through processes of collective individuation which cultivate singularity, not individuality. This concept of collective individuation opens avenues for considering a new form of political activity and questions the very grounds on which experience has been connected to the politics of everyday life to date. This new form of political activity – outside politics – involves the insertion of those who have been excluded within the political domain *as* the illegitimate, unrepresentable actors they are.

Outside politics work with – not against – the excess, indeterminacy and incommensurability of experience.

Experience, politics, metamorphosis

We locate outside politics in the context of the other prevalent forms of political engagement, in Chapter 7. Firstly, political activity which takes the state as its object is underpinned by an idea of experience as universal. Universal experience privileges political strategies which address the institution of the state as *the* way to do politics. An alternative approach, micropolitics, takes the limits of state politics as its point of departure and posits an idea of experience as situated and differentially constructed through a subject's positioning in the world. Micropolitics privilege the everyday and cultural realms as sites of transformation, and commonly involve putting experience to work as situated experience. Micropolitics fracture the ongoing processes of capture entailed in state politics. Yet, seen historically, micropolitics have also been one of the means through which the neoliberal state (and post-Fordist regulation) has reinvented itself and continues to disseminate into social and cultural life. We consider a third concept of experience – continuous experience – and discuss the political strategies of imperceptibility and dis-identification as the means of working with the excess and indeterminacy of outside politics.

In Chapter 8, we discuss how things, people, situations are affected by continuous experience but not as it is interpreted, represented or declared. Rather, continuous experience is dispersed, never unified. It interrupts and tarries with time; continuous experience refigures spaces as it moves through situations carrying an unrepresentable excess of sociability. Through readings of Cassavetes' film *Opening Night* and Sebald's book *The Emigrants*, we suggest that this excess is neither mystical nor extraordinary. Like the shared desire for metamorphosis in Herzog's film, this excess is carried with experience as it circulates amongst people, things and situations. It travels in continuous experience, materializing and moving people, allowing them to connect with, instead of repudiating disparate and unexpected trajectories.

Working with continuous experience entails refusing clichéd subject positions in the absence of alternatives, anticipating and orientating towards non-existent, contingent possibilities which may never come about. Importantly, here, the everyday is not a site of stasis to be contrasted with extraordinary moments or spaces of transformation – as in Herzog's *Grizzly Man*, the everyday is already strange, indeterminate, continuously transforming, becoming. The concept of continuous experience provides a way into working with and fuelling processes of socio-political transformation, processes that are already occurring: the outside politics of those who exist within the very hegemonic modes of regulation which are unable to represent them. Thus, we put forward the concept of continuous experience as the singular itinerary of each of us, not in the attempt to claim that this is what experience is, but as a tool for contributing to the open agenda of outside, imperceptible politics.

As we worked on developing the notions of continuous experience and outside politics we produced additional chapters in which we discuss: the relation between continuous experience and emerging responses to questions of embodiment as well as to current research in neuroscience; post-colonial theory and the geopolitics of continuous experience; the relevance of remembering, anti-memory and time for continuous experience, and; outside politics and the contemporary reconfiguration of political sovereignty. We decided to include these chapters in a second (forthcoming) volume of *Analysing Everyday Experience*. Our focus here, in the first volume, is on making the case for analysing experience: it can make a crucial contribution to political transformation which entails disrupting unitary subjectivities, circum-venting univocal integration and contributing to the formation of plural historical actors. Hence, this first volume illustrates how experience, as Eagleton (2005, p. 24) puts it, is both supremely important and deeply untrustworthy. Its importance lies in the imaginary relationships we have with the real conditions of our lives, and these cannot be elucidat-ed through experience itself.

Part I
The Problem of Experience

1
Interrupting Neoliberal Subjectivities

Hazardous experience

Could our appetite for ingesting and divulging experience really be unlimited? We read more biographies and autobiographies now than ever before. From therapeutic encounters, to talk shows, reality TV, webcams and through to qualitative research, we are increasingly interested in absorbing the ordinary and extraordinary details of people's lives. Think for example of StoryCorps, the US oral history project which celebrates shared humanity and collective identity by inviting a quarter of a million people to interview people they know in purpose built 'storybooths' located throughout the country. People invited to participate in the project are informed that their involvement is likely to lead to personal development because 'listening is an act of love' (StoryCorps, 2005). Is this the promise which is keeping us so busy in the discovery of experience? What of the politics of experience? Is there a risk that the proliferation of self-representation diverts attempts at political engagement into the personal realm? Or does the turn to experience contribute to the blurring of personal and political realms and to the development of new forms of political engagement? Is our interest in experience affording us more or less coherent subjectivities and identities? Should we be feeding this appetite or trying to stymie it? We have good reason to be wary. In many cases the turn to experience is a reductive one, the only strategy for political engagement it offers is the affirmation of identity – one's own or others.

Identity politics and the current interest in experience are intertwined. One, now familiar, version of the present holds that as multinationals increasingly undermine the authorities of states, globalization is fuelling a sense of personal powerlessness on the part of many people.

3

At the same time communities and institutions, which may previously have offered some insulation from the inevitable limitations of the liberal selves, are fragmenting (for example, Brown, 1995). Together, the demise of grand narratives about progress and state sovereignty, and the proliferation of identity-based political strategies, cast experience as a means of restoring coherence in the face of fragmentation. However, when experience is invoked as the *basis* of political claims, it is introduced as something which must, at all costs, be affirmed. Then, to question experience becomes, not a mark of interest, but an attack on identity. But why has self-affirmation come to stand in for other possible modes of political engagement which involve working with experience? This question has been answered in different ways. For example, Foucault offers a critique of identity politics as a naïve approach to the machinations of power. A Nietzschean reading suggests that a weak and pervasive mentality of resentment resulting from a thwarted will to power gives rise to stifling self-insistence. From a psychoanalytic perspective, the reluctance to question experience could indicate a psychic inability to deal with ambiguity, a situation problematically resolved by splitting good from bad, self from power (for example, Kristeva, 1986). Clearly, there are fertile grounds for contesting reductive approaches to the politics of experience.

Social and cultural research is not immune from the affirmative approach to experience deployed in identity politics. When social research conceives of politics as identity politics, it can easily lapse into a redemptive humanism. In the absence of an alternative approach to experience, this work cannot contribute to rethinking the pervasive notion that we are really liberal subjects in various states of imperfection, constantly trying to better ourselves. Such research cannot then identify and contribute to ways of being which could challenge neo-liberal practices and policies as they unfurl.

What is invoked in the politics of self-affirmation is a notion of subjectivity as transparent and ultimately knowable: that is, at any point in time the subject can see and know himself, and what he knows can always be represented (in language and practice). Subjectivity is reduced to conscious self-knowledge which is in turn reduced to that which can already be articulated. Because the subject is visible to himself/herself, there is nothing indefinite or unclear about self-knowledge. Insistent attempts at self-representation for political ends risk incorporating this solid, misplaced self-belief and a concomitant restricted, narrow notion of experience. Experience becomes what can be known and represented at any point in time. It becomes the possession of an individual, something fixed. What is lost here is any sense of the unfinished and elastic processes through which subjects come to be placed in social reality (de Lauretis, 1984). When experience is reified and perceived as knowable we overlook the role interpretation, rereading and self-doubt might play in constituting experience – and we miss experience which exceeds interpretation. In other words, we neglect the creation of experience in intersubjective collaboration and in the processes of social relations. Approaching experience as fixed does not equip us to question even our most formulaic and superfluous self-representations. The price of affirming identity is the inability to imagine any other mode of being, the inability to initiate a different way of relating to oneself and others. This leaves us vulnerable to becoming clichés of ourselves. In response it may be tempting to discard experience altogether, on the basis that it is not a useful means for intervening in our current socio-political realm. Rather than follow such a path, we want to propose an alternative approach to experience. Firstly, in this chapter, we consider the repudiation of experience as an object of interest for social researchers. We argue that, although this repudiation can be understood as arising in response to the reduction of political activity to self-affirmation, it fails to intervene in the proliferation of the very concept of experience it criticizes.

Experience as the object of research

Attempts to grapple with or repudiate experience have fuelled long-standing debates within the humanities and social sciences. The role of these debates in the development of disciplinary knowledge and boundaries is more evident in some disciplines than others. For example, although it is not that hard to trace the historical importance of contested experience in the emergence of psychology, it is frequently obscured as people are inducted into the discipline. The received historical account of psychology emphasizes the foundational role of experimentation and goes on to oppose the possibility of a scientific psychology with the study of experience. This is despite the fact that the work undertaken by the man traditionally heralded as the father of psychology, Wundt, questioned any such opposition. In the late 19th century, Wundt was deeply interested in experience. He tackled the double-edged legacy of Kant's thoughts on 'inner experience' or 'mental life': that is, although experience is vitally important to understand, because it is cast as an essentially interior matter, it cannot be grasped by scientific means. The popular version of Wundt's role in the birth of psychology is that by devising experimental procedures for studying psychology and, by placing these in a laboratory setting, he made the necessary moves for a scientific understanding of psychology. But what is peculiar about this account is it typically neglects the *object* of Wundt's work – people's 'inner experience'.

This version of psychology's history does inform us that, over time, Wundt effectively lost the debate over the contentious object of experience. As one who moved psychological research into the laboratory setting, his ongoing influence is indisputable. But his work on experience made no great contribution to the rapid development of the discipline in the early 20th century. This 'success' relied on the construction and analysis of an altogether different object of knowledge: that is, an aggregated, collective subject who can be accessed and known through statistical procedures (Danziger, 1990; Holzkamp, 1980). Experience does not feature as an object of interest in psychological studies of the aggregated subject – it is still cast as a hindrance to scientific psychology (see Chapter 6 for another perspective on collectivity). The turn away from experience can be traced – not to behaviourist repudiations of interiority – but to the earlier influence of Galton's 19th century work on mass testing of the population. Mass testing promised to have useful applications in real life settings, particularly in schools and in selection for the military (Danziger, 1990). That is, the rapid proliferation of psychological knowledge was enabled by developments in applied fields, and not through any resolution of the problem of experience. The resolution, if the behaviourist rejection of experience can be understood that way, came after the fact of psychology's expansion – hence this is a case of epistemological debates, not leading, but trailing in the wake of developments in applied psychology. It is in this sense that the emergence of psychology can be said to be founded on the repudiation of its own object, experience. However, if the success of Wundt's work has only been partial, the same can be said for the efforts to shift the psychological gaze away from experience altogether. Much clinical work has continued to revolve around attempts to understand experience, for example. And – even if marginalized within in the discipline – the influence and proliferation of psychoanalytic thinking in everyday life and ways of understanding ourselves has been considerable (for example, Parker, 1997). The matter of experience is not entirely closed in psychology, but its constitutive role in the development of other disciplines is more readily evident, in cultural studies for example.

Contesting the authenticity of experience

In the 1950s and 1960s, early cultural research work contested cultural elitism by working on social histories of the lived experience of ordinary people – (for example, Hoggart's [1957] *The Uses of Literacy*). By disputing transcendent notions of experience, cultural studies sought to understand the historical and cultural production of specific varieties of experience. Following the Marxist legacy, it was proposed that 'social being determines consciousness' (Williams, 1980, p. 31). The concept of experience became a vehicle for approaching both that consciousness and the conditions in which it emerged (for example, Thompson, 1968). Importantly, culture is understood here as part of the ongoing, everyday activity of people who are trying to act on their lives, rather than relegated to art galleries, theatres, the literary cannon and other hallowed domains of life (Williams, 1965; Thompson, 1968). Here, understanding culture involves analysing the role of lived experience in the development of everyday practices. Experience provides a window to both the individual and the social realms.

Experience takes on an authenticating function; it is the grounds from which knowledge is developed and the yardstick against which it can be evaluated. This form of social history repudiates any notion of history as a grand narrative of evolutionary progress in the domains of technology, economy or social administration (Hall, 1981). Importantly, in what has come to be known as the culturalist strand of cultural studies, experience is not the sum total of practices and modes of domination, but also contains the seeds of resistance (for example, Williams, 1980). This position has spawned research on concrete daily practices and encouraged engagement with everyday life. However, its humanism – evident in the assumptions made about agency and in the emphasis on the authenticity granted to experience – has been criticized, initially from a structuralist perspective. For Lévi-Strauss (1972), for example, understanding culture involved analysing the internal relations between signifying practices rather than taking authentic experience as a point of departure. And Althusser (1971) argued that the real conditions of our lives are not necessarily represented in the conscious meanings we ascribe to experience, rather they act on us through subconscious categories. What is important about experience, then, is the imaginary relationships we have with the real conditions of our lives, and these cannot be elucidated through experience itself. Thus, whilst culturalists defined both consciousness and culture as collective affairs they 'stopped far short of the radical proposition that, in culture and in language, the subject was "spoken by" the categories of culture in which he/she thought, rather than "speaking them'" (Hall, 1981, p. 29).

Like Wundt, cultural studies scholars have grappled with the distinction between experience and any attempt to reflect on or explain experience. From a structuralist (and post-structuralist) perspective, experience is always and only an effect of cultural and social production. Moreover, because it may not reveal the cultural processes through which it has been produced, it cannot act as the grounds for developing an explanation of the processes through which it has been constituted. The reception and impact of this kind of critique on cultural studies can been traced in the work of Stuart Hall who, in 1969, saw lived experience as the focal point of cultural studies research (Pickering, 1997). A decade later, in describing the 'two paradigms' of cultural studies, Hall (1981) still acknowledged the political rationale for culturalism but recognized its problematic emphasis on experience. He argued that the importance of culturalism lies in its emphasis on the role of consciously directed political struggle. However, because culturalists fail to acknowledge the historical production and specificity of 'agency' they invoke a naïve humanism in their attempts to explain socio-political change. To the extent that structuralism decentres experience it provides a path around the essentialist authenticity of experience and back towards understanding the workings of ideology – processes which are largely unrepresented in consciousness. However, whilst culturalism mistakenly ontologizes the prerequisites of political action – conscious, agentic attempts to read and act on one's experience – structuralism can no longer grapple with their occurrence or relevance at all (Hall, 1981). In overlooking the importance of people's struggles to engage in political action, structuralist and post-structuralist accounts offer a limited view of political and social change. This unresolved tension over the meaning and relevance of experience continues to be a highly productive force in the field of cultural studies (for example, Clifford, 2000; Seigworth & Gardiner, 2004; Sandywell, 2004).

Debates about the role of experience have continued in the humanities as well as social sciences. For example, the link between casting experience as the foundation of self-knowledge and the limitations of identity politics is widely recognized, particularly in the wake of queer interventions (Scott, 1993/1991; Butler, 1990). For example, in synthesizing post-structuralist critiques of identity-foundationalism with social history's emphasis on elucidating difference, Scott argues that any approach to experience as inherently meaningful forecloses attempts to understand difference as socially and historically produced. Difference cannot be properly understood through a foundational approach to experience because '[m]aking visible the experience of a different group exposes the existence of repressive mechanisms, but not their inner workings or logics; we know that difference exists, but we don't understand it as relationally constituted' (Scott, 1991/1993, p. 401). This raises questions over whether it is possible to interrogate difference without reinscribing it in the fetish of identity; that is, can difference be a means to anything other than the proliferation of identities?

Over the course of the book, we will trace a politically useful means for working with experience, one which both works with and breaks the terms of a culturalism-structuralism debate. But our starting point involves taking a closer look at the place of experience in this debate. We do this by turning to a particular reading of Foucault's later work, commonly known as governmentality studies (for example, Burchell, Gordon & Miller, 1991; Rose, 1996a, 1996b; Dean 1999). In considering the insights governmentality theory offers about experience, as well as the unnecessary constraints it places on attempts to elucidate experience, we are treating this approach as a case-study of the contemporary fate of experience. Broadly speaking, the analytic strategy of governmentality theory is to historicize, albeit in a very particular manner, refusing any linear relations of determinacy between events, and privileging the contingency of relations to the self as they emerge and travel between different realms of life. Rose (1996a), for example, argues that understanding subjectification requires an exegesis of the relations between practices of governance and social administration on the one hand, and historical shifts in modes of relating to the self on the other. Notably, this focus on technologies of governance is described in opposition to culturalist attempts to understand contemporary modes of subjectification by mapping their emergence in relation to cultural and social shifts. Neither do analyses of experience appear promising from the perspective of governmentality studies. In fact, research which focused on experience is assumed to be naïve, and fail to take account of historically specific constructions of subjectivity.

Governmentality studies substitute experience with an alternative object of research: discourse. This has been a useful and productive move. However, we argue that much is unnecessarily jettisoned when the diversity of approaches to experience is conflated and opposed to the proper understanding of subjectification as emerging in the technical aspects of governing relations with self and others. The effect of this kind of repudiation of experience is that it cannot address the pervasive reduction of political engagement to self-affirmation. Moreover, by simply theorizing the problematic individualism of contemporary usages of experience, governmentality studies become an inseparable part of the problem. Instead of moving beyond the limitations of experience as it is currently being employed, this approach has become one of the major theories to underpin and sustain neoliberal individualism (Papadopoulos, 2003). Following the trajectory of governmentality theory amounts to abstaining from the terrain where the battle is being fought.

Contesting the relevance of experience

Governmentality theory usefully foregrounds the importance of offering a historical account of the processes through which experience has been constituted as an object of reflection, discussion and interest. Experience is not thought as ontologically prior to the historical and social processes through which it is produced. From this perspective, it is not only a particular kind of experience – such as the experience of 'being addicted' (see below) – that is historically constructed, but the very notion of experience as a thing or process in and of itself. Hence, in contrast to culturalist positions, governmentality theorists suggest that positing experience as the grounds for resisting domination fails to challenge many contemporary modes of domination and regulation. Instead, when the move towards interrogating experience as a means of resistance is historicized it can be seen as part of a broader cultural turn inward for the source of meaning (the psy-complex, Rose, 1985). It has contributed to a therapeutic culture, and to propagating a specific version of freedom – not radical freedom, but the depoliticized, individualistic freedom to realize our latent potential through actively working on and shaping our lifestyle or our interiority (for example, Cruikshank, 1993). Located in the tradition of structuralist and post-structuralist critiques of experience, governmentality studies suggests that it is fundamentally misguided to posit experience as an object through which we can gain insight into historical shifts in particular ways of relating to ourselves and others. We have already indicated that researching experience *can* certainly be a navel-gazing dead end, but we want to lay the ground for challenging this as the only and inevitable way of working with experience in social research. Our aim in this book is to contest the hasty conflation of all interest in the category of experience both with an individualistic political trajectory and with a naïve conception of social and historical change as originating in consciousness.

In problematizing experience, governmentality theory provides a keen analysis of the relationship between subjectification and the socio-political realm. Hence, our interest in developing this case-study of the fate of experience is not to simply negate governmentality studies' account of experience. In addition to offering a powerful diagnosis of pervasive humanist accounts of experience, governmentality theory has contributed to elucidating the particular ways in which subjectification and discourse are connected in neoliberal times. Our aim is to build on this by considering modes of being which interrupt neoliberal individualism.

Lived experiences of liberal individualism

Increasingly, we are enjoined to think of ourselves as autonomous, unitary, rational actors with capacities for control and with responsibilities for our own destinies (although the distribution of such capacities is by no means equal). We continue to develop psychologized ways of understanding ourselves as individuals who cannot be understood without recourse to our interiority. This psychologization of life makes (some) sense of the otherwise idiosyncratic appeal on the part of Bush to the US public. In January 2003, Americans were asked to support a war against Iraq on the grounds that Saddam Hussein is the sort of rare person who cannot be helped by therapy. In addition to the idea that failing to be a good target for therapy can be used as part of an argument for a 'just war', there is an implicit message in Bush's statement: that most significant problems we encounter *can* or should be resolved through this very particular form of therapeutic salvation. This indicates the extent to which we are coming to understand ourselves as objects of psychological knowledge, first and foremost. Knowledge of interiority is being prioritized over and above understanding the social, economic, material and political relations in which we find ourselves. One outcome is that it is difficult to make sense of ourselves outside of these liberal individualistic terms. Or more precisely, to be recognized as anything other than a rational, autonomous, unitary subject risks being pathologized. Simultaneously, we are faced with impoverished notions of the social realm, it is frequently invoked as nothing more than the product of individuals' activities (for example, as indicated by Thatcher's famous denial of the existence of society [Thatcher, 1987]).

Addictive investments in liberal individualism

Yet, alongside this deployment of notions of individual autonomy and rationality and empowerment, we find that the self-same liberal individual is under increasing threat. This coexistence of proliferation and threat is evident in the recent history of the very idea of addiction

(Keane, 2001). Before the turn of the 20th century, the reason why someone might compulsively act against his or her own will was first explained in terms of something inherent in substances: addiction stems from drugs themselves, for example. But as the notion is deployed in disparate realms of life this logic starts to fall apart (Sedgwick, 1992). Today, talk of being addicted to food, shopping, exercise, work and sex is all fairly commonplace. Yet attempts to suggest that there is something inherently addictive about food, shopping or sex, are easily questioned. Instead, another rationale for addiction has emerged – the problem pertains to relations with the self and with others. For example, the emerging literature on sex addiction explains this addiction, not as a problem with sex itself, but as the result of addicts' objectification of others (Keane, 2001). Hence, rather than suggest that reformed addicts abstain from sex altogether, conquering one's addiction involves cultivating appropriate sexual desires and practising the right kind of sex. Addicts must develop a particular self, one who realizes that really sex is all about an expression of love in the context of a monogamous relationship. In the case of sex addiction, the irony of locating addiction in the self is that the 'cure' repeats the problematic objectification of others. The cure assumes that partners' desires are always and only of the healthy variety, and partners with desires which fall outside of this normative notion of sexuality are always understood as victims of the addict's objectification (Keane, 2001).

In the deployment of addiction discourse, the idea that addiction stems from particular damaging substances is becoming weaker and weaker. At the same time, the notion of addiction itself is proliferating in epidemic proportions – and addiction has been fittingly characterized as 'an epidemic of the will' (Sedgwick, 1992). This epidemic confronts us with subjects who might be other than the liberal ideal. It taps into and fuels anxieties around the active, autonomous subject who strives for and achieves freedom. We could suggest that these anxieties are increasing as people realize the impossibility of embodying the ideal of autonomy, that is, that the growth in addiction represents a threat to liberal norms. However, the proliferation of anxieties about rational, autonomous control does not necessarily weaken this normative notion of subjectivity, it can strengthen it. That is, the multiplication of anxieties about failures to exercise free-will indicates the *allure* of liberal modes of subjectification. Anxieties about the demise of autonomy and the increase in practices designed to promote autonomy (such as self-help groups) extend the same notion of the subject; that is, a subject who is always already anointed with an inner voice or space, and with the capacity to access this inner space and so discover his or her own truth (Cindy Patton, 2000). The notion of addiction affirms the idea that the truth of subjects can be known and represented. It illustrates the impasse which we face now: attempts to understand subjectivity only shore up liberal individualism (Papadopoulos, 2003). Or is it an impasse?

Living autonomy – experiences of HIV treatments

We want to approach this apparent impasse from another angle, by discussing the problematic place of liberal individualism in both everyday experience and in attempts to research and understand such experience. The particular moment through which liberal individualism is explored below is an instance of attempting to manage HIV. This instance is located in the HIV epidemic as it is developing in the gay community in Sydney, Australia. In New South Wales (NSW) over 85 per cent of HIV positive people are men who have been infected through sex with men. We will say more about the specificities of the HIV epidemic in Sydney in Chapter 4 and Chapter 5. For now it is important to know that, in addition to predominantly impacting homosexually active men, there is a relatively low rate of HIV infection in Australia (similar to the UK, the prevalence rate of HIV in adults is estimated to be around 0.1 per cent, as compared with 0.6 per cent in the US [UNAIDS, 2004]). This picture is probably due to a combination of factors: a large gay community who have close connections with gay community in San Francisco (meaning that there was advanced warning of the strange illness amongst homosexually active men that was yet to be named HIV); early prevention efforts arising from the gay community and strengthened by alliances with government and researchers; the ongoing development of community lobby groups and agencies; the early introduction of needle exchange programs resulting in low rates of transmission amongst injecting drug users; and an immigration policy which selects migrants on the basis of HIV negative serostatus. Our broad concern in turning to the contested terrain of lived experience of HIV is to understand the terms and practices through which HIV positive people might engage with, be constrained by, move beyond or be produced through medical technologies. Rather than posit some notion of 'illness identity' and seek to understand how people relate to it (for example, Crossley, 1999; Frank, 1995), here we are interested in elucidating the devices of 'meaning production' through which experiences of illness are fabricated (Ariss, 1997; Dean, 1994; Rose, 1996a).

Medical practices and technologies loom large at moments in some people's accounts of their experience. For others they have always remained, or have been reined into, the background. People taking HIV treatments are faced with negotiating a highly complex and rapidly changing terrain. Since the 'protease moment' in 1996, many of these changes have been largely due to medical advances in treatments. The advent of Highly Active Anti-Retroviral Therapy (HAART, later modified to ART before becoming known as ARV treatment) has meant that people who can access the drugs, and who respond to the drugs, may come to live HIV as a chronic illness. In Australia, all citizens and permanent residents have access to HIV treatments at a minimal cost through a combination of federal health schemes. The system is not without its difficulties. Ease of access can be constrained: only specialists or specialized general practitioners can prescribe and monitor ARV treatment; some doctors charge upfront fees; and these fees may not be fully reimbursed through the federal healthcare system; drugs can only be purchased from hospital pharmacies (although currently a limited number of local chemists are participating in a pilot project to improve accessibility of ARV treatment in NSW). Aside from doctors' bills, the annual cost of triple combination therapy to the patient is no more than $600 – less for those on very low incomes. Non-residents, on the other hand, have huge difficulties in accessing treatments, making it virtually impossible for all but the very wealthy. And for HIV positive migrants to switch from non-resident to permanent resident status is only possible in exceptional circumstances.

Beyond problems of access, ARV treatment continues to present serious challenges to those who have can avail of it (for example, in the form of erratic and uncertain efficacy, or serious side-effects). More than a decade after the introduction of ART, its use is somewhat more predictable and there are more avenues for discussing and managing its uncertainties. But the instance described below occurred within the first three years of the introduction of ART. In this initial period, there was a flood of information (highly technical and covering a diverse array of drugs with unpredictable outcomes and different uses) accessible through gay press and community agencies as well as medical sources. This information was simultaneously received with both a tremendous sense of hope and the exhaustion of having 'seen it all before' and seen it end badly. Only a few years prior, much hope had been placed in drug trials to investigate the benefits of using an existing drug, AZT, for treating HIV. The suspension of the trials was suffered as a massive and life-taking setback by many. AZT was to have been the breakthrough in the management of HIV. Thus, the general euphoria over the announcement of HAART was clouded by anxiety and caution on the part of many HIV positive people.

In contrast to this anxiety, early medical advertising for HAART seemed cool and serene. It focused one's attentions well beyond the intricate details of drug regimens: the sky was now the limit. For example, in the US advertisements there was a predominance of lone men atop large mountains with expansive views of other large mountains and big skies. In Australia there was a white bird flying solo in clear blue skies. Despite the differences between the pharmaceutical campaigns announcing HAART, the message was the same: the horizon is yours, talk to your doctor to access your future. Representations of HIV as a collective affair were markedly absent in these campaigns or, as in one US advertisement, were literally buried in time: a printed headline announcing the success of HIV treatments was placed over an artistically 'aged' black and white image of the quilt project. Death and its collective remembering were rendered unnecessary episodes, now firmly in our past. By the late 1990s, the future of HIV was represented as unmediated by collective or community responses. This future belonged to the liberal individual, capable of availing of the opportunities provided by medicine, and the uncertainty of treatment outcome was masked.

Not surprisingly, the tensions between the proliferation and inadequacies of the liberal subject were also evident. Analyses of medical discourse suggested that positive people were being enjoined to take control of their lives by taking treatments and held responsible for the uncertain efficacy of drugs (Race et al., 2001). Still today, taking HIV treatments means participating in a highly experimental science in the making, a science in which one is not simply dominated by medicine. Being enjoined to discourses of patient empowerment can mean actively participating in the constraint of HIV experience. We want to give a sense of this. The following memory was written by Luke (a pseudonym) who was participating in research about modes of HIV subjectification. In Chapter 3 we discuss the methodology employed in this research in close detail. The memory below was written by Luke for the purpose of analysing it with a group of other people who were currently taking HIV treatments. The cue, 'taking charge', was suggested by another person in the group, as a potential lead into interrogating personal experiences of HIV treatments; everyone wrote a memory in response to this cue. People involved in this memory-work research were asked to write in the third person and they were asked to pick one particular incidence of the cue (as opposed to giving a general account), and to try to describe it in as much detail as possible (Haug, 1987, 1992; Crawford, Kippax, Onyx, Gault & Benton, 1992). A week later Luke returned with this:

> Luke, 'taking charge':
> *"Taking charge", he thought, a memory about taking charge. Possibilities started coming to him, one after another: the one when he'd started organising all the doses in the morning so he'd know he'd taken them; the one when he'd enlisted the help of friends to remind him to take those previously organised doses; the time when he'd begun marking both in his diary, and on the calendar the tablets for side-effects he had to take only once a week – and more – how he'd figured out if he took his meds [sic] with the World Health Organisation Rehydration mixture,* the difficult one went down easier; how if he always ate the yoghurt the naturopath recommended with his morning dose ... well – the ways, and times, he'd taken charge seem to go on and on – but he couldn't pick one, and then when he did pick one – and then another – he couldn't seem to write it. "What the Hell's this", he thought "I can write – this is not complicated". Then he realised in spite of all the ways and means he'd taken and devised to take charge, he didn't feel in charge, he just felt trapped; and he could only write it like this.*

The memory articulates a powerful paradox. People are enjoined to be candidates for liberal subjectivity, to act as if self-mastery is always possible. Yet that sense of being in control is perpetually elusive. Moreover, although the effort can be consuming there are limits to the pleasures to be gleaned from the mysteries of digestion and sleep, and from developing a capacity to relate more and more aspects of one's life to a medical regimen. Yet, because the language of autonomy assumes that control is always achievable, it is virtually impossible to articulate and make sense of experiences like Luke's in terms other than personal failure.

Much of the discussion of treatments in this memory-work group touched on the broader debates in Sydney over shifts in HIV community

---

* WHO rehydration mixture counter-acts the dehydrating side-effects of one of the drugs commonly prescribed as part of combination therapy.

and identity in the late 1990s (and in Chapter 5 we consider people's experiences of these debates as they have developed more recently). For some, developments in treatments constituted another threat to HIV community. In the past, treatments activism and lobbying had provided a focal point for gay and HIV community engagement. Focusing on the inadequacies of medical practices and knowledges worked as a means of making connections between people. But the 'treatment breakthrough' of 1996 could be understood as strengthening the ever-present moves towards medicalizing HIV identity and towards silencing positive people's experiences. That is, medical success could mean that there is not the same interest in listening to the experiences of positive people. (Notably, research on British doctors' experiences of HIV medicine since 1996 suggests that doctors also experience the ambiguity of medical advances: more routine consultations mean that they have less opportunity for developing close connections with their now relatively healthy patients [Rosengarten, Imrie, Flowers, Davis & Hart, 2004]). Post-ART, doctors are focused on monitoring the efficacy of treatments through test results (viral load, t-cells, liver function) not on the intricacies of how people actually manage to incorporate treatments into their day to day lives. Read in this light, the memory serves as a classic example of the excruciating experience of being at the receiving end of dehumanizing medical practices; a desperate account of the inadequacies of the liberal subject in the face of medical authority. The implicit message of such a reading is that medicalization is at the root of problems like Luke's. This justifies a politics revolving around the affirmation of HIV identity as a response to medicalization. Although this reading of the memory was considered in the group discussion, it was not the only position discussed. In fact, whilst there were several other memories which were read in terms of an opposition between medicine and experience, Luke's memory was understood as particularly significant because it troubles this binary.

Unlike the traditional victim of oppressive power (in this case that power is medicalization); there is nothing passive about Luke. Rather he actively develops a set of practices to respond to his situation. But these practices are akin to the bars in the cage which comes to trap him, bars *of his own making*. Luke is deeply complicit in his own regulation – the problem he is describing is not just that of the liberal subject who fails in his aspiration to self-mastery. It is the lot of the neoliberal subject who enacts his own regulation through his attempts to wrest control over his life. The step from the memory to justifying self-affirmation as a politically effective means of responding to medicalization (the first reading) is not automatic. This second reading foregrounds the author's puzzled acknowledgment of the complicity of the neoliberal subject. It is an open problem for which no response is being suggested. Moreover, this second reading illustrates the inadequacies of casting of experience as the authentic grounds on which resistance to power and ideology rests. There can be no clear separation between Luke's experience of trying to take control and his investment in forms of self-regulation which constrain him. That is, it is no longer possible to oppose the authenticity of Luke's experience with the oppressive forces of medicalization.

Experience and socio-political change

Rather than take a foundational approach to experience and claim Luke's memory as indicative of a particular identity, it can be thought in terms of the problem to be explained (Scott, 1991/1993). In this reading, refusing the account as evidence of HIV identity, refusing the idea that what it necessarily means to be HIV positive (on treatments) is to 'feel trapped' or to succumb to the forces of medicalization, the problem to be explained is the predicament of neoliberal subjects who enact their own regulation through attempts to realize a liberal notion of freedom. As discussed earlier, this neoliberal noose of subjectivity is the focus of much of the literature on governmentality (for example, Dean, 1994, 1999; Rose 1989, 1996a, 1996b, 2002). Governmentality studies are interested in productive power, power which operates through expert knowledges (for example, medicine, psychology) producing the will to voluntarily adopt the regulative functions of government in people's attempts at self-improvement. This mode of subjectification acts as a vehicle for a range of late-capitalist, neoliberal practices and policies of government and regulation. The problem now, as Nikolas Rose points out, is we are compelled to be free.

This means that understanding the relations between the subject and power 'is not a matter of lamenting the ways in which autonomy is suppressed by the state, but of investigating the ways in which subjectivity has become an essential object, target, and resource for certain strategies, tactics, and procedures of regulation' (Rose, 1996b, p. 152). Governing through people's attempts at self-improvement involves both translating people's aspirations into forms of regulation and proliferating new aspirations. Historically, the psy-disciplines, partly through their focus on experience, have provided means for connecting personal experience with the means of its governance. From the perspective of governmentality theorists, experience is discursively constituted, and discourses 'are embodied within complex technical and practical associations and devices that provide "places" that human beings must occupy if they are to have the status of subjects of particular sorts' (Rose, 1996b, p. 53). Experience is given meaning (or its meaning is contested) through subjectification. Rather than understand subjectification as a process of conferring meaning or positioning in narrative (an approach widely adopted by psychologists, for example), governmentality studies posits its occurrence 'in a complex of apparatuses, practices, machinations, and assemblages within which human being has been fabricated, and which presuppose and enjoin particular relations with ourselves' (Rose, 1996b, p. 10). This suggests that, to the extent that analysing experience relies on the interrogation of shared systems of meaning, it is not a good way of understanding subjectification. In order to understand the relationship between the sociopolitical realm (for example, current governmental, professional and institutional policies on HIV care and prevention) and emerging modes of subjectification (for example, the practices described in Luke's memory), we need to avoid conflating conscious self-representation of experience and the often unspoken, unconscious embodiment of discourse.

Experience is an effect of discourse, a by-product, given meaning by the illusory 'I' or author of experience. Subjectification cannot be understood by recourse to experience. Rather governmentality studies entail historical analyses of both transformations in modes of relating to ourselves as particular kinds of subjects (for example, as HIV positive) and of ways in which particular conceptions of these relations travel from one domain of life to another. These approaches to transformations in modes of relating to the self (and others) usefully explain the effectiveness of contemporary neoliberal modes of governance: they harness and work through the interpretation of experience. Subjects of neoliberalism come to understand and to interpret their experience in particular ways – and not others. Luke knows the limitations of autonomy, he rails against it, yet it is hard to articulate his experience outside of it. However, whether approaching subjectification through the analysis of practices, apparatuses and assemblages *necessarily* involves repudiating experience hinges on the particular concept of experience involved. We want to suggest that experience is more than an effect of discourse or discourses, and more than the product of a subject's positioning in multiple discourses (Davies & Harré, 1990). One response to the contested role of experience in the culturalist/structuralist debates is to identify emerging modalities of experience which, although they are produced through our contemporary socio-political conditions (and discourses), cannot be reduced to them (Virno, 1996). If we adopt the position that researching experience is essentially conservative, we effectively shore up the notion that experience *is* a given, a fixed empirical reality. Moreover, we lose the capacity to understand an important element of historical change – shifting, continuous, collective experience (see Chapter 8). Whilst governmentality theory offers a possible understanding of the present, because it repudiates experience as an object of analysis it cannot elucidate the connections between immanent processes of becoming and socio-political change (Deleuze & Guattarri, 1988). Ultimately, the cost of jettisoning a close examination of the complexity of experience is to deter research which can engage with and contribute to emerging modes of political engagement.

We are not suggesting that researching lived experience is the *only* way to consider socio-political change. For example, in her reading of GlaxoSmithKline's UK campaign launching the HIV drug Trizivir, Rosengarten (2004) considers the modes of political engagement which are being opened as well as those being foreclosed. The advertisements feature groovy and racially diverse 'youth'. They are cast as demanding consumers, but consumers whose lifestyle needs are being met by GlaxoSmithKline. Trizivir is not a new drug, but a repackaging of three HIV drugs in one. This simplifies the task of adhering to a daily regimen. The advertisements represent happy customers. But why so happy? Rosengarten points out that, at the time of its launch, Trizivir was known to have serious side-effects (common to most HIV drugs) and because its impact on long-term viral suppression was *unknown*, there was a possibility that poor viral suppression could lead to drug resistance, making Trizivir a risky choice. The advertisements – together with the uncritical reproduction of their message in media reports – invoke a mode of engagement which risks being politically tangential in this specific context. The activities which were absent not only from the campaign, but from the public discussion prompted by the campaign, included pushing drug companies for less toxic, more effective drugs. (Rosengarten notes that it is always possible that working on lifestyle could enable treatments activism, but unlikely if 'being groovy' is simply equated with being politically active.) In contrast to the analyses entailed in governmentality studies which culminate in a general diagnoses of the problem of regulative freedom, this analysis of the Trizivir campaign discusses different modes of striving for freedom and returns us to debating the limitations and possibilities entailed in specific kinds of freedom. But it is precisely this step, from broad critique to theorizing different and new modes of political engagement, at which many social researchers baulk.

Interrupting neoliberalism

We want to suggest that, by jettisoning experience as an object of analysis, governmentality theory misses its own target – that is, deploying a more effective means of intervening in the proliferation of a particular notion of liberal (or neoliberal) subjectivity as an autonomous project of self-invention. This is not an impossible target. Consider, for example, autobiographical work which tests the liberal assumption that processes of reflecting on interiority and analysing experience lead us to a deeper understanding of the subject, to the truth of subjectivity (for example, Gallop, 1988; Walkerdine, 1990; Gillian Rose, 1995). The alternative to the totalizing diagnoses offered by governmentality theorists does not involve re-embracing a concept of experience as the authentic grounds from which knowledge is developed. Rather, it is possible to build on the notion of experience as discursively constituted and the important insights this has enabled (for example, Mos, 1996). Luke's memory, for example, can be approached in terms of the discursive production of liberal and neoliberal subjectivities. Certainly, there is the risk that approaches to discourse which start from experience will return to celebrations of the subject's agentic capacity to draw on discourse to rework himself (for example, Prilleltensky & Nelson, 2002). This is because, in and of itself, the move to discourse as an approach to experience fails to rework the relationship between discourse, experience and subjectification, and most importantly it fails to disrupt idea that experience is the basis for privileged self-knowledge (see Chapter 4 for a fuller discussion of this relation).

With the emergence of new forms of regulation and new subjectivities, the limitations of familiar modes of political engagement are becoming increasingly apparent. The insistence on identity-affirmation occludes interrogation of the particular ways in which harnessing identity (such HIV identity) can be more or less politically effective at any given moment (for example, Race, 2001; Butler, 1992). The discursive turn, illustrated in our discussion of governmentality theory, helps to identify the inadequacies of identity politics. We are increasingly subject to a mode of regulation which operates both through people's attempts to translate the personal into the political and through attempts to live the personal as political. Hope is delivered in the form of broad-based claims about 'inventing ourselves differently' (Rose, 1996b, p. 197). Yet, investigating the specificities of how this may or may not be occurring is discouraged if it involves returning to the uncertainty and incompleteness of lived experience. The concept of experience is cast as an accompanying slave of or 'silent witnesses' to the unfolding of neoliberal geoculture. In contrast, our interest in experience stems from the way in which it can disrupt the coherence of positions and situations which deploy this neoliberal politics. This possibility does not stem from experience thought as the basis for resisting self-regulation, but arises through working with a notion of experience as dispersed, continuous and exceeding representation.

Going beyond conflating experience with discourse involves considering the plasticity of experience, its corrigibility, its inherent sociability. Only then is it possible to approach questions of subjectivity without (implicitly) offering answers which invoke the truth of the subject. When we negate this promise of truth and account for the possibility that experience can exceed representation, exceed discourse, it is possible to begin to understand subjectification *without* being compelled to invoke the notions of development and self-actualization on which the deployment of the neoliberal subject is premised. Only then can analyses of experience add to our repertoire of strategies for rethinking the present.

Experience as excess

The political importance of experience has been invoked in other guises. In *A Room of One's Own*, Woolf insisted:

> ... it is fatal for anyone who writes to think of their sex. It is fatal to be a man or woman pure and simple ... It is fatal for a woman to lay the least stress on any grievance; to plead even with justice any cause; in any way to speak consciously as a woman. And fatal is no figure of speech; for anything written with that conscious bias is doomed to death. It ceases to be fertilized ... it cannot grow in the minds of others ... The whole of the mind must lie wide open if we are to get the sense that the writer is communicating his experience with perfect fullness. (Woolf, 1929/1993, p. 169)

At the same time as aspiring to represent the 'fullness of experience', Woolf scuttles any hope of achieving this through representations of identity. And by approaching her subjects through fragmented angles and unfinished, conflicting moments of self-awareness and absorption in the world, she challenges readers over any desire for a truth of the subject. We do not value her writing because of her character's capacities for comprehensive self-representation. No seamless *coherence* of identity or subjectivity emerges in the struggle of her writing. Woolf is mistress of distraction, intrusion, interruption and unsteady, peripheral vision. Yet, what Woolf evokes in her work – experience which cannot be narrativized, cannot be reduced to an identity – frequently confounds social researchers. The problem for social researchers is readily understandable: how it is possible to analyse that which exceeds representation in words and language? Any such possibility hinges on the concept of experience being employed.

At the outset of discussing such a concept we want to suggest two things. Firstly, there is nothing essentially private and interior to experience (Toulmin, 1985). Experience is malleable, it can be reread, and reworked. Investigating the points where experience begins to congeal and solidify can serve as a point of departure for challenging the utility of clichéd modes of being. That is, when public self-representations are politically ineffective, theorizing experience can contribute to new modes of political engagement. Concomitantly, shrinking from experience can amount to the failure to test the elasticity of the socio-political realm (Gillian Rose, 1996). Secondly, experience can undo one's authoritative relationship to oneself. In subverting the idea that the truth of subjects can be known and represented, and that self-invention is an activity which can be mastered, the self-realizing, self-liberating modes of subjectification entailed in neoliberalism are called into question. Once we are no longer compelled to shore up the 'cover-story' of truth, we are free to explore different forms of satisfaction and self-invention (Phillips, 1999) – the kinds of diversity and contingencies that biography tends to gloss in the attempt to 'explain' its subject (discussed in Chapter 3). This could lead to elucidating modes of subjectification which involve seeking ways beyond the limited project of articulation (the focus of the following chapter), as well as modes of subjectification which open subjects to the disruptive relations in which they find themselves (examined in Chapter 4 and Chapter 6). Or perhaps theorizing experience could lead to insight about modes of subjectification which are faithful to socio-political changes which have yet to be realized, may never be realized (Badiou, 1999), ways of being which break with linear time and engage with continuous experience (Chapter 8). Challenging the socio-political conditions of globalized, neoliberal late-capitalism is not a matter of finding a new ground for resistance – but of refusing a dichotomy between regulative practices, technologies or discourses on the one hand and regulated experience on the other. This returns us to the task of understanding the specificity of regulation and to the ways in which everyday experience proliferates and subverts the active, rational subject of liberal and neoliberal policies and practices.

Reworking the concept of experience on the terrain of its immanent malleability and sociability allows us to participate in the emergence of new forms of collectivity and new forms of social relations. Social and political change is not a matter of regulation, it depends on the formation of fluid yet forceful historical subjectivities. Of course regulation is crucial for social order and political stability, and this is the perspective governmentality studies adopt. But our interest and our focus throughout this book will be to offer a possible account of experience which can contribute to the creation of historical subjectivities, fostering transformative processes against and beyond existing forms of regulation. We will argue that these historical subjectivities emerge in and through experience. This is something which was a central concern of the cultural studies since the 1960s and 1970s. The next chapter considers this theoretical tradition, especially the concept of articulation. We discuss the promise of articulation as a means of grasping sociopolitical change and, through exploring its limits, argue that there is an excess of experience – experience which is never articulated but which can nonetheless erupt and force change at particular moments.

2
The Political Project of Articulation

The 'studies-discourse'

In the historical formation of our socio-political organization there is a recurring pattern of exclusion – exclusion of certain communities, social groups or collective identities. Exclusion is a multi-layered phenomenon. There is the symbolic production of the 'other' community, combined with its discursification, that is, the definition of the features and characteristics of that community, and the naming of what matters each time you encounter the supposed other. This discursive-symbolic production orders our perception, classifies what and how we see – images, colours, sounds. In addition, there is the effacement of the other both from the social imaginary and from political institutions: this occurs through criminalization, incrimination of deficiencies in the form of psychological processes, and through refusal of social and political rights. And there is the material displacement and exploitation of the other community – through border-making, withholding of passports, and the organization of detention. Finally, the strongest form of exclusion involves the material extinction of the other, destroying the conditions of existence, the physical space, the archives, the infrastructure, death, killing, and genocide. Do analyses of experience contribute in any way towards confronting these multi-layered practices of exclusion? In this chapter, we address these questions through consideration of a particular critical turn in academic discourse, one which has been chiefly initiated by cultural studies and executed in gender studies, science studies and cultural studies (Haraway, 1994) – the 'studies-discourse'. Through a reading of Luis Buñuel's film *Tristana*, we consider tensions over the concept of experience which is invoked in the studies-discourse – that is, between experience as that which (at least potentially) can always be modified and usurped into neoliberal political projects and notions of experience which take seriously the fundamental exclusions (from both symbolic and material realms) lived by many.

The 'studies-discourse' appears as emblem and reminder of inter-textuality, of theory-in-the-making, multiplicity, transdisciplinarity, and of social intervention and accountability. It is concerned with difference and differentiation, with opposing both finalism and any idea of a coherent representational tactic. Importantly, it promises no redemption. The 'studies-discourse' is marked by an opposition to posi-tivist thinking in the social sciences as well as to the proliferation of anti-theoretical sentiments in the Left, so called Left conservatism (Connery, 1999). In this chapter we consider a particular approach to experience widely used in the 'studies-discourse': articulation. We sug-gest that at the very moment that it claims to give voice to the experi-ences of the other and to processes of social exclusion, the concept of articulation risks privileging some aspects of experience and further consigning others to invisibility. We argue that 30 years after the first appearance of cultural studies and the 'studies-discourse' articulation needs to be rethought. The materiality of social exclusion needs to be foregrounded in attempts to elucidate the growing hostility, resentment and incomprehensibility between different communities, state authori-ties, and transnational organizations of contemporary geopolitics.

The political strategy of articulation

The 'studies-discourse' is concerned to reorganize symbolic-material arrangements so as to enable the self-expression and the empowerment of excluded communities. Research stemming from this tradition has been important in the proliferation of a particular interest in and approach experience: the enunciation of experiences of marginaliza-tion is cultivated; experience is linked to socio-historical trajectories (Scott, 1991/1993); and 'auto-ethnographic' research practices are val-orized (Pratt, 1992). It is the process of articulation which captures the moment which is so crucial for gender and cultural studies, that is, the moment when the rearrangement and reconnection of existing modes of thinking and acting gives rise to material empowerment and to the entitlement to speak.

When the concept of articulation is taken up in gender studies it is used to further the project of contesting gender normativity and hetero-sexist hegemony 'by rendering the symbolic increasingly dynamic, that is, by considering the conditions and limits of representation as open to significant re-articulations and transformations under the pressure of social practices of various kinds' (Butler, 1997, p. 23). And, similarly, in cultural studies articulation is used to rework the opaque and resistant notion of ideology into something increasingly flexible and transformable:

> Thus, a theory of articulation is both a way of understanding how ideological elements come, under certain conditions, to cohere together within a discourse, and a way of asking how they do or do not become articulated, at specific conjunctures, to certain political subjects. Let me put that the other way: the theory of articulation asks how an ideology discovers its subject rather than how the subject thinks the necessary and inevitable thoughts which belong to it; it enables us to think how an ideology empowers people, enabling them to begin to make some sense or intelligibility of their historical situation, without reducing those forms of intelligibility to their socioeconomic or class location or social position. (Hall, 1986a, p. 53)

The articulation of experience, following Stuart Hall, involves putting different ideas and practices together in order to facilitate and valorize a commonality which creates counter-discourses, oppositions and alliances, and which generates voice and movement (Bhabha, 1994; Clifford, 2001; Hall, 1986a, 1986b; Slack, 1996). In this sense, articulation is productive of socio-political change. Importantly, voice and movement do not shape collective practices by cultivating abstract identifications, but by working on the level of the micropolitics of everyday life experience. The battle to change the conditions of hegemony involves building lines of action by laboriously restructuring what has been seized and forged by repressive authorities.

In this account, the politics of articulation are realized when desires and contentious politics materialize in social and cultural life. Following Clifford, for example, articulation 'works' when the indigenous people of new Caledonia, who had been named as 'canaques' by the French colonial power, 'make claims under the banner of their historical and cultural diversity', change the signifier 'canaques' to 'Kanaks' and form a movement for engaging themselves in the post-colonial conditions of the late 20th century (Clifford, 2001, p. 472). And as words travel through different sites in the global economy of immigration, so also the word 'canaques': transformed to Kanake, it was used in the post-World War II West-Germany as a generic pejorative term for 'foreigners', while during the nineties it experienced a resignification and is now used to recapture anti-racist, 'kanakian' resistance to the assimilationist polices of the German administration and governing parties: Kanak Attak (www.kanak-attak.de). The logic of articulation entails transfiguring the conditions for socio-political action by undoing fixed representations of social communities, transforming the texture of everyday experience, and by changing the relations of participating communities to knowledge production.

But despite the important role played by the studies-discourse in general and the concept of articulation in particular in untackling the relation between experience and exclusion, it seems that these approaches may be inadequate for addressing current geopolitical problems and current forms of violence. How is it possible that silencing and extinction coexist so perfectly with the proliferation of articulation? In whose name does the 'studies-discourse' speak and in which socio-political conditions is it situated? Which experiences can be articulated and reconfigured in counter-hegemonic political practices and which remain out of sight? In this chapter we argue that what remains out of sight is in fact a whole other side of our world – World 2 – a world which is radically incommensurable with the approach to experience entailed in the studies-discourse.

Tristana

What we want to do first is to situate the conditions of World 2's concealment by following some different, often disparate paths, in the studies-discourse. We will track these paths using a narrative borrowed from Luis Buñuel's film *Tristana*, made at the end of 1969. We quote from his autobiography:

> After *The Milky Way*, I became interested in Galdós's epistolary novel *Tristana*. Although it's certainly not one of his best, the character of Don Lope is fascinating, and I thought I might be able to switch the action from Madrid to Toledo and thus render homage to the city I loved so much ... The film was shot in Toledo, except for some scenes in a studio in Madrid ... If, as in *Nazarin*, the main character is a faithful copy of Galdós's, I made considerable changes in the structure and atmosphere, once again situating the action in a more contemporary period. With Julio Alejandro's help, I added several personally meaningful details, like the bell tower and the mortuary statue of Cardinal Tavera. Once again, I haven't seen *Tristana* since it opened [in Madrid and Rome in 1970], but I remember

liking the second half, from the return of the young woman with the amputated leg. I can still hear footsteps in the corridor, the scrape of her crutches, and the febrile conversation of the priests over their cups of hot chocolate. (Buñuel, 1983, p. 246)

Toledo is a rather small city, an old city where tradition seems to be immovable, where the uphill lanes lead to the cathedral and the winding streets are seized by honourable men and couples preserving family values and social security. It is a city which gives you the feeling of 'confinement and containment' (Edwards, 1995, p. 57; Higgin-botham, 1979). 'Everyone in Buñuel's film is locked into geography, bounded by authority, surrounded by the constraining walls of history and forced into implacable social rituals' (Partridge, 1995, p. 215). After the death of her mother Tristana (Catherine Deneuve) stays in the house of Don Lope (Fernando Rey). At first sight he seems a liberal, open-minded gentleman living from his declining fortunes with Saturna (Lola Gaos), the house servant. Don Lope appears at the begin-ning as the guardian and protector of the innocent Tristana. And, as is often the case, humanism transforms rapidly to its opposite. During the six years of his life with Tristana, Don Lope occupies all the central motifs ingrained by the prevailing drastic female-male asymmetry: hypocritical mentor, demanding lover, oppressive husband, moralizing father, and rapist. After two years Tristana starts seeing Horacio (Franco Nero), a young bohemian artist who asks her to marry him. Tristana refuses to marry but stays with him and they leave Toledo together. Now Don Lope is alone with Saturna again, his foreseeing, tireless domestic servant. Saturna is the one who maintains the whole house-hold, she keeps things going, knows how a bourgeois household works and what the turbulent souls of Don Lope and Tristana demand; and she can offer it. As the anticipating, diligent servant of Don Lope, Saturna appears to be the opposite of Tristana. In fact she is one of the presuppositions of Tristana's life. Not so much because there is an alliance between them – Saturna always remains loyal to Don Lope – but because she is represented as a creative problem solver responsible for everyday reproduction.

One day Saturna announces to Don Lope that Tristana is back in Toledo. She is seriously ill with a tumour and she wants to return to Don Lope's house. He accepts her believing that because of her sickness she won't be able to leave him again. After having arranged Tristana's return to Don Lope's house, Horacio disappears from her life. The tumour deteriorates and her leg is amputated. Tristana starts overtly displaying her rejection, detestation and defiance of Don Lope. But despite her revulsion she accepts him in marriage. Don Lope becomes more and more conservative and conformist. He, the liberal, who sent a policeman in the wrong direction while he was chasing a thief (because 'the police represent the principle of strength and a man such as I always defends the weaker party' [Buñuel & Alejandro, 1971, p. 23]), the one who refused clerics entrance to his house and who used to denigrate religion, the one who used to belittle couples on the street for smelling of 'the sickening odour of marital bliss' and for their 'bovine resignation' (Buñuel & Alejandro, 1971, p. 52) subsides into conformity and befriends priests (Buache, 1973). The more Don Lope becomes a caricature of a liberal gentleman, the more Tristana transforms into the unspoken authority in the house. If Don Lope dominates the overt organization of the space, she dominates the unseen space of intersubjective relations. Don Ambrosio, one of the priests who comes to drink chocolate in Don Lope's house, diagnoses 'something satanic in this resentment' of Tristana (Buñuel & Alejandro, 1971, p. 130). In the end, Don Lope is lying sick in bed and asks her to call the doctor. She picks up the phone but she does not call the doctor. Don Lope dies. She opens the window.

Questioning articulation

This is the plot. Now the questions: Could we regard Tristana's act as a form of articulation in the monosexual and oppressive universe of pre-civil-war Toledo? Are Tristana's metamorphoses – silence, desire for/ seduction into a better life, finally negation – transformations which ensue from her increasing awareness of the mechanics of gender oppression? Or are they just different motifs of the same theme, namely that her lived experience is ordered and constrained by a male code? These questions allude to a long discussion in feminism and gender studies. If Tristana is acting to liberate herself from patriarchal dominance, by reconfiguring and imploding the sexual logic of patriarchy, then we encounter a world in which liberation appears to be a matter of individual initiative first and foremost. Social and cultural research which promotes action (and engagement in power relations) over mourning fosters such an understanding of agency (Brown, 1995). But, as we indicated in the previous chapter, it seems that despite the worthiness of this idea, it shares a problematic affinity with the structure of politics in a neoliberal world carried out by self-assembling, self-asserting, self-liberating individuals or isolated communities. And in this world, only some who engage in practices of self-liberation are emancipated. The possibility to speak is offered to few and withheld from the many. Agentic acts may work, or they may well fail. Sexual difference feminism offers a powerful analysis of the fact that in the liberal universe only some reach the sublime: it draws our attention to the radical insuperable dichotomy between the sexes, constituted on the symbolic level, which overrides any attempt to reverse existing asymmetries (Irigaray, 1985a, 1985b). But this critical insight contains some well-known, disturbing problems: what to do with the ahistoricity of sexual difference feminism, how to reintroduce time and change into the symbolic, how to expand gender distinctions to address other situated differences, how to take account of the fact that each one of the sexes is not one (Butler, 1990)?

This is the first set of questions. Their discussion raises a second set, that is, questions more closely related to the problem of the invisibility of some experiences: who is the subject of articulation in the cultural politics of the neoliberal era? What is revealed by articulation – is it socio-cultural structures, personal experiences, collective experiences or discourses? What does articulation leave aside? What is the relation between 'the world' and World 2? World 2 is partly outside of the prevalent pattern of articulation. World 2 is this world which remains unarticulated, a world of grief, incoherent pleasures and resentment. Here, articulation often feels cold, distanced, impossible. How can we approach this world?

The obligation to speak and the problem of articulation

Tristana's suffering arises from the fact that she is obliged to speak using signs, practices and rituals which are elements of a masculinist symbolic-material universe in which she is absent. Of course, Tristana can speak this language and she can even change the conditions of this language, but that does not mean that she can articulate herself through this language. The concept of articulation allows us to trace how normative matrices of interaction and coercive structures of existence can be modified. In fact articulation is exactly that: the rearrangement of an order of practices and signs from which new orders occur. A theory of articulation necessarily assumes that the actors involved – in this case Tristana, or on the social level various communities – *can* articulate themselves in ways which express and to a certain degree reorganize the symbolic/material realm. As discussed above, articulation is conceived as a means of realizing the malleability of the symbolic-material realm

(Butler, 1997), or of challenging determinist accounts of ideology (Hall, 1986a).

But is Tristana's behaviour an act of articulation? This question can only be answered in the affirmative if we take the standpoint of an independent observer. Moving into Tristana's own position however, we can see that she is *obliged* to speak, to verbalize her experiences and to act. As she eats peas she hesitates which one of two similar peas she shall eat. Walking with Saturna through the small streets of Toledo, Tristana asks her which one of two similar streets they shall take. And Don Lope refuses to answer the question which one of two identical pillars of a colonnade he prefers because they are the same (Buñuel & Alejandro, 1971). Tristana responds: 'No two pillars are ever the same. If you look carefully you can always see the difference. I always choose between things – between two grapes or two bread rolls or two snow-flakes ... because there's always a little something which makes me like one of them more' (Buñuel & Alejandro, 1971, p. 52).

Tristana lives in a world filled with obligations to choose, to speak, to act. In other words, she lives a world which demands the visualiza-tion of experience. In this world she has limited access to the grammar of the socio-material and symbolic conditions in which she is embed-ded. It is true that she is involved in constructing them, and that she can radically negate them – as she does in the end – Tristana can manipulate the conditions of her coercion and domination, she can change things. She can do all that, but only because she is obliged to act. In the grammar of her existence there is no space to have a break, to rest: to cease and go with time, to be in the flow of time, to tarry with time, to dwell on moments of time (Theunissen, 1991). Tristana's activism is essentially reactive in the Nietzschean sense. It ensues from her attempt to avoid the pressure of time, from resentment, anger, sorrow, sometimes from fear. And she is obliged to respond to all that, she cannot choose silence because she is already silenced. Approaching Tristana's actions through the lens of articulation allows us to capture the moments of socio-cultural agency and agential relationality in her existence. But this lens fails to reveal *why* articulation happens, the conditions which give rise to, and limit, her involvement in socio-political transformation. This has some consequences.

When we approach current cultural transformations through the lens of articulation we commit a sort of epistemic fallacy: we define the world in terms of our knowledge of it. And also we trim down experience to what can be verbalized and become knowledgeable. But the world is not the accomplice of our knowledge! As Foucault says:

We must not resolve discourse into a play of pre-existing signifi-
cations; we must not imagine that the world turns towards us as a
legible face which we would have only to decipher; the world is not
the accomplice of our knowledge; there is no prediscursive provi-
dence which disposes the world in our favour. We must conceive
discourse as a violence which we do to things, or in any case as a
practice which we impose on them; and it is in this practice that the
events of discourse find the principle of their regularity. (Foucault,
1981, p. 67)

Our knowledge of the world is a knowledge which positions us in constellations of power. It is contaminated through practices of claiming
power and attaining power. Certainly, it is the case that Tristana
speaks, the marginalized and excluded speak (here we use speak as a
generic term for positioning, being present to oneself and to others,
being there, acting and intervening, perceiving, classifying and producing). But if we fail to differentiate between the *obligation* to enunciate
experience and an act of *articulation*, we risk making an elision between
the immanent unfolding of an action and a specific notion of political
action. That is, we reassign a quality to the acts of others which is pertinent to political engagement thought to hinge on the compulsion to
speak (or in other words a specific form of self-identity based on the
will to hear-yourself-speak).

The interpretation of Tristana's acts presented here can and must
rely on a theory of articulation. This would be the only way to address
issues of engagement and strategies of emancipation. But at the same
time Tristana is in fact prohibited from articulation. Tristana's acts are
driven by an obligation to take seriously her resentment against Don
Lope's mannerly oppression, by the obligation to cope with the shame
she feels – not only for herself but the shame for the behaviour of
others, for Don Lope's hypocrisy – by the obligation to alleviate her
disgust for her own situation, finally by the obligation to take care of
herself.

If the voice of the world is a voice amplified by the will to hear-yourself-speak, to hear your own experiences, the voice of World 2 is driven
by carefulness, shame, disgust, and resentment. It is Améry who elucidates how resentment enforces the desire for change and how it elabor-
ates the entanglement of individual and social history:

And I enter into the realm of German history and historicity as I
speak further of the victim's resentments. I am obliged, however, to

define their objective task. Perhaps it is only concern for my own purification, but I hope that my resentment – which is my personal protest against the antimoral natural process of healing that time brings about, and by which I make the genuinely humane and absurd demand that time be turned back – will also perform a historical function. Were it to fulfil the task that I set it, it could historically represent, as a stage of the world's moral dynamics of progress, the German revolution that did not take place. This demand is no less absurd and no less moral than the individual demand that irreversible processes be reversible. (Améry, 1964/1980, p. 77)

Obliteration, seduction for a better life, and pleasure

Tristana's primordial condition is a condition of obliteration. She is indistinct in the masculine economy of Toledo. At the beginning she acts in complete accordance with a patriarchal code which is designed to maintain male domination. She is identical with this code. The first sexual encounter with Don Lope, after his transformation from guardian to father to lover, is a very ambiguous scene. Tristana acts as if she wants to be seduced, there is no direct physical force. There is something mechanical about Tristana in this scene. She enacts her existential fate: she is a part of a sexual economy which – in every particular moment – reproduces a radical male-female asymmetry. Tristana's woodenness in this scene speaks to the fact that she is fitting into a ubiquitous phallocentric discourse of femininity. Her femininity is not there, it is external to the specific socio-cultural constellation of meaning in which she is embedded.

Sexual difference feminism is useful in foregrounding this prior exclusion. Irigaray, for example, offers a radical rejection of the fiction of an omnipotent subject capable of changing the conditions of exploitation and domination. There is no possibility of a positive articulation through simply inverting the primordial female-male asymmetry. Despite the idealistic connotations of this version of feminism, there is negative vision at work here which is extremely useful. This is the position that, from the outset, individual existence is marked by incommensurability – for example, the incommensurability of Tristana's femininity with patriarchal fantasies of femininity. In the beginning was incomprehensibility – the incomprehensibility of Tristana's femininity in the world of Toledo. Each and every articulation is already signified by this primordial obliteration. Enunciation of experience, articulation, is always governed by something prior.

It is hard to tell if the feelings which are enfolded in this existential condition can be conveyed. These include the feeling of impulsive rage against obliteration which simultaneously creates tenderness and warmth; the condition of irreparable bitterness, felt alongside a deep desire to connect and to share with others. (Gilroy interprets Du Bois's idea of double consciousness – later we'll come to this again – as 'a means to animate a dream of global co-operation among peoples of colour' (Gilroy, 1993, p. 126). In this reading agency is derived from the very moment of obliteration. It is obliteration and exclusion which produce desire and communication. This insight may be particularly hard to take up in our current socio-political conditions which foreground our self-speaking, self-liberating capacities above all else; but it is not a particularly new insight.

> As soon as I desire I am asking to be considered. I am not merely here-and-now, sealed into thingness. I am for somewhere else and for something else. I demand that notice be taken of my negating activity insofar as I pursue something other than life; insofar as I do battle for the creation of a human world – that is, a world of reciprocal recognitions. (Fanon, 1967, p. 218)

Fanon speaks here in the first person positioning himself as part of a future world of mutual acceptance. Primordial obliteration, if acknowledged, produces localized action, secular visions, fleshly desires, and the motion of material bodies. Thus, any attempt to respond to the challenges of sexual difference feminism by reinstalling a coherent historical actor (for instance, in the form of 'the' woman) completely neutralizes the power of the negative vision at work in this position. Such a move only succeeds in reinstating a way of thinking which pertains to phallocentric transcendental fantasies of a progressive dialectical process in history, and in elaborating the healing superstitions of modernity immanent in the idea of a coherent, self-identical experiential subject (see Chapter 7).

Tristana's revolt against Don Lope, Tristana's love for Horacio, Tristana's activity are all forms of her desire for consideration. This desire ensues from her experience of obliteration but never overcomes it. Tristana's action is culturally and historically localized in the society of Toledo. Her engagement in strategies of praxis is not so much an act of articulation, it is rather a consequence of her obliteration. Recognizing Tristana's act as a response to a primordial obliteration gives rise to a different account of articulation. That is, we can combine the insights to be gleaned from (a) the powerful negative vision of sexual difference feminism (whilst opposing its forgetfulness of the historicity of domination) and (b) gender constructionism (whilst opposing its complicity with the neoliberal matrix of socialization) with (c) an acknowledgement that the condition of irreconcilable obliteration and incomprehensibility is the condition in which the other, here Tristana, starts to speak and to articulate herself. Now, the moment of articulation is the moment in which a person or even a community is seduced by a possibility of a better life, the possibility of inclusion, of being considered.

The desire for consideration is a seductive and captivating one because it multiplies itself and reproduces itself in life by making life liveable. This is the moment in which the fury resulting from primordial and irreversible obliteration transforms itself into its opposite: it generates pleasure and hope. In Tristana's case, the invitation to engage oneself in the dynamics of power and social change is coextensive with the distribution of hope in conditions of an unconditional hopelessness imposed by a radical female-male asymmetry. The seduction for a better life and for consideration, the contest of power structures, the pleasures, the multiplication of sexual practices, the calculation of interdependencies and the establishment of alliances, all take place in and involve the concrete field of everyday existence, the actuality of existential presence. Articulation is this particular form of seduction, combining and rearranging the dynamics of the power with an embrace of everyday life, and a tolerance of what is real.

Amputation and finiteness

Although speaking, acting, and verbalizing experience is always a discursive occurrence, the obligation to speak one's own experiences ensues from a primordial obliteration. Articulating – that is, putting into words as well as reconnecting and rearranging the socio-material conditions of existence – embraces many different pre-verbal and non-verbal forms of action, but none of them is pre-discursive. The notion that there is a primordial obliteration at work is not a metaphorical one. That is, we are not invoking a transcendental understanding of language, but rather suggesting that 'language has been granted too much power' (Barad, 2003, p. 801). In order to discern the importance and the limits of a theory of articulation, we have to link the discursive phenomenon of articulation to the materiality of this primordial obliteration, and to make this link without relapsing into nostalgic explanations which mystify as they evoke a presence 'beyond.'

The primordial obliteration which obliges articulation is based on a contradictory state of being: on the one hand, there is the very bodily feeling of the necessity and the yearning to be present and to intervene; on the other, there is the sheer impossibility of being present because of your bodily shape, a passport, a language, lineage, religion, race, or your engagements in 'remaking geographies and scales' (Tsing, 2000, p. 350). The concept of articulation is important to the extent that it unveils moments of intervention, but in so doing much is overlooked. Failures to manipulate power are occluded by the concept of articulation. Here we are thinking of mundane failures which occur simply because you fail to make the right choices at the right time, or perhaps because in order to make the right choices you would have to change in ways that are alien to your body and habitus, or because your limbs are just not strong enough to cross the borders into the glorious new world, your skills do not allow you to use high-tech weapons, your face is not white enough, your pronunciation is unclear and distorted by a strong accent – not to mention the whole problem of language politics (Pennycook, 2001). The theory of articulation is based on the very liberal notion that, *in principle*, we are able to reconfigure existing relations and to enable a better life. And of course many of us are. But not all. This basic impossibility of the problem of articulation does not disrupt, but it is inextricably interwoven into, the liberal project (especially in its neoliberal expression).

The impossibility of articulation stems from the fact that disarticulation and effacement are necessary elements of any project of articulation. There is always more to experience than can be put to work. That which remains unarticulated – World 2 – is nothing more and nothing less than bodies and experiences which simply do not match. But World 2 is not an attempt to incorporate these bodies into our discourses. Don't panic: 'The fears of Nietzsche and Scheler actually were not warranted. Our slave morality will not triumph' (Améry, 1964/1980, p. 81). World 2 is neither against articulation nor for more articulation. It simply shows that there is yet much to be done. The significance of articulation is that it cultivates memory and perception and a feeling for questions of hegemony. Its impossibility is that bodies do not always facilitate, they are weak, unwilling, resisting, vulnerable, uncertain. Fanon captures this:

> And then the occasion arose when I had to meet the white man's eyes. An unfamiliar weight burdened me. The real world challenged my claims. In the white world the man of colour encounters

difficulties in the development of his bodily schema. Consciousness of the body is solely a negating activity ... The body is surrounded by an atmosphere of certain uncertainty. (Fanon, 1967, p. 110)

Later in the same chapter called 'The fact of blackness' Fanon continues:

> I was responsible at the same time for my body, for my race, for my ancestors. I subjected myself to an objective examination, I discovered my blackness, my ethnic characteristics; and I was battered down by tom-toms, cannibalism, intellectual deficiency, fetishism, racial defects, slave ships, and above all else, above all: "Sho' good eatin'." On that day, completely dislocated, unable to be abroad with the other, the white man, who unmercifully imprisoned me, I took my self far off from my own presence, far indeed, and made myself an object. What else could it be for me but an amputation, an excision, a haemorrhage that spattered my whole body with black blood? (Fanon, 1967, p. 112)

Fanon introduces the metaphor of amputation in order to describe how obliteration is always present as a bodily feeling, steering your movements through discourse, geopolitical positions, socio-cultural spaces, how obliteration makes you vulnerable to exclusion. For Fanon this bodily feeling is of course the effect of the white man's discourse, but at the same time it is more than a construction, it is a 'fact,' governing being in the world.

Tristana returns to the house of Don Lope when she is ill. She asks Horacio, her ephemeral lover and the promise for a better life, to bring her back. But why? Why is she orchestrating her own subordination, the amputation of her own desire? Under the pressure of the obligation to speak Tristana initiates acts of liberation against the masculinist economy in which she is embedded during her life in Don Lope's house. These acts could have been partially successful in initiating change, but what kind of change? As soon as we perform freedom we participate in the regulation of society, we participate in the reformation of structures of domination. We know that feminism is not feminism, we know that there are feminisms which show their complicity with different modes of oppression: class, colonial, racist, homophobic. We know that well-intended actions can contribute to repressive regulatory state institutions (de Lauretis, 1987, 1988). Similarly, if we investigate the cultural studies-discourse we see how attention to cultural differences always entails a double movement. It reconstitutes a particular (minority) community as a specific form of collective subject, casting it as capable of claiming inclusion in social and political regimes of power (Rosaldo, 1993). And, it simultaneously renders a community amenable to management through its codification (Marvakis & Papadopoulos, 2002). Researching cultural difference is a Janus-faced enterprise: it empowers social communities at the same time as fabricating knowledge which enables the management of social domains of existence where minorities and cultural communities are present. Notably, knowledge of cultural difference serves not only as an instrument for regulation from above but also as the means for the self-regulation and the ordering of social relations of the communities themselves.

If the obligation to speak and to articulate experience is nothing other than the involvement in contested power relations with uncertain outcomes, there can be no guarantees that communities (or individuals) acting under this logic of remain clean, indisputable or morally pure. We are not objecting to this involvement in power and politics. Neither do we advocate a 'proper' process for engaging in power relations. Rather, our concern is to take seriously the failures, defeats and injuries incurred through positioning in such relations. Moreover, we want to argue that, although the cultural studies approach to the problem of experience is indispensable, it is insufficient for understanding experience. Tristana's move into her own subordination is one example, but there are many.

The moment we want to take seriously is the moment when you resign from your position, terminate your efforts, relinquish claims to power, abandon hope. And even if this only lasts for a short time, it reveals the vulnerability of your embodiment, it reveals how you are other than a social agent, and it reveals experience which is excluded from the political project of articulation. We cannot begin to understand why Tristana asks Horacio to bring her back to Don Lope without turning to this moment. Tristana participates in the amputation of her own desire because she feels this very moment of finiteness returning her to the most contained and disgusting realm of coerced subordination. Of course it is not that outside of Don Lope's environment Tristana has escaped the masculinist economy of oppression. But what happens is that Tristana's illness and amputation interrupt any possibility for hope and desire.

There is a fear of the finiteness of the self, of its incompleteness, transitory nature, its imperfection which multiplies the effects of the primordial obliteration already inscribed on the body. What turns obliteration into the obligation to speak is that the will to interfere and the will for a better life are always situated in the here-and-now, in your immediate lifeworld. But the obligation to speak is transformed into acts of radical negation at moments when you lose yourself in weakness and helplessness, when you are absorbed by the suddenness of life events (Bohrer, 1998), when you lose not only your capacity to play the game, but also to hope.

It is this being-towards-death which makes obliteration visible and painful. We already know why articulation is good. The point is that it is helpful to know when articulation is impossible: in the ontology of finitude and temporality, articulation is impossible when obliteration re-emerges and violently disrupts any hope of seduction into a better life. In this moment experience entails much more than that which is given in the immediate experience of one's own presence, it becomes fluid. It can go so far as to involve the experience of dissolution and death, its own negation.

Survival, loss of hope and the inevitability of disparity

Extinction is not a singular event in the geopolitical and cultural mechanics of domination. What is particularly important for this argument is, not the act of extinction as physical effacement, but the lived experience of damaged survival. It is in conditions of damaged survival that certain communities or individuals devote themselves to a discourse of negativity. The logic of negation is caused by the loss of hope. The opposite of obliteration and silence is not articulation, but hope. Hope does not overcome obliteration, but makes it possible to inhabit a lifeworld marked by obliteration. Thus, the loss of hope amounts to the amputation of desire – or better – it is when desire is defined directly by obliteration. The amputation of Tristana's leg is the physical pronouncement of the amputation of her desire, of her capacity to revolt, of her hope for revolt. It is this state of being that brings her directly to acts of radical negation: obliteration, loss of hope, radical negativity. And in the same way that the transformation of hope into mere 'thingness' leads Tristana to operate in terms of a radical negativity and to allow Don Lope to die, the loss of hope for cultural communities leads to radical incommensurability and to the inevitable disparity between the world and World 2.

On being thrown into a concrete geopolitical or social situation, communities or individuals encounter the world as an opaque horizon which gradually – through the projection of their fantasies, hopes, and desires – attains shape and structure. This moment of structuring one's lifeworld, this very moment of imagination is always anchored in one's own specific, contingent perspective. The contingency of one's own experience of the world renders imagination subject to constant change. Imagination of the world is constantly under threat from events which interrupt attempts at realization and push communities or individuals to conceive of themselves as being-towards-death (be it a military campaign, a financial crisis, torture, poverty, political oppression, or a serious illness such as that of Tristana). In conditions of pervasive structural inequalities and asymmetries, in conditions where primordial obliteration systematically undermines any attempt at successfully playing the game of power, any damaging event undercuts the capacity to project and to structure the opaque horizon of the future. Thus, the loss of hope and the amputation of desire mean that imagination becomes an individual affair, incapable of being shared with others. You are encapsulated in your own experiences, you are stuck with fixed interpretations of your experiences. Experience becomes a given, its continuity between bodies and events is threatened (see Chapter 8). Hope and imagination are relational qualities of being-in-the-world and of experiencing the world. They exist only – continuing the assault on the Heideggerian terminology – in the realm of the 'Mit-Sein', being-with. Thus, this moment on which obliteration works is not the point of articulation but the moment when hope and co-constructive imagination are shared. It is the moment when experience stops being an individual affair, and becomes continuous. This is what Tristana seeks after leaving Toledo with Horacio and this is what Tristana loses when she returns. Of course her primordial obliteration, her trajectory in the realm of a masculinist economy of desire, the deep incommensurability of her femininity with any of its given articulations cannot be 'solved' or questioned. What she questions with her practice of articulation is the encapsulation of her desire and any notion that her imagination is untranslatable. The most valuable and remarkable moment of the studies-discourse (and of a theory of articulation) is exactly that: they render the horizon of our praxis amenable to common inscriptions and projections.

Thus, hope and imagination have nothing to do with redemption or salvation. In a world pre-formatted in terms of a primordial obliteration, salvation and healing are meaningless superstitions. Hope means having the ability to hope with others (individuals or communities). And the loss of hope foregrounds the incommensurability of experience.

Tristana's return to Don Lope's house under the pressure of a life threatening event places her in a situation of inevitable and growing disparity between her expectations and her life conditions. In a similar way, cultural communities follow paths which become increasingly difficult to share with other communities. What we experience is not so much a scarcity of hope and imagination but an unbounded incommensurability of hope between different regions and cultural spaces.

This incommensurability does not refer to an insurmountable divergence between the semantic or discursive means used by different communities to understand the world. The theory of articulation is particularly good at encompassing geopolitical constellations of similarity and difference, of intercultural exchanges and displacements, of unfinished 'histories of people in transit, variously empowered and compelled' (Clifford, 1997, p. 2). The incommensurability between the world and World 2 is not the outcome of a shortage in interactions and translations between different locales and contexts. It is the result of a growing incapacity and hesitancy to share imagination and hope. It is the result of blocking the flow and continuity of experience, closing it down to a mere individual and transparent capacity. Forging localities from very different materials, intersecting different cultural paths, communicating different notions of belonging, all these become increasingly typical of communication processes in an increasingly interconnected social landscape. There is no lack of communication. But there is often a shortcoming in the ways we conceive future, its promises, its speed, and its anomalies. As Ang (1997, p. 58) says, although 'there are no longer cultural incommensurabilities in such a hybridized world' there is a form of incommensurability that 'pertains to the residue of the irreducibly particular that cannot, ultimately, be shared.' This form of incommensurability refers, not to the semantics and politics of intercultural transactions, but to how we imagine the world in which we can live. The worlds of the other are understandable, at least partly, but meaningless. You cannot imagine yourself there. They exist as fictive names made up for novels you never read, as pure facts in these thick world almanacs which you find regularly in Safeway's shelves or on old postcards in the flea markets of the metropolises. Often you encounter them in the subtitles of today's headlines. The feature pages of the *New York Times* dedicate articles to these worlds now and then. But you never read them and you will never go. These worlds are meaningless because they have nothing to do with your hopes. This is the disparity between the world we know and in which we dwell and World 2.

World 2

Tristana's radical negativity which leads her to refuse to summon a doctor for Don Lope when he is dying could be read as her triumph over her oppressor (Edwards, 1995; Partridge, 1995; Tsuchiya, 1990). But this enthusiasm seems to be misplaced. Tristana continues to exist in a society which is and will continue to be overtly regulated by a masculinist economy of gender relations and sexual desire. The death of Don Lope – the morally inevitable death of Don Lope – leaves her carrying the shame of his practices; he is no longer there able to take up the responsibility for his acts, to restore, to re-make. Feeling embarrassment for the other's deeds is a very agonizing emotion – you can not easily get rid of it. But in addition, very soon after these events (the filmic time covers a period of six years, 1929–1935) the Spanish Civil War will ignite (and the conservative and catholic Toledo will be a scene of heavy fights between the Republican forces and Franco's army). In 1939 the Popular Front and the anarchist movement will surrender to General Franco's army, an army provided with weapons by Hitler's Germany and Mussolini's Italy. The Spanish civil war, this prelude to World War II, will end with the establishment of a dictatorship which lasted 36 years. And it is not only because Buñuel made the film during the Franco regime with all the expected difficulties (Aranda, 1976; Higginbotham, 1988), that Tristana's story seems to comment on the social mechanics of Spanish conservatism and its genealogy. The film is the negative story of an oppressive society written in the language of its cultural practices – an enterprise which characterizes Buñuel's cinematic writing ever since *L'Age d'or* (1930) and is in the same vein as de Sade's *Justine* and Goya's *Los Caprichos*. In the language of cultural negativism, *Tristana*'s microcosm seems to contain *in nuce* central aspects of the socio-cultural workings which resulted in the defeat of the Republican forces and the Spanish anarchist movement. In this sense, Buñuel's cinematography could be seen as a minuscule fragment of a project which is not intended, in Orgel's words,

> to tell a history of how anarchism was repressed (although it surely was), but rather to show how it was produced in popular, political, and intellectual imaginations as a particularly dangerous kind of social movement and the effects this had not only for the movement itself, but also for more general understandings of social resistance. (Orgel, 2001, p. 2)

Reading *Tristana's* experience of radical negativity only as an act of liberation and articulation fails to take account of the violence which pervades the asymmetrical configuration between the sexes, an asymmetry which was and continues to be persistent in Tristana's life. In contrast, it is possible to read Tristana's radical negativity as unveiling how this enduring asymmetry uncovers worlds and opens forces, undoing articulation. In this reading, Tristana experiences the exhilaration of liberation not at the moment of Don Lope's death but earlier, after recovering from the operation when she seems to have decided that there is no possibility for action other than negativity. We see Tristana standing on the balcony of her bedroom, leaning on her clutches, opening her 'dressing gown in a haughty and imperious manner' (Buñuel & Alejandro, 1971, p. 133). The camera presents her from below as a grinning mutilated Virgin Mary statue exercising blasphemy and pleasure over the deprived male gaze. Incompleteness, incomprehensibility, negativity become sacral. Consecrated finiteness, this is World 2.

The claim of a theory of articulation and of the 'studies-discourse' is that they can conceptualize contemporary cultural transactions and understand the affairs of under-represented communities and social actors. And of course a theory of articulation can certainly contribute here. But when events violently dislocate social actors from their attempts at political enunciation and social emancipation, a different perspective comes into view. It is a perspective which is almost ineffable, a perspective which reveals a second world resisting its discursification. It reveals also a surplus of experience which is there as a potential but resists its transformation into a fixed and transparent meaning of the self. World 2 is a world which revolts without saying why, it is a world which exceeds any of its given positive articulations in the coordinates of a neoliberal matrix of existence. World 2 is an insurgency against the idea that we can all emancipate. Don Lope invokes the natural law of the free individual: 'Passion must be free. It is the natural law. No chains, no signatures, no benedictions' (Buñuel & Alejandro, 1971, p. 2). It is this liberal logic on which he grounds his whole aesthetic of life and existence and through which, in the final analysis, he cannot realize himself. Tristana revolts against this. World 2 opposes this fantasy of an overall and limitless emancipation inherent in the mythology of liberalism. World 2 is enclosed in finiteness, temporality and historical time. It always carries with it a centre, a reference to obliterated meanings. World 2 is elusive but usually very close. Often it is just an effect of our own disorientation. Distortion is always there, sometimes deceptively faraway, but always rooted in your materiality. Moreover, it produces materiality and life in unprecedented ways (a productivity which is elucidated in Haraway's [1995] cyborg manifesto, for example). In World 2 there is always a there – a body which does not help, a place which you desire, a land which is ending, an experience which cannot be articulated.

Certainly, there is a value in approaching experience as the stuff of articulation, that is, in invoking a (necessary) discourse of excessive visualization, of new options, new paths of action and enunciation, new connections to other experiences, transparency and presence. This is all fine. The problem is that there is more to experience than can be elucidated by this discourse. World 2 is shy. World 2 is always elsewhere. In *The Black Atlantic*, Gilroy (1993) delineates life as lived in the realm of double consciousness. World 2 is a multiplication of that, it has countless 'consciousnesses', limitless experiences. World 2 is marked by experience which breaks with the fetish of language, meaning, and individualism. In the next chapter, we will take up this issue and will start to conceptualize experience as an inherently collective affair. The final chapters of the book will develop an account of experience which not only acknowledges but also moves beyond the theoretical legacy of cultural studies, described in the present chapter. In Chapter 6 and Chapter 8 in particular, we will develop a framework of politics which takes account of the unfinished project of articulation and the immanent potential of World 2. We will call this framework of action and experience outside politics, that is, politics which do not simply envisage the development of alternative hegemonic strategies but attempt to thoroughly rearrange the conditions on which our political projects and visions are formulated. This is, in fact, also the political project of World 2. World 2 is not a counter-discourse, it is not hegemonic, it eschews alliances and alignments. But World 2 is not really opposing the theme of hegemonic politics; it just takes it to the end (and beckons to post-liberal culture). World 2 is not the other story of experience or the critical story of modernity and post-modernity, it is simply the negative story of modernity and post-modernity. World 2 is a project without emancipative strategy but with fanaticism and 'impulsive' (Adorno, 1983) humanism: World, which is understood, is negated. World 2 is unexpected, violent, contentious, inventive. World 2 is a world against stable traditions, be they mainstream or critical (or their derivatives). World 2 is the negation of the contemporary world, a contemporary world which like Toledo – as Buñuel has said of a city once loved and now deprived of mystery and intimacy (Aranda, 1976, p. 241) – 'is old and stinks of piss.'

Part II

Working with a Moving Target in Social Research

3
The Collective Subject of Memory-work

The problem of politically engaged research

We would hazard a guess that, although academics may not have self-consciously set out to master this particular skill (and may even see academic research as standing in opposition to 'sensationalist journalism'), many working in the humanities and social sciences can now write a good headline. Particularly one announcing disaster. *Feminist accused of sexual harassment!* shouted Jane Gallop (1997), when she needed to unhinge the way feminist critiques of sexual politics had morphed into moralizing criticisms of sex. *Caught in the neoliberal noose* we wrote ourselves in analysing the predicament of people taking responsibility for decisions about unpredictable and relatively untested HIV treatments. And, as we try to see beyond these headlines, we find a throng of exclamations: *No escape! Structuralists and poststructuralists alike trapped by the logic of our own theories and actions! Fools to have thought we could ever offer anything anyhow! Complicit Interpellations! Tainted academics further embroiled as they try to stop uncontrollable regulation!* There is striking futility both railed against and proliferated in these banners. Reading through ever more careful analyses, and listening to increasingly tightly crafted lectures which return us to our current predicament cast as a colonizing and immoveable force, we have to ask: *Does it have to be this way?*

As discussed earlier, the problem is that the terms social researchers use (and criticize) to understand the emergence and operation of contemporary modes of self-regulation and experience – agency, autonomy, responsibility – serve to proliferate and strengthen the forces we are trying to rework. In the previous chapter, we argued that the political project of articulation initiated primarily by cultural studies seems

49

to run into the dead end of privileging a very particular form of experience and neglecting other forms which challenge the very foundation of our current political praxis. This difficulty is more apparent in and crucial for discursive approaches and governmentality studies where even attempts to make the domain of subjectivity the focus of inquiry can be understood as an extension of neoliberal governance and regulation (see Chapter 1). Although these conceptual tools seem to offer little in the way of understanding how we might actively participate in initiating radical socio-political change today, they are defended on the grounds that they accurately capture the machinations of power in our societies (and this is particularly apt for governmentality studies). But this melancholy has a conservative appeal – it lets us off the hook of working out how to act, of risking the uncertain move beyond our particular interest to one more general, of developing connections between people and interests, of actively working on the political dimensions of social research. In this chapter, we approach the broad terrain of the relationship between research and politics from the viewpoint of methodology.

If we accept that social research is not simply a matter of representation, but involves (knowingly or unknowingly) intervening in and constructing our current social and political conditions, we are then presented with a set of questions about how this happens in the process of researching experience. In this chapter, we turn to these questions by discussing a specific methodology, memory-work (Haug, 1987, 1992). Hence this chapter further elucidates the production of the written memories and analyses what we discuss in Chapter 1, Chapter 4 and Chapter 5. However, we have devoted a specific chapter to this methodology because it provides a useful point of departure for considering anti-foundationalist approaches to experience. We outline the rationale and method of memory-work, emphasizing the way it *undoes* the subject of linear, causal, biographical narratives. Memory-work invites consideration of experience as collectively produced, a notion which is foregrounded in Haug and other's (1987) original introduction to the method. Two decades later, it is both necessary and possible to reconsider and rework the notion of collectivity (the focus of Chapter 6). In turning to memory-work here, we are not trying to advocate its use on the grounds that it is a superior methodology for researching experience – memory-work is not a fixed method, rather it was envisaged as an open set of tools, tools which would require replacing and refining in response to different configurations of the both experience and the socio-political realm. Thus, memory-work offers fertile ground for considering the relationships between experience, social research methodologies and socio-political change.

Power in and of social research

Because social researchers are involved in a set of practices which construct and regulate objects and people even as they aim to liberate, there is a need to consider the power both in and of social research. How are researchers complicit in the regulation of people's lives? Can research avoid simply reproducing versions of reality which it set out to resist or rework? Is it possible to intervene in forms of regulation in which we are already complicit in order to produce new objects which reflect different visions of social reality, past, present and future? These are all questions about how we can work with rather than shy away from the political dimensions of research, and they are certainly not new (for example, Wetherell & Potter, 1992). Notwithstanding its vital importance, the ongoing discussion about the question of power in research – how power is played out between researchers and researched – risks inadvertently drowning out an equally important focus: the power of social research. In the literature on social research methodology, discussions about techniques for intervening in the power relations inherent in social research (for example, for empowering participants) are common (for instance, Massat & Lundy, 1997). Less attention has been devoted to the relationship between social research and ways of intervening in the socio-political realm beyond the research process itself.

Any attempt to harness and work with the power of social research introduces the problem of expertise. If academic expertise is a means of exercising power and influence over others (not only those who participate in research, but those who constitute its audience) the past two decades have seen a proliferation of attempts to develop research methods designed to share power and acknowledge different forms of expertise (for example, Lather & Smithies, 1997). The imperative to acknowledge different forms of expertise and to involve different actors in the production of academic knowledge is evident well beyond discussions of methodology – consider the increasing move towards funding researchers who involve research partners (such as government departments, commercial entities or community agencies) in the planning and design of their work. This important shift foregrounds the difficult question of representation: is social research a means of representing everyday experience first and foremost? From a methodological viewpoint, many have responded to this question by attempting to identify methods which promise the best possible means of representing experience (for example, Clandinin & Connelly, 2000). When questions of method revolve around how best to frame research participants involvement so that the research can 'give voice' to their authentic experience (for example, Hones, 1998), the foundational notion of experience being invoked limits possibilities for understanding sociopolitical transformation (Butler, 1992). Discussion of these difficulties has lead to the recognition that, instead of simply positing social research as a neutral vehicle for the inclusion of disempowered groups, it offers *particular* and limited modes of representation, and it may well involve shaping and changing the identities of those to which it aims to give voice (for example, Prior, 1997). If we consider the power involved in social research as productive, as opposed to simply oppressive, it is evident that research can create new modes of exclusion in the same moment that it enables new forms of inclusion.

Social researchers have embraced discourse as an object of social research, in part, because this move provides an exit point of sorts from the quagmire of representation. Here, research produces knowledge of discourse not knowledge of people or subjects. For example, focus group discussions with men can be analysed with a view to what they can illuminate about discourses of masculinity, not the actual men participating in the discussions (Wetherell & Edley, 1999). Men's talk is a pathway to discourse, rather than to their authentic experiences of masculinity. In this sense discourse provides a way of avoiding the problem of representation (and, by implication, the problem of expert knowledge of subjective experience). But it does not, in and of itself, deepen researchers' efforts to understand or work with the power of research: a melancholic uptake of discourse can serve as a justification for avoiding this problem altogether. Memory-work is interesting in this regard, because the methodology requires that researchers and researched approach experience as contestable so that they can participate in the rethinking and reworking their present socio-political conditions.

The rationale for memory-work

Memory-work does not provide a neat solution to these questions about the links between academic work and the broader social and political realm. It does go some way towards providing a way of working with experience without falling into the trap of defending and affirming experience *per se*. And this is a real trap for those who are interested in approaching experience as more than a by-product of discourse. In contrast, memory-work is an attempt to work with experience in such a way as to question the connections between experience, subjects and modes of appropriation. Experience is simultaneously envisaged as socially produced and amenable to being reworked or re-interpreted.

The women who developed memory-work, Andresen, Bünz-Elfferding, Haug, Hauser, Lang, Laudan, Lüdenabbm Neur, Nemitz, Neihoff, Prinz, Räthzel, Scheu and Thomas, came together in the eighties as a group of German, Marxist feminists wanting to research female sexualization (Haug, 1987). The fundamental difficulty they identified with the work they were encountering – be it psychoanalytic accounts of feminine sexuality or Foucauldian genealogies – was a tendency to apply theory to experience, to subsume experience under theoretical positions. The effect of prioritizing theory over experience like this is to distort and flatten the multiplicity and diversity of experience. They disputed the transcendent understanding of theory implicit in this relation, and the positioning of researchers as inexplicably free of their own subjective experiences in the moment of theory production.

Inadequate accounts of experience perpetuate the problematic opposition between objectivity and subjectivity. In contrast, 'objectivity' can be understood as dependent on subjectivity (Deutscher, 1983). Haug and others were already working in a Marxist tradition which disputed this opposition: from a Marxist perspective subjectivity is understood as produced through and working on the objective conditions of existence (Holzkamp, 1984; Tolman, 1994). They aimed to build on this insight by challenging the opposition between objective, transcendent theory and subjective, bounded experience. This meant returning to experience in the attempt to cultivate different approaches to the relationship between experience and knowledge. So, they took experience as a starting point – of sorts.

They wanted to unhinge and destabilize entrenched power relations between objective researchers and subjective researched. So they enacted the impossibility of subject-object distinctions by making themselves both the researchers and researched of their own work (Willig, 2000). They began to theorize their own experience and to devise tools for doing this. They saw experience as collectively produced, and to facilitate identification of and intervention into these processes, they decided to do work as a group. They wanted to do research which had an explicit political value, which enabled intervention in problematic modes and processes of sexualization. Their goal was to initiate social change rather than document it, or bemoan its absence. But why intervene by taking experience as a point of departure; an alternative would be to start with social practices, structures or discourses? Importantly, they thought of individuals as actively appropriating social structures. Rather than being passively determined by our social contexts – we actively take them on, make sense of them, weave ourselves into them and in so doing become who we are. So the constraints of the social realm cannot be thought independently of our experience with them. Haug and others were interested in 'experience as [the] lived practice ... of a self constructed identity'; they understood experience to be simultaneously 'structured by expectations, norms and values' and to contain 'an element of resistance, a germ of oppositional cultural activity' (1987, p. 42). As with Hall's (1981) insistence on the insights of both the culturalist and structuralist/post-structuralist approaches to experience, memory-work involves working with the tension between these two positions (but the attempt to do this is not without its problems, as discussed below). Whilst their articulation of memory-work is bound to the terms of identity and resistance, we will be arguing that the methodological tools they developed are useful for interrogating the dissolution and fragmentation of identity (Clifford, 2000).

Haug and others were part of a much broader move to recognize the personal as political. They had participated in the feminist consciousness-raising movement, and wanted to build on it. In this regard, they did not see themselves as discovering or revealing the previously excluded personal sphere, they went beyond the call to simply identify the personal as political. Rather, they recognized that as researchers they were not providing a neutral channel for representing the personal in political terms, but they were involved in constructing the relationship between personal and political realms. Memory-work is an attempt, not to reveal the political dimensions of experience, but to put experience to work by translating it in ways which intervene in the production of socio-political conditions. That is, the political efficacy of research hinges on the particular ways in which it enables and enacts translation between the personal and public. As they began to draw on their own experiences in undertaking research, they identified concepts and processes which work against effective translation. Foremost amongst these is the notion of determinism – social or psychological. If they lapsed into explaining their experiences as determined by the past, they found that they closed down ways of thinking about and translating between public and personal realms. Rather than think of the subject or self as the sum of his or her experiences, they countered any notion of the past as causal 'of today's person' (1987, p. 46–7). Instead they set out to refuse the compression of diverse experiences into evidence that we have always been becoming who we are now.

So although Haug and others wanted to draw on their experiences, they foregrounded many of the hazards entailed in doing this. In particular, they were aware of the risk of nailing people down to the accounts they give of experience, fixing identities and subjectivities in the process. This meant devising ways of theorizing experience which open possibilities for rethinking who we are now (tools which, we want to suggest, might be extended and used to even refuse the question), for asking how people appropriate the social realm, and for initiating change by identifying and devising different modes of appropriation. To the extent that biographical and autobiographical accounts offer linear, causal explanations of individuals as products of our past experiences (Phillips, 1999), they tend to occlude the very social processes which need to be interrogated and to shore up a notion of the subject that memory-work seeks to challenge – as coherent, unitary and masterful – making the present seem inevitable. So there is a sense in which biographical coherence needs to be treated with suspicion as its very logic is afforded by the fact that the narrative tends to reproduce clichéd notions of subjectivity or identity and occludes elements of experience which are not captured in normative accounts.

Whilst Haug criticized biography *per se* as the misguided means of offering overly psychologized, linear, coherent explanations, this is not to say that there is either a theoretical or methodological necessity to approach biography in this particular way. For example, the idea of biography and autobiography as a process of excavating interior, psychological space undertaken for the purpose of accessing the 'truth' of the subject is subverted in the (largely feminist) genres of ficto-criticism, autobiographical theorizing and anti-narrative (for example, Gallop, 1988; Probyn, 1993; Waldby, 1995; Gillian Rose, 1995). In Chapter 8, we draw on Sebald's fictive biographies of emigrants' lives to elucidate the singular, dispersed and continuous dimensions of experience. However, acknowledging the limitations of linear, biographical accounts for theorizing socio-political change poses a fundamental challenge to another methodological approach common in social research: narrative analysis (for example, Kleinman, 1988; Riessman, 1993; Frank, 1995). To the extent that narrative approaches invite participants to 'tell their stories' and involve giving linear explanations of subjectivities, they occlude understanding of experience which may appear meaningless from a given perspective, but which nonetheless may materialize in significant ways (for example, consider Tristana's radical negativity, discussed in Chapter 2, an experience which cannot be apprehended through a politics of articulation). Because Haug and others were interested in theorizing experience for the purpose of understanding and intervening in processes of change, they devised tools which effectively challenge any notion of the individual subject as unitary, fixed, or determined.

The subject of memory-work

It is evident then, that in contrast to social research which contributes to an image of the person as fixed, unitary, bounded, self-knowing – that is, a phallocentric subject (Irigaray, 1985a) – in memory-work it is the fluidity and malleability of experience which is of interest. Co-researchers bring experience to the group, not in order to assert a particular version of subjectivity (for example, being a woman means being subjected to a patriarchal regime), but as a means of questioning the necessity and the construction of aspects of subjectivity (for example, in what ways does the appropriation of sexuality affirm or question this patriarchal regime). To the extent that memory-work avoids casting experience as a fixed property of the individual, the process can be a means of challenging hegemonic notions of subjectivity, not just in the analysis of empirical data but in their production (Gillies et al., 2004; Gillies et al., 2005).

The subject of memory-work is distinctly non-unitary. Unlike many humanist depictions of agentic subjects, memory-work does not assume that the subject's interiority is transparent to him or herself. This is evident in the practice of memory-work: although the idea that 'I know myself ' is challenged (for example, through the practices of writing in the third person, of taking the gaps and absences in memories as objects for analysis, of insisting that authors do not have the ultimate authority of interpretation over their own memories), it simultaneously allows the functional value of claims to 'know myself' (for example, in affirming the value of negating others' inadequate interpretations and in emphasizing the importance of making oneself better understood, see below). Rather than interrupt the 'pure' practice of representation, this ambiguity of positioning, knowing yet not knowing oneself, can fuel the group analysis of memories (Stephenson, Kippax & Crawford, 1996). In this sense, memory-work can be thought as enabling a strategic use of the self-knowledge for the purposes of ultimately questioning the phallocentric, individual, unitary subject and developing a socio-historical account of particular modes of relating to and knowing oneself (Spivak [in an interview with Rooney], 1994). Self-knowledge is always questionable.

Generalizing from experience

Haug and others (1987) argued that because experience is collectively produced, a specific experience is potentially generalizable. They did not mean that a given experience could be directly applied to other individuals' experience, or that two different experiences would have the same meaning. Rather, because subjective experience already contains objective socio-political conditions, analysing it can illuminate our understanding of these general conditions. The epistemological underpinnings of this insistence on generalizability can be better understood if we consider how positivist and post-positivist science have colonized the notions of generalizability employed in social science. From a positivist perspective, scientific laws are generalizable to the extent that they describe relationships between abstract entities, that is, aggregates which have been abstracted from a number of cases. These laws do not account for the actual relationships between unique cases. Hence cases which cannot be explained by a particular law can be explained away by the fact that there are 'always exceptions to the rule', their existence does not necessarily weaken the rule nor do they necessitate further interrogation (in fact, many statistical tests cannot be undertaken until 'outlier' or exceptional cases have been excluded from the data set). But this specific notion of generalizability only flourished in the early 20th century following the proliferation of statistics and positivist science. Previously, generalization was commonly understood as arising from either the theoretical or empirical interrogation of the convergences and divergences between particular cases, cases which were thought to be different instances of universal laws. In this understanding, universal laws cannot be formulated without attention to the specificities of real cases and it is exactly this specificity which they seek to explain. Importantly, here generalization is understood not as a move 'from the concrete to the abstract, but from the abstract to the concrete: the equation of the abstract and general is rejected from the outset. The ultimate aim [is] ... to start with the abstract and make it general by tying it back to the concrete' (Tolman, 1994, p. 139). It is in this sense that memory-work involves interrogating the potentially generalizable dimensions of experience.

The practice of memory-work

In order to undertake politically meaningful work through researching experience, Haug and others felt that they had to work against everyday ways of naturalizing experience. They had to find new ways around their empathy with each other, as well as their moralizing reactions to the accounts offered in the group, both responses which inhibited their ability to question the taken for granted. As mentioned, memory-work is not supposed to be a fixed unchanging set of practices. But, to give a sense of what might be involved, we will use a set of guidelines drawn up by Crawford and others (Crawford, Kippax, Onyx, Gault & Benton, 1992) in their development of memory-work to research gender and emotion. Very basically, groups form out of a common interest in researching a topic, and meet regularly over a period of weeks, months or years, analysing a series of memories. The guidelines for writing memories are:

1. Write a memory
2. of a particular episode, action or event
3. in the third person
4. in as much detail as is possible, including even 'inconsequential' or trivial detail (it may be helpful to think of a key image, sound, taste, smell, touch)
5. but without importing interpretation, explanation or biography

(adapted from Crawford et al., 1992, p. 43).

The idea is to pick a 'cue' for remembering (for example, 'taking charge' as discussed in Chapter 1) and to write about a specific event, not a general account. This allows examination of the particular ways in which appropriation works, the points at which alternate meanings and practices are overlooked. It is also important not to go for the jugular, to try to avoid really obvious cues which are likely to evoke stories that people are likely to be over-rehearsed (Haug suggests that 'losing one's virginity' is an example of this) or already coded as somehow foundational to one's identity ('being diagnosed HIV positive' may be an instance of this for many positive people). Writing in the third person is a curious technique. It is an invitation to co-researchers to observe aspects of themselves. Rather than simply perform or affirm coherent selves it serves to release people from self-justification, facilitating the emergence of apparently incoherent or meaningless details. So writing as 'she' or 'he' instead of 'I' enables co-researchers to entertain the possibility that their experiences could be understood and lived differently. Theoretically, this technique is linked to a critique of self-identity, of approaches to subjectivity which assume individual unitary coherence. By writing in the third person, memory-workers occupy at least two distinct positions – the 'she' of the written memory and the 'I' which re-emerges in the group discussion (Stephenson, Kippax & Crawford, 1996). This separation works to create a space to interrogate what otherwise might be treated as the sacred domain of the unitary individual. The rationale for concentrating on giving the fullest description possible, including apparently inconsequential details, and avoiding self-explanation is similar. The idea is to try to avoid producing a fully justified account which resists unravelling, but to include as many details as possible so that the processes of appropriation are amenable to analysis. Typically, groups decide on a cue, then go away and think and write about them, returning with the written memories.

Crawford and others have suggested the following guidelines for group discussions:

1. Each person expresses opinions and ideas about each memory in turn, and
2. looks for similarities and differences between the memories, and looks for links between the memories whose relation to each other is not immediately apparent. Each person should question particularly those aspects of the events which are not readily understandable, but she or he should (try) not to resort to autobiography or biography.
3. Each person identifies clichés, generalizations, contradictions, cultural imperatives, metaphors ... and
4. discusses theories, popular conceptions, sayings and images about the topic.
5. Finally, each person examines what is not written in the memories (but what might be expected to be), and
6. rewrites the memories

(adapted from Crawford et al., 1992, p. 45).

As memory-work groups discuss the accounts they try to realize their generalizability, to contest and develop the potential of abstract ideas and theories by linking them to concrete experiences. This means that the analysis proceeds by trying to denaturalize the account, to avoid reading it as part of the author's individual biography and to see it as a snapshot of the social processes through which we are constituted as particular kinds of selves. The notions of both memory as a psychological capacity and one's life-story as a linear, relatively coherent sequence of events are deconstructed. In stark contrast to the broader, foundational, turn to experience evident in much social and cultural research, Haug and others did not position experience as evidence. Experience is the matter to be questioned, the problem to be explained (Scott, 1991/1993). This is why experience is a starting point *of sorts*. It is not the unquestionable bedrock of subjectivity or identity (Butler, 1992).

Discussing personal experience in the group is a way of identifying and resisting the orthodoxies and self-censure in which co-researchers tend to engage. By focusing on the details of and gaps in the accounts, together with the value-laden language in which they are expressed, reading the memories involves an analysis of processes of appropriation. Hearing one's memory being discussed in the group can prompt authors to realize their 'communicative incompetences' – that is, the gaps and absences which lead to confusion and misreading, the turns of phrase which seem to invite particular evaluations. Rewriting the memories means that misreadings can be clarified. In addition, the group discussion can result in the incorporation of new insights into the rewritten memories. For these reasons, we have included this guideline about rewriting memories. In practice, the work discussed in this book did not extend to rewriting memories, for reasons to do with our different understanding of the potential of collectivity (as discussed in Chapter 6). We tried to clarify misunderstandings in the group discussion and to take account of these clarifications in the analysis, but we found that working with the accounts which had been written prior to the group discussion was a useful strategy for foregrounding and working with difference within the group (as discussed below).

The group discussion moves between the details and idiosyncrasies of the written accounts and the identification and interrogation of broader social norms, institutions, structures or discourses (Willig, 2000) which may elucidate the memories, or may constrain understanding of them. So, for example, in the discussions about 'taking charge' of medical regimens (see Chapter 1) accounts of the emotional difficulties and frustrations people confront were analysed in the light of the dominant discourses available for public discussion of HIV treatments (for example, discourses of medical authority and patient empowerment). The point of the analysis is not simply to identify the imprint of a hegemonic discourse on people's experience. The aim is to understand the available and emerging modes of appropriation and their effects, not only on everyday experience, but on shaping or interrupting particular discourses. For Haug and others, the effect of theorizing their experiences in this way, was that they began to think of themselves as 'living historically'. What they had previously thought to be the natural sequences of their lives, started to appear as historically constituted avenues for interpreting and managing the material and social realities in which they were immersed. They began to see themselves as women of their time and women able to act on their time.

In describing memory-work so far, we have been largely faithful to Haug and others' initial account (with the exception that the original authors do not draw on discursive accounts of experience where our account does). Yet, they anticipated that it would change in response to different research questions in different socio-political contexts (Johnston, 2001). The memory-work projects discussed here involved rethinking and reworking these tools. In part, this reworking was necessary because the memory-work groups of HIV positive people were initiated by researchers (in collaboration with community organizations) and, although people were invited to participate as co-researchers, they did not write about the group discussions. Thus, the responsibility for an important element of the analysis stayed with the original researchers. But more importantly, the work discussed here focused on a different topic, and took place in another hemisphere and a couple of decades after Haug and others devised the methodology. This meant that the experiences were being questioned in a very different political climate. In line with Haug and others' initial eschewal of methodological fetishism, we are not trying to 'refine' the tools on offer with the aim of elucidating procedural gaps or clarifying analytic procedures. Instead, we are stretching and breaking with the original formulation of memory-work in response to new or increasingly evident configurations of the socio-political domain – configurations which demand different ways of working on the connection between collectivity and socio-political change. Before discussing this further, we want to turn to the place of collectivity in the work of Haug and others.

The collective subject of memory-work

Memory-work jettisons three popular ways of conceiving of the subject in social and cultural research: the unitary, rational subject who can be understood in terms of his/her linear development; the aggregate subject, characterized and approached as a passive, mass of characteristics dispersed across a population (Danziger, 1990); and the psychoanalytic subject whose capacities for action and self-knowledge are hindered by unconscious repression. In their place, memory-work posits a collective subject. This subject is comprised of beings who, knowingly or unknowingly, strive to locate and relocate themselves historically and socially. On foregrounding collectivity, it becomes evident that the knowledge produced through theorizing experience is not about interiority, but pertains to the socio-political domain. Memory-work seeks to denaturalize the given of experience, to understand how we have come to be and how we could be otherwise. The focus is on tensions and shifts in collective experiences and the extent to which different possible transformations could bring about alternate futures.

Tensions in the subject/s of memory-work

Although memory-work posits and works with a fluid, non-identical subject, the subject of *Female Sexualization* differs from the radical subject of structuralist and post-structuralist movements which were occurring alongside the development of memory-work. Like the culturalists in social history and early cultural studies, Haug and others baulked at the proposition that the subject is spoken into being through language. For example, Haug repeatedly argues that written memories have the potential to reveal 'the ways in which individuals construct themselves into existing structures' (1987, p. 41), implicitly suggesting that the subject exists (in some sense) *before* the process of its social production. That is, in Haug's account the subject is being cast as ontologically prior to her own construction (Grosz, 1994). Adhering to this notion of the subject enables memory-workers to insist on the agency of subjects – a response to the overly passive, individualizing and depoliticizing notions of the subject which are not uncommon in social research. But, the difficulty with positing agency as an ontological capacity of subjects is that we lose the opportunity of understanding how agency itself is constructed and distributed in better or worse ways, more or less even (this question is further discussed in Chapter 4). We have suggested that these tensions over the extent to which the subject is socially and historically produced can be productive in the group discussions. However, when we follow them through into the notion of the collective subject entailed in memory-work, they become increasingly problematic.

The collective subject is fundamental to memory-work because it is thought to enable socio-political change. Change is possible because individuals actively appropriate social structures: the point of the analysis is to find the times and places where there may be, or have been, some flexibility in these structures and to consider ways in which this flexibility might be acted on. By arriving at shared understandings of the appropriations of social structures, Haug argues, memory-work enables resistance and reworking. The outcome of the process is the development of: 'a collective subject capable of resisting some of the harmful consequences of traditional divisions of labour' (Haug, 1987, p. 58). Socio-political change hinges on this 'collective subject', the 'we' of memory-work.

Crucially, the path to collective resistance is possible because individual experiences, the details of the memories, are potentially generalizable. For some (after decades of post-structuralist work), this claim to generalizability may seem at odds with an emphasis on the value of idiosyncratic details. It might be pointed out that attempts to generalize inevitably result in exclusion. However, whilst memory-work foregrounds the potentially problematic and exclusionary dimensions of universal notions, as discussed above it does not baulk at generalization. The political value of this stance hinges on the notion that 'politics begins not when you organize to defend an individual or particular or local interest, but when you organize to further the 'general' interest within which your particular interest may be represented' (Gillian Rose, 1996, p. 4). Memory-work refuses the severance of the particular from the general.

How does collectivity emerge and function in practice? Memory work is portrayed by Haug as a blurring of individual boundaries: 'Our work begins ... from the premise that the differences in our various areas of experience will have produced and will carry with them specific and distinct boundaries and separations, and that our collective work will make it possible to soften the edges of those rigid boundaries' (p. 58). By no means is collectivity equated with consensus. Discussions are described as 'vehement', and the process of rewriting is supposed to, among other things, provide an opportunity to explore and communicate across differences between group members. Exploring differences in memory-work groups generates rich material for further analysis but, in place of a 'blurring of boundaries', in practice we want to suggest that it is always possible that it can lead to the entrenchment of positions, the blank refusal to integrate alternate interpretations of memories. Does such intransigence figure as a threat to the notion of collective subjectivity? Although Haug describes disagreements, they do not feature as part of the workings of collectivity and there is an implicit suggestion that it is through their resolution that collectivity emerges. The emergence of a collective subject in the group discussions seems relatively unproblematic. When the resolution of conflicts is characterized as a matter of 'personal stability' (p. 57), it is implied that the absence of agreement results form personal instability, rather than the incommensurability of particular positions. There is no explicit discussion of how unresolved difference can be a productive part of the process.

The barmaid's pleasure and the problem of collectivity

Like all concepts employed in the social sciences, the meaning and use of 'collectivity' has to be situated historically. The promise of collectivity may appear more problematic now that the oppositions between practices which constrain and those which liberate, between isolated, politically powerless individuals and powerful, politically capable collectives have been deconstructed. However, we want to suggest here (and argue more fully in Chapter 6) that working with a concept of collectivity can be a productive means of moving beyond the mere 'recognition' of difference; it can enable new forms of connection between people and new ways of relating both to others and to oneself. But in what sense is this different to the notion of collectivity entailed in the original account of memory-work?

Haug and others decided to undertake collective questioning of experience, so as to harness the power to work against the more habitual, individualistic way of relating to experience – that is, seeing experience as arising from and representing the truth of one's inner being or past history. They recognized that such psychologization of experience inhibited women from acknowledging and analysing the commonalities in their lives and from there, working back to a deeper political understanding, not only of the social production of female sexualization, but of the active roles that women themselves play in this process. But, undertaking collective analyses of experience is not a straightforward affair. Collectivity can both enable and limit the process of socio-political transformation. The tension, between exploring and eliding difference within memory-groups, is more than a matter of practice; it brings us to the heart of current epistemological and political difficulties with the very notion of collectivity. And it is a tension Haug and others must have faced, if not explicitly discussed in their group meetings. For example, in a chapter about 'the slavegirl project',

Andresen, Haug, Hauser and Niehoff explain that the group had been writing about the objectification and commodification of women's bodies. They discussed the skill women (are expected to) develop – an ability to tread a fine line between being sexual beings and being loose women. When they decided to write about this issue, one woman returned to the group with the unexpected. She wrote a glowing account of herself working in a bar on a hot day. The only woman in the company of male customers, she decided to play some music and started to dance *'excessively, ecstatically', happily ignoring [or bearing] the way 'all eyes were turned in [her] direction'* (1987, pp. 149–50).

On first reading the memory, the other group members noted the seeming absence of any conflict over her performance. And it was pointed out that, although described in terms of pleasure, the incident could be read as an unambiguous account of the *problems* of objecti-fication, the very problems they sought to deconstruct. If we follow the account of memory-work as a process which elucidates 'our active par-ticipation in social structures that gives them their solidity ... more solid than prison walls' it is not hard to understand how such an account might be read (and was read in the group) as an instance of a woman's involvement in her own entrapment (Haug, 1987, p. 59). But the author refused to subscribe to such an interpretation, insisting that her memory was about the *pleasures of transgression*. This led to a discussion about transgression and freedom. The others in the group are reported as deciding that the author simply could not recognize her objectification as such The problem, it seemed, was that she was drawing on an inad-equate account of freedom, traceable to Freud, who thought that freedom was a matter of transgressing the constraints of civilization. What the author's own interpretation of her experience ignored was both the futile isolation of some forms of transgression and the freedom to be gained from realizing the malleability of social rules by working with them, instead of breaking them outright. Thus, the author's insist-ence on affirming the pleasure she experienced in dancing was ex-plained as a problem of the paucity of tools for understanding and practising real freedom. The insight which emerged from the group analysis of the memory was that the attainment of freedom from sexual objectification is a matter of forging ourselves *in relation to* the con-straints of our situations. In contrast, attempts to simply transgress these constraints only blind us to their ongoing operation – and this explains the author's persistence in remembering her experience as one of pleas-ure. This reading suggests that, had she only had a better way of under-standing freedom, she would have remembered this very differently.

Despite the importance of elucidating different possible relationships between freedom and constraint, this analysis is deeply disconcerting. The author's pleasure is cast in terms of false consciousness. Her experience is subsumed under a broad theoretical position in which transgressing the rules about overt displays of sexuality only ever makes women more active (not less, nor differently active) in the unfettered reproduction of patriarchal norms. This is an instance of memory-workers doing exactly what they had set out to avoid – glossing over the complexity of experience. We do not learn how the author of the memory came to accept this new reading. Did she wholeheartedly agree, or did she harbour a critique of the others' inability to theorize the complexities and transformative powers of pleasure? Did she feel like her experience was being subsumed by a reading which upheld bourgeois morality at the expense of interrogating what she was offering to the group? Someone left the group before their book was published – was it the author of the barmaid memory? If she did have any lingering attachment to her initial interpretation, it is subsumed by the authorial 'we' recounting the group discussion. It is impossible to discern whether this 'we' represents seamless coherence and agreement, productive diversity, uncomfortable inclusions or smoothes over outright differences in positions or even a break in the group.

The collective analysis of memories can be a powerful means of silencing and excluding people. There is no ultimate bases from which 'good' exclusions can be distinguished from bad, nor should memory-work groups seek to articulate them. It is not the fact of exclusion with which we are concerned here, but the way the process is neglected. Whilst Haug acknowledges that speaking as an 'I' necessarily occludes the complexity of subjective experience, the barmaid's tale suggests that it is equally the case that speaking as 'we' glosses over the contradictions of collective experience. Rather than play it safe, and avoid collectivity, is it possible to rework memory-work so as to take account of the fact that 'the alchemy of collaboration does not merge the two authors into a single voice' but transforms them into 'the chorus of a multitude' (Hardt [in an interview with Dunn], 2000)?

The problem with collectivity that we are raising is not new. For the past two decades, the collective 'we' of social research and political practice has been deeply questioned. Feminist politics illustrate this well.

All determinations [of sexual difference] ... have foundered on the shoals of fictional essentialism, false universals, and untenable unities. In addition to these theoretical interrogations, political challenges to feminisms that are white, heterosexual, and middle class by women who are otherwise have made strikingly clear that 'woman' is a dangerous and depoliticizing metonymy: no individual woman harbours the variety of modes of subjection, power, desire, danger and resourcefulness experienced by women living inside particular skins, classes, epochs, or cultures. 'All that is solid melts into air' – the sanguine 'we' uttered in feminist theory and practice only two decades ago is gone for good. (Brown, 1995, p. 166)

All attempts to describe or work with a collective feminist 'we' confront the imperative to include different experiences, subjectivities or identities. As suggested by Brown, the limits of essentialist theories and the increasing awareness of histories of exclusion which continue to unfold through representations of 'us' and 'we', indicate the need to rethink any idea of collectivity as an aggregate of individuals who concur by virtue of a shared identity or history. But inclusion of difference in and of itself does not enable collectivities to operate in more just or equal ways, nor does it necessarily undermine hegemonic modes of regulation. The additional challenge is to recognize how, even collectivities that enable us to work with and through and across differences, can be the very site where new forms of regulation unfold. Now, late-capitalist, imperial sovereignty operates not only through exclusion but through *inclusion* of difference (see Chapter 6). In such cases, what use are 'we'?

The Marxist notion of collectivity entailed in memory-work helps to question the proliferation of liberal and neoliberal individualism. To reconsider collectivity now does not necessarily entail returning to individualizing, depoliticizing alternatives. Rather, adopting the radical openness of enacting collectivity as a *process* returns us to the work of addressing, rather than downplaying, the difficulties and problems entailed in attempts to forge, sustain and develop socio-political change.

Rethinking collectivity

The two of us wrote Anti-Oedipus together. Since each of us was several, there was already quite a crowd. (Deleuze & Guattari, 1988, p. 514)

We have described how collectivity figures as the basis for socio-political transformation in memory-work as it was initially developed. But, if the inevitable radicalizing potential of collectivity is questioned and recast as a potential which may or may not be fulfilled, the challenges of under-taking memory-work are reframed. How can we realize collectivity as transformative; how can we prevent collectivity ossifying into the status quo? What does an anti-foundationalist collectivity look like or how is it enacted? One possible move is to argue that, it is not only commonalities that give rise to new understandings, but attempts to recognize differences among and between memory-workers *as* difference which can enable socio-political change. Importantly, foregrounding difference can subvert the consolidation of particular identity categories on which political action is often based. For example, as feminist and queer debates have demonstrated, interrogating difference can threaten the stability of the identity category 'woman' (De Lauretis, 1988; Scott, 1991/1993; Butler, 1990, 1992, 1994). In place of identity-politics this way of working with difference calls for anti-foundationalist feminisms or coalition politics – forms of self-consciously risky politics which must remain exposed to hijacking because change necessitates openness. This offers an interesting possibility for repositioning collective subjectivity (Spivak, 1990; Burman, 1994). When memory-workers question the basis of collective subjectivity, examining difference *as* potentially incommensurable difference, they are trying to contribute to change. Now collectivity is a coalition working together, not on the basis of common identities, but because they have a shared goal (from which they may envisage different future benefits and different future paths) and recognize the necessity of pooling their efforts to attain it. The emphasis shifts from collectivity as an outcome to collectivity as a process.

The premise of this interest in difference is, of course, that many are excluded access to the socio-political realm on the basis of their religious affiliations, race, sex, sexuality, ethnicity or some other marker of their identity. But, as discussed in the following chapter, the risk of relying on the inclusion of difference as a strategy for change in and of itself is that we end up with practices of recognition which are severed from practices of redistribution (Santos, 2001). Such domestication of difference has, in part, provided the rationale for the move from 'identity' to queer politics, for example (Butler, 1990; Rubin, 1984). In their analysis of the modes of biopolitical regulation and resistance emerging in our late-capitalist, globalized world order, Hardt and Negri (2000) argue that today difference and alterity are easily recouped – contemporary imperial power operates through the recognition and inclusion of difference. We are being ruled, not through the exclusion of difference, but through its hierarchical inclusion. As with the agency of individual subjects, now the value and limitations of differences which operate in and through collectivities hinge on the social and historical practices through which they have come to be included (as well as attempts to rework these practices).

Questions about the link between collectivity and socio-political change can be pursued by considering different modes of connecting and relating, both within and between collectives. In this regard, the distinction made in political theory between 'the people' and 'the multitude' is pertinent now, because it offers a way of understanding how collectivity can become a vigorous, multiple, productive source of creativity (Virno, 2004), as opposed to a move towards sameness. The power of 'the people' is enabled and constrained by a shared identity. Relations within such collectives are dictated by the need for similarity, and difference is the marker or relations with 'others'. In contrast, the multitude involves 'an open set of relations, [it] is not homogeneous and identical with itself and bears an indistinct, inclusive relation to those outside of it. Whereas the multitude is an *inconclusive constituent relation*, the people is a constituted synthesis that is prepared for sovereignty' (Hardt & Negri, 2000, p. 103, emphasis added). The relations being described as existing in the multitude are marked by singularity, openness and inconclusiveness. And the possibilities entailed in emphasizing openness evoke the Marxist account of change with which memory-work began. Marx distinguished between emancipation (the inclusion of more people into the same problematic socio-political realm) and liberation (the reworking and reappropriation of the very terrain on which the socio-political realm has developed). In reworking memory-work it may be possible to aim for the latter. Instead of refining the methodology to achieve greater accuracy or faithfulness to a particular procedure, we want to keep wrangling with problems of generalization and to concentrate on the socio-political possibilities of research.

In practise, the transformative potential of collectivity emerges as memory-workers attempt to move *beyond* the limitations of individual positions. Clearly, this was never thought as a matter of adopting a perspective of objective transcendence. But we want to contest any idea that memory-work should involve individuals constituting themselves as a collective 'people' with the limited goal of emancipation. Instead, the value of practising collectivity lies in the partial joining of embodied, situated knowledges (Haraway, 1991). In this sense, collective processes do not comprehensively represent the subjectivities of individuals involved, nor is this their aim. Collectivity is a matter of becoming – or unbecoming – as opposed to being, as we will argue in Chapter 6 (Deleuze & Guattari, 1988; Michaels, 1990). The transformative potential of memory-work analyses does not stem from the capacity to resolve (or gloss over) difference. Working with the memories as situated accounts entails interrogating the specific conditions under which a particular strategy emerges as politically effective. It means cultivating partial connections between experiences, adopting a 'mobile positioning' in the attempt to understand the situatedness of different interpretations, an understanding which will always be incomplete (Haraway, 1991; Stephenson & Kippax, 1999). Thus, the potential of collectivity entailed in memory-work hinges on the interpellation of the group as a differentiated, 'autonomous mass of intelligent productivity' (Hardt & Negri, 2000, p. 344). Difference is important, as we will argue in the next chapter, not for its own sake, but to the extent to which it can enable the flow of singularities, and the transgression of boundaries that have previously closed off concrete entry points into reworking the socio-political realm.

4
The Sociability of Experience

From the particular to the general

> According to what logic can particularism flourish severed from the universal? (Schor, 1995, p. 16)

Is it possible to develop and find terms which are adequate to connecting with and affecting others – not through recognition and similarity – but across difference? This emerges as a pressing question in contemporary efforts to forge new forms of political participation. For example, Hardt and Negri argue that 'one of the central and most urgent political paradoxes of our time [is that] in our much elaborated age of communication, *struggles have become all but incommunicable*' (2000, p. 54). Radical political struggles at the end of the 20th century – Tiananmen Square, the Los Angeles riots, Zapatistas, counter-globalization protests, the French riots (November 2005) etc. were like 'burning flashes' on the global sky failing to connect to each other. The means for translation between them had not yet emerged.

In this chapter we want to approach this general problem by focusing on the particular experiences of HIV positive gay men of embodying infectivity. The success of HIV prevention strategies can be attributed to the fact that, through emphasizing positive and negative men's 'mutual responsibility' for HIV transmission, they shore up the connections between different actors in the gay community. Yet, experiences of 'feeling infectious' question any notion of a shared understanding of 'mutual responsibility'. Foregrounding what is mutual or shared in social relations overlooks the essential ambiguity of connections between people. Of course, the absence of either shared understandings or clear recognition of the other's position can give rise to confusion, but it is also an important element in the development of *new* ways of connecting. Transfiguring relations, working with mis-recognition and incommensurable difference, open new possibilities for working in and on the socio-political domain.

Feeling infectious and shared responsibility

We want to tackle the question of the relation between experience and sociability through the analysis and discussion of a version of memory-work (as discussed in Chapter 3) which we used in order to understand the ways in which changing medical treatments for HIV enable and limit people's engagement with themselves, with others and with 'community'. Although the research involved working with several different groups of HIV positive gay men (see Chapter 5), the accounts discussed here come from one particular meeting of four men (between their early 30s and mid-50s). These men were professionals living middle-class lifestyles; they all lived within easy reach of inner-city gay Sydney and were actively involved in the 'gay community' (both through leisure and through participation in community organizations). At the time the group met, two of the men were on combination therapy and two were taking a break from treatment. The group met five times over a period of several months, and the cue 'feeling infectious' was chosen for the fourth meeting.

When the group discussion turned to infectiousness, it was evident that there are no ready meanings at hand, even after 20 years of the epidemic. This is not surprising: the meaning and significance of infectiousness is elusive and continues to change. The introduction of ARV treatment has contributed to this shift. Treatment successes have triggered changes in the meaning of a HIV diagnosis. More specifically, research conducted in Sydney suggests that HIV treatments newly differentiate men along the lines of positive or negative serostatus (Rosengarten, Race & Kippax, 2000; Kippax & Race, 2003). HIV negative men, unless they are in a relationship with a positive man, typically have relatively little understanding of the complexity of ARVs. Whereas positive men faced with making 'consumer-choices' about HIV treatments, are inducted into a vast, complex and shifting field of knowledge concerning drug types, drug combinations, drug efficacy, drug-resistance, toxicity and viral load. The men involved in this memory-work group discussed different ways in which they were confronted with the chasm between themselves and HIV negative others, and the problems which disclosure presents (that is, telling others whether one's serostatus is positive or negative or unknown). The cue 'feeling infectious' was chosen, and people produced and discussed written accounts of such instances. Drawing on the group discussion and on some of the other memories of infectivity, we want to set the scene for an analysis of one particular account, and to give a sense of the range of issues and different positions discussed.

The capacity to infect others with HIV can be more confronting than the threat HIV poses to one's own health. For example, Jim explained that it was only at a point of 'feeling infectious' in relation to another that the embodied feeling of being positive started to become apparent to him:

> Jim: ... when I first became positive I really put on a brave face ... Like weirdly enough this experience [of unprotected sex] was probably the first time I really began to deal with my status in the sense of really feeling what it feels like to be positive and the full sort of implications for that. And um I don't think I ever really acknowledged it before.

But here 'acknowledgement' can come in the form of a 'double-negation' (Jim's words). 'Being infectious' can be a virtually unspeakable state.

> Jim: ... for me it [unprotected sex with stranger of undeclared status] was such a horrifying experience that I couldn't imagine anybody sort of even vaguely empathising, y'know it was just something that was plain bad and um I did it. ... it just put me into a state of complete speechlessness. Unable to sort of *be* ...

He had met a man of unknown serostatus, in a sauna, who left Jim in no doubt about his desire for and the pleasure he derived from having unprotected anal intercourse with Jim (saying 'now I'm happy' as they parted). Jim explained that ordinarily he would have little discussion with people after a sexual encounter in a sauna, but on this occasion he could not leave things there. He extended an uncharacteristic, non-verbal invitation to leave the sauna together with the intention of opening a possibility for talking about what had occurred. But the man refused, or seemed unaware of, the invitation. And nothing was said:

... that was really sort of the most difficult thing about it, because it was a feeling of complete speechlessness that I couldn't declare myself or assert myself or, um I was actually sort of like debarred from saying well I knew this um, y'know was the case. I had just never felt like that before. Like completely sort of precluded from, from speaking ... I felt I had some *duty* to say something.

The context of Jim's speechlessness, his being 'unable to *be*', is a complicated one.

Condom-use, the long accepted and promoted norm for homosexual men in Sydney, has been part of a broader 'sex-positive' response to HIV on the part of gay community. This response is informed by the need to promote shared responsibility for HIV and to contest potential exclusions of HIV positive men. The use of condoms precludes the need to exchange information about serostatus; it avoids (often moralizing) interventions in the anonymity and fleetingness of some sexual encounters between men. But it is not the only HIV prevention strategy adopted. Since the initial promotion of condoms (a response which proceeded knowledge of and a test for HIV), there have been many important technological advances; for example, in the form of a test for HIV status, and later a test for viral load, more effective HIV treatments which can reduce viral load, more effective treatments and prophylaxes for opportunistic infections, refinements of knowledge about the risk of transmission and the introduction of post-exposure prophylaxis (PEP) – a high dose of HIV treatments taken after possible exposure to the virus as a means of avoiding subsequent infection. They have all been incorporated into the development of prevention strategies (for example, Race, 2001) and it no longer makes sense to assume that serostatus is irrelevant to sexual practice. Researchers have documented an increase in rates of unprotected anal intercourse between casual partners in Australia (Van de Ven, Rawstorne, Crawford & Kippax, 2002; Van de Ven, Rawstorne, Treloar & Richters, 2003). But these changes cannot be simply explained in terms of an increase in 'unsafe sex'. They signal the emergence of new strategies – some safer than others – which include: unprotected sex between positive partners (validated on the basis that concerns about reinfection and drug resistance have not been substantiated, or are not serious enough); withdrawal; unprotected receptive anal intercourse – on the part of positive men; and unprotected insertive anal intercourse – on the part of negative men. HIV serostatus and clinical markers such as viral load are becoming increasingly salient in men's negotiation of unprotected sex and HIV transmission in instances of condomless sex is reduced – although not eliminated – by the harm reduction strategies that such medical information enables (Van de Ven, et al., 2004). More recently there has been an increase in HIV incidence (NCHECR, 2004).

In this shifting context, it is not surprising that the memory-work group discussion about 'feeling infectious' involved examining the tension between the widespread uptake of social and sexual practices which promote shared responsibility and inclusion on the one hand, and experiences of feeling separated by serostatus on the other. The written accounts provoked questions about the extent of responsibility one can or should have for others, and the point at which the other can or should be granted the ability to participate in decisions. There were very different positions taken in relation to the division between positive and negative men. At one extreme 'shared responsibility' can mean that each individual takes responsibility for himself – there is no need for positive men to take responsibility for others. (This position is not so 'extreme' as might be imagined, in the sense that it emerged in discussion of specific sexual contexts which have evolved as sites where positive men have casual sex with other positive men). Alternately, there are moments when the burden or 'shared responsibility' is experienced as falling squarely on the positive partner's shoulders. For example, the account Mark wrote in response to the cue 'feeling infectious' described the guilt he felt after having safe sex with a casual partner. The sex had been 'very safe' ('it wasn't sort of the full glamorous sex' – it had not included penetration), and Mark felt that they had both had a 'wonderful time'. The next morning Mark and Sam were lying in bed 'talking nonsense', implicitly exploring the possibility of things developing. Then, Sam punctured the 'afterglow' with: 'by the way, how do you feel about it, the bug?' Mark responded by disclosing his positive serostatus. No relationship eventuated. About his feelings of guilt, Mark wrote:

> Not having informed Sam about his HIV status and being cornered into a confession a day later, when talk about possibly more dates had started, he felt so dreadful and guilty for days. Not worth the anguish, so [Mark] decided then, to be more forthcoming in future. Soon he experienced the other side of this "truth and bare" decision: being rejected. That hurts. In moments like these, he certainly feels "not the same as".

The culture of safe-sex does not always preclude the felt necessity for disclosure. Serostatus matters, and not just in the sense that it represents the possibility of HIV transmission. Even in situations where transmission is virtually impossible, serostatus can interrupt the development of social (not only sexual) relations:

Jim: So for you is feeling infectious ... more about being different to other people than about the possibility of actually infecting someone?

Mark: Yeah. But now actually it feels that there is a possibility of rejection only because you're HIV positive ... it's nothing to do with looks or type or whatever ... the *ease* of having conversations or connecting with other people is a hurdle ...

Embodying HIV can inhibit sociability, even when it is unspoken. 'Feeling infectious' can involve a paradoxical responsibility for others. Taking on responsibility for infection through disclosure can interrupt and sever relations with other men – attempts to care for others can render the problem of care irrelevant. The stifling, isolating weight of this responsibility is conveyed in Robert's written account:

Robert, 'Feeling infectious':
He lay awake in bed, just staring up at the ceiling. Unable to sleep, thinking about what happened the night before. They had met at a work "do"; right from the start it was always going to be a one nightstand. The other guy was visiting from overseas, no chance of anything deep. All had gone well, they went out for dinner, drinks afterwards, and in fact they'd ended up quite drunk and back at the other guy's hotel room. They immediately got into it, all over each other like a rash. The sex however was appalling, a mix of no lube, no condom, too drunk and one stupid question. And of course right in the middle of things he asked him, when they thought for a split second about not using a condom, "well you're not positive or anything ...are you?" and he replied "umm ...actually I am."

The inevitable honest answer, why do you always insist on the honest answer? That killed the moment. They never did anything, anything remotely risky, but nonetheless the moment was destroyed and now he was lying awake in bed while the other guy slept like a baby, feeling totally empty. He'd been awake for hours worrying what the other guy would think of him, how he would respond, what he would say when he woke. Would he think less of him? Drunk or out of it was the only way he seemed to be able to let himself do it these days. He'd never felt so totally different, like an alien, another species, something that could only hurt or kill. All the rhetoric about this being everybody's responsibility went straight out the window. When all was said and done it was his responsibility, he was the one who would be blamed if things went wrong, got out of hand or they had done anything. He was the one that would always have to be careful and take control. He felt like he should be wrapped in plastic, locked in a room. He wasn't safe, never could be safe. He should be kept away from others cause things had always gone wrong for him, how else had he gotten into this position? It was then he decided this was all too hard, too much angst; it was better just never to do it again. The words of an old friend from years ago came back to haunt him "it spits poison now".

Robert's account conveys a sense of infinite loneliness associated with disclosure. And the response – not to disclose – can invoke a state of non-being (it '*was all too hard*'), of being frozen and suspended beyond reach but in the midst of other people's sexual relations. The different forms of isolation which arise in Robert's and Mark's accounts – and Jim's speechlessness – serve to question the reach of public policies which have been advocating 'shared responsibility'. It is against this background that we want to consider Damien's memory.

Damien, 'Feeling Infectious':
Damien had wandered around for a month post diagnosis without sex drive, surviving on sleeping tablets as a coping strategy. He travelled to London and was encouraged to go out to The Hoist, a club in Vauxhall, by a good mate. Damien arrived and had a great conversation with a number of rough-looking Germans, one of whom he went home with. As the fumbling began it was clear condoms were not on the agenda, and suddenly the thought of sharing his experience – one to that point of desperate aloneness – with this nameless man, was exhilarating. The thought of being infectious felt like control – it felt like power in a sea of powerlessness. The appalling reality that this is what happened to me struck me deeply.

Damien tested HIV positive several years after the 1996 announcements about the breakthrough in treatments, and the incident occurred soon after his seroconversion (that is, the point of HIV infection). The account evokes the loneliness of traversing the distance between being HIV negative and positive, between sleeplessness and drugged sleep, between home (Australia) and away (London), between having lost his sex drive and found it again, between feelings of '*desperate aloneness*' and the desire to '*share his experience*', between power and '*a sea of powerlessness*', between this sexual encounter he is describing and his reflections on a past encounter ('*the appalling reality that this is what happened to me*') in which he unknowingly had sex with a positive person and was subsequently diagnosed HIV positive. The exhilaration accompanying the feeling of having the power to infect another is interrupted by the vivid connection he experiences between his own desire and that of another man, the man who he thinks has infected him. The desire to rupture their (his own and this other positive man's) isolation derails him, a movement which is accompanied by an intense sense of power.

How can we understand this account and Damien's subsequent discussion of it? During the memory-work group, Damien discussed feeling 'incredibly empowered and in control' in this moment – 'one of the most malevolent experiences in [his] life'. Moreover, he expected it to be (and remain) an encounter with an initially 'faceless and featureless' other. But months later, out of the blue, this other contacted him from the other side of the world to let Damien know that he remembered the experience as 'incredible' – still without knowing that 'it was incredible for a whole set of other reasons as well which [Damien] didn't share with him'. In what follows, we open a trajectory between the specificities of Damien's account and general problem of developing ways of acting on and in compelling, memorable and risky relations – the matter of which may never be overtly declared or fully understood.

There are at least three different approaches which can be taken in order to elucidate – not simply the 'meaning' of the experience which is being articulated here – but how the account refigures the very trajectory of a particular experience and troubles hegemonic discourses of HIV. We could adopt an essentially affirmative stance, insisting that subjects have agency and seeking to trace the apparent misdirection or absence of Damien's. This approach is problematic because, as we discussed in Chapter 1, it seems to propagate the autonomous, assertive self entailed in neoliberal practices of subjectification. Secondly, we could read this memory insisting that the real agents of change lie, not in the subjectivities of agentic beings, but in the practical and technical organization of life. Transformation is a haphazard and chance affair, something which cannot be grasped by considering people's meaning-making efforts. This stance, which is related to social constructionist, discursive and some post-structuralist approaches, usefully directs our attention beyond Damien himself to the organization of sexual subcultures. Bypassing subjective experience and focusing on the technical organization of life can certainly be an important step in understanding changes in social and sexual practice. Yet, relegating experience to a mere epiphenomenon neglects the role experience plays in the malleability and emergence of new modes of sociability. A third, approach to this account entails *forging* pathways for risking the move from the specificity of Damien's 'feeling infectious' to the general problem of responsibility for oneself and to others. This raises questions about the ways in which flows of power are harnessed and challenge established modes of relating. Here experience is an interesting, erratic and contingent player in refiguring sociability.

Affirming agency

The affirmative approach to experience entails studying people as agents who are active in constructing themselves as subjects and contribute to shaping the social contexts in which they live. Here, agency is conceived as an 'ability or volitional activity' which hinges on reflexivity (Prilleltensky & Nelson, 2002, p. 6). Insisting on agency as the cornerstone of any theory of personhood (for example, Shotter, 1984; Harré, 1983; this is also central, if only implicitly, in the theories of risk, for example, Beck, 1992) has been a vitally important chapter in social research. In particular, theories of the subject which emphasize agency have been developed with an emancipatory intent: they counter the dominant practice of investigating people as passive objects and have been embraced as a means of researching the domain of subjectivity whilst redirecting it from its historical path of constraint and oppression. As a result there has been a proliferation of research, practices and therapies which attempt to deploy agency as a means of self and social transformation. The affirmative approach to experience provides a valuable counter-move to research which, by explicitly excluding the relevance of subjective experience, implicitly asserts the value of some people's experience over others. However, as discussed in Chapter 1, promoting agency may be a problematic solution for the problems we face *now*, when neoliberal modes of regulation hinge on an almost compulsive faith in individuals' agentic capacities.

Seen historically, the move to affirm agency has shored up liberal and neoliberal forms of governance, contributed to a cultural turn inward for the source of meaning, and propagated the freedom to partake in the processes of our subjectification. Understanding agency as a situated concept foregrounds the relationship between the concept of agency as a capacity and a liberal political rationality which enables and constrains particular modes of relating to self and others (for example, Sennett, 1976). 'Cultural psychology', for instance, emerged with the aim of representing the experience of people who have been previously overlooked, and it does do this (for example, Cole, 1996; Rogoff, 2003; Shweder, 1991). Yet, it simultaneously operates as a colonizing force, imposing dominant psychological categories and concepts on those whose experience it strives to represent (Marvakis & Papadopoulos, 2002). That is, the inclusion of new forms of experience can have unintended effects: it can extend the domain of neoliberal regulation to include the very forms of autonomy and empowerment that social researchers have tried to proliferate.

This is the problem with which Foucault (1988a) presents us as he tracks the move beyond sovereign power – a power which might be identified as existing in a specific, separate body (the sovereign, the 'seat of power') and which is exercised over subjects – to disciplinary and bio-powers. Rather than being oppressive, disciplinary power is productive. It exists, not in institutions like the state which we can resist (or not), but in the very relations through which we construct ourselves. This means that disciplinary power cannot be simply opposed by resisting some outside force which is imposed on us (a problem which is further discussed in Chapter 6). The agentic, autonomous subject is not the antithesis of disciplinary power; rather it provides the means for regulation. In examining Luke's memory and the memory-work group's discussion of the difficulties people encounter in taking ART, we considered the emergence of this paradox (in Chapter 1). In such situations, HIV positive people are frequently addressed as agents living in conditions of risk who must 'take control' of their lives – which is typically exactly what people want (and are trying hard) to do. But this imperative simultaneously fits with, and extends, contemporary neoliberal practices of health management which constitute patients as individually responsible for health (for a thoughtful analysis of this issue see Greco, 1998). What gets overlooked in affirmations of agency of this kind is the fact that, frequently, people who are unable to control drug regimens or drug efficacy are lacking neither the desire nor the inventiveness to strive for control. Yet, the affirmation of agency entailed in discourses of 'patient empowerment' makes it is almost impossible to consider the *limits* of an individual's control. In this context, promoting agency can be productive in different ways: it supports people in what they want to do and it can lead to good results; it simultaneously extends individual responsibility beyond reason, and inhibits the development of alternate ways of relating to difficulties encountered in taking ARV treatment – from managing regimens through to drug failure.

The deployment of agency, thought as a volitional activity, cannot account for the ways in which 'the "I" draws what is called its "agency" in part through being implicated in the very relations of power that it seeks to oppose' (Butler, 1993, p. 122). We lose the opportunity of understanding how agency itself is constructed and differentially distributed. And we cannot comprehend how specific kinds of agency can be *disempowering* (as in Luke's account of 'taking charge', or in Jean Améry's [1964/1980] discussion of the fate of the intellectual in Auschwitz discussed in Chapters 2 and 5).

Adopting the affirmative stance makes it virtually impossible to pursue an analysis of Damien's memory without knowing what happened next (we know that in the moment of this sexual encounter he was confronted with the possibility of unprotected sex, but we do not know what Damien then did). If the sexual encounter continued regardless of HIV transmission it might be possible to elucidate why – by identifying barriers to condom-use, for example. Or, if we learned that, after the moment described, Damien consciously drew on a safe-sex strategy we might try to connect some aspect of this experience with the enabling of agency. But because we do not know we cannot elucidate agency (either enabled or constrained) and we are left with little else to say. Thus, research which takes the affirmation of agency as its point of departure can only erroneously forgo mining experiences like this account of 'feeling infectious' for a deeper understanding of modes of subjectification which may be emerging, solidifying or being reworked.

Being unable to elucidate Damien's account through this narrow notion of agency is problematic. It means bypassing an opportunity to intervene in the polarized explanations of the contemporary changes (described above) in safe sex culture and practice in Sydney – and it shores up the misunderstanding that experience is nothing more than material for illustrating existing understandings. Of these polarized approaches, the first insists on the 'responsible' and caring terms in which relations between gay men are conducted, through the identification of 'cultures of care' (Hurley, 2003; Weeks, 1998). The second points towards the absence of responsibility and the erosion the social bond between gay men (Worth, 2004; Watney, 1994). Both positions invoke a liberal rationality and, by assuming prior knowledge of what constitutes the social bond, they fail to grapple with important aspects of this experience: the contentiousness, the incompleteness and the unpredictability of this moment. Neither of these explanations of shifts in safe sex practice work with experience as an emergent, unfinished process. Before we open up the notion of sociability entailed in this approach to experience, we want to turn to a second set of tools on which social researchers might draw in considering Damien's account.

The turn to discourse

> Whilst all political rationalities are dependent upon some conception of the nature of the person to be governed, attempts to found politics in human nature never close political arguments. (Rose, 1992, p. 542)

The turn to discourse as an object of social research foregrounds the unforeseen and unpredictable nature of socio-political transformation. Change does not stem from a human capacity for agency. Nor are political ideologies understood as causal forces. Instead, there are responses to situated problems – responses which give rise to new and often unintended consequences, sometimes fuelling existing political rationalities and ideologies. Here, subjectification is understood as the end-product of 'a complex of apparatuses, practices, machinations, and assemblages ... which presuppose and enjoin particular relations with ourselves' and with others (Rose, 1996b, p. 10). This post-structuralist position is concerned with free-floating assemblages, in place of deterministic structures. Assemblages emerge through the fluid and contingent alignments between different actants, practices, ideologies and political rationalities. They cannot be understood as the product of a single logic, they are multiply determined and constantly shifting (Collier & Ong, 2004).

An example of the importance of tracking the contingent and unintended pathways of change comes from Miller and Rose's (1995) account of the rapid proliferation of a new subjectivity for workers in the North-Atlantic – the enterprising subject. The lack of international competitiveness on the part of manufactures in the North-Atlantic became a problem in the 1980s. By chance, this problem arose at a particular time when it was possible to offer a solution comprised of a number of distinct components. Firstly, companies drew on a managerial discourse which promoted the value of harnessing worker's agency (around since the 1960s). In addition, they drew on the then current political investment in enterprise. Taken together, these two moves lent 'a new political salience ... to an entrepreneurial identity ... [and] opened a fertile territory for the development of a variety of programs for reinvigorating personal and economic existence' (Miller & Rose, 1995, pp. 454–5). In turn, the elaboration of entrepreneurial subjectivity in the workplace invigorated the development of political strategies for managing a whole host of social questions, extending beyond questions of work (for example, into unemployment, Dean, 1999).

Notably, discursive explanations of the kind we have sketched here can be advanced without recourse to experience: there is no need to inquire into what it feels like, or what it means to be an entrepreneurial subject, for example. Moreover, taking experience as a point of departure is understood as misleading because attempts to trace the meaning of experience in narrative or language are seen as solidifying the very regime of the self they seek to question, that is, the psy-complex (Rose, 1996b). Productive assemblages, or discourses, may never enter the consciousness of subjects, they may never be given meaning, but nonetheless they organize the possibilities for our attempts to render life meaningful and to direct action. They can only be appreciated by bypassing questions of meaning and considering, instead, 'the practices that *act upon* human beings and human conduct in specific domains of existence' (Miller & Rose, 1995, p. 428, emphasis added).

Importantly, this refusal of meaning radically questions the conservative tendencies of affirmative approaches which – to the extent that they locate socio-political change as originating in agentic actors – imply that good things result from good, well-executed intentions. In rejecting any *a priori* capacity for agency, discursive analyses open the possibility for considering the construction and uptake of specific modes of agency. For example, a very particular kind of agency is conferred through entering into discourse of entrepreneurial subjectivity (or lost through refusal or inability to do so), privileging some forms of engagement with the world above others.

Seen from this perspective, no matter how interesting or eloquent Damien's account, it only leads us away from the real site of action; for example, the haphazard, contingent technical and practical organization of sexual subcultures. Examining the account institutes the deceptive belief that what is described can be employed to illuminate our understanding of the processes of change, real or potential. It may be granted that a particular experience like Damien's could serve as an illustration of cracks in discourses of 'shared responsibility' or 'cultures of care', but it cannot help us to understand how these fissures have emerged or can it illuminate the fault lines they are following.

Is it possible, however, to approach experience without anchoring it to the idea that narrative or meaning-making are privileged sites of socio-political change? We want to argue that, not only is it possible, it is important to do so. The approach to discourse we have described sidesteps the productive ambivalences of experience. The effect is, not only to neglect, but to mute the radical, creative impulse to collectively rework our current circumstances. Any reading of the moment evoked in Damien's account is more than an illustrative or descriptive exercise. We propose, using the words of Michel de Certeau (1997, p. 199), that social research is the 'art of transportation and intersection.' The alternative we are suggesting entails 'the sober, rational and realistic evaluation of historical systems, the constraints of what they can be, and the zones open to creativity', it involves identifying 'not the perfect (and inevitable) future, but the face of an alternative, credibly better and historically possible (but far from certain) future' (Wallerstein, 1998, pp. 1–2). If we take it that, although dominant, neoliberal modes of regulation are not compelled by a given, natural overarching law of change, we can be satisfied with neither retrospective diagnoses nor projects of self-affirmation, rather we have to search out and identify the *particular mechanisms* of change and stasis. This returns us to the specific ways of connecting with others which might subvert relations of power and contribute to both the identification of emerging assemblages and to the formation of new ones.

A third approach, then, to analysing Damien's account involves developing ways of interrogating the relation between particular experience and a malleable socio-political realm (Kippax, 2003). In doing this, we introduce a third term – sociability – to consider social relations with others and with oneself. Sociability can be thought without reinstating a self-affirming 'I' as the origin of intersubjectivity. Instead of taking intersubjectivity as an unproblematic given, we are seeking to understand the specific ways in which people develop inclusive connections and counter the increasing exclusions of large numbers of people from participating in society (Santos, 2001). Forms of sociability which try to counter exclusion involve working with the ambivalences and dangers that lie within relations *as* within, rather than splitting and excluding (Gillian Rose, 1996). More specifically, the modes of connection which are of interest are those which contest the codification and homogenization of experience by remaining open to the unpredictability of events, and through cultivating the singular trajectories of experiences (Lazzarato, 2004a; see also Chapter 6 and Chapter 8).

Transfiguring relations

> ... it takes three to make a relationship between two. (Gillian Rose, 1996, p. 10)

The shift beyond condom-use demands examining (not papering over) cracks in 'shared responsibility'. Rather than read Damien's experience as an instance of the 'failure' of communication or responsibility, we can start by considering a fundamental paradox of communication: meaning is elusive and ambiguous (Diprose, 2003). We can even say that sometimes it is not necessary for communication. What this suggests, is not the impossibility of shared meanings or understandings, but that moments of recognition and understanding are always, simultaneously, moments of misrecognition and misunderstanding (Simmel, 1950, 1910–11). Moreover, social inclusion is not (only) underpinned by sharing identifiable meanings – the emergence of productive connections between people hinges on openness to the ambiguity of communication. Likewise, the development of sexual and social relations between gay men in Sydney involves more than the presence or absence of 'shared responsibility' or 'mutual recognition'. Working with the excess of social relations allows social researchers to grapple with the productive ambivalences of communication.

Embodying infectiousness

Casual sex between men frequently involves a highly codified and ritualized set of practices (Race, forthcoming; Smith, 2004). The successful uptake of condoms was read as signalling the development of a culture of responsibility amongst gay men (Weeks, 1995). 'Safer sex' is not the continuation of 'anything goes libertarianism', Weeks argues, but heralds the development of new forms of mutual responsibility: 'the discourse of safer sex is precisely about balancing individual needs and responsibility to others in a community of identity whose organizing principle is the avoidance of infection and the provision of mutual support' (1998, p. 44). But many of the experiences of 'feeling infectious' discussed in the memory-work group question any notion of a unitary 'community of identity'. Serostatus can re-emerge as relevant, not only because new safe sex strategies continue to develop, but simply because it matters to some people. This was hammered home to Mark when he tried to talk to Sam about the fact that he had not disclosed his serostatus prior to their safe-sex encounter. The conversation occurred a few days later:

Mark: I said "you know I really feel so bad about this," he said "you should," but actually he said "actually you shouldn't because nothing happened but I just want to know" and he said "I don't even know if I'm HIV positive, negative," he said "I prefer to think I'm negative." He said "I haven't been tested for it so I'm possibly in the same boat as you are." But he only said that more or less to make me feel better, y'know. And yes we saw each other just as friends, we never had sex after that.

This desire, 'just to know' more about a sexual partner than Sam may know about himself is just one way in which the unity of interests between positive and negative men can be severed. Different forms of exclusion emerged in the course of discussing memories of 'feeling infectious'. For example, the exclusion of positive men arose: when Robert described feeling '*like he should be wrapped in plastic, locked in a room*'; when Jim found himself 'speechless' and 'unable to *be*'; and in Mark's account of rejection and feeling '*not the same as*'. Negotiating HIV can also lead to the exclusion of negative men. For instance, Jim noted the development of positive-positive sexual cultures, saying: 'in a way being positive gives you access to something that negative people don't have access to if they want to remain negative. You can have unprotected sex. Just because I know so many positive guys who don't use condoms with each other because they know that they're positive'. Inclusion and exclusion can occur when actions are read as 'disclosing' – irrespective of actors' intentions. For instance, Damien explained that before he started having sex with this man in London, there was a group encounter. Like Damien, the others involved were not from London – they were mostly Germans and an American. The American man was moved to the periphery on the basis that some of the others read his condom-use as an indication HIV-positive status (Damien did not).

We can read Damien's memory as an account of the embodiment of the materiality of an experience of HIV – an experience which exceeds the linguistic or narrativized meanings of HIV which are ready at hand. Damien is simultaneously struck by the 'appalling reality' (of his own past and) of what it is to be *capable* of infecting another. Being positive can involve negotiating sexual encounters with others who – although they must know that the possibility is present – seem unconcerned by or incapable of imagining infection. For example, Damien, speaking about a time prior to seroconversion, said that 'the assumptions I was making [then] ... are completely different from the assumptions I now make ... Then I thought the person doing the fucking would not possibly infect me because they wouldn't'. A partner's apparent lack of interest can ward off attempts to speak about infectiousness (as Jim describes, on the part of the man he met in the sauna). Damien remembers doing this himself prior to his own seroconversion. He was about to engage in unprotected receptive anal intercourse with a stranger in a sauna who:

> Damien: said to me "you don't want this, don't do this [have anal sex without a condom]" ... And at the time I thought "oh for god's sake", at the time I was actually really irritated. Because I thought "well I'm actually quite enjoying that and all of a sudden it's, I wasn't going to let you come up my arse but I wasn't going to let you do this".

For positive men, being confronted with a partner's disinterest in or ignorance of infectiousness can leave one isolated in the concern about transmission, and making this concern a shared responsibility may not be possible. Yet, whilst infectivity can be virtually unspeakable in contexts where this division between positive and negative men emerges, it is not immaterial.

Damien's memory 'forces us to think' about modes of connecting which – although they may be unspeakable – still have a material force and play a role in transforming social relations (Deleuze, 1994, p. 139). Damien finds himself in incommensurable relations with others and with himself. In this moment, the possibility of ascribing meaning to his encounter seems to evaporate. The memory offers no linear narrative in which Damien recognizes a problem and self-consciously seeks a solution. The account jarringly shifts from third back to first-person at the point where Damien describes the feeling of power he now has in this encounter in London and places this in relation to the past (imagined) feeling of another man in another country, the man who he thinks has infected him (*'The appalling reality that this is what happened to me struck me deeply'*). This disruption suggests two distinct, but co-existent, modes of being – the positive man still is the negative man. The incommensurability of experience is important in tracing the trajectory from this written memory to the different modes of relating between gay men in casual sexual encounters and, to sociability more broadly. Transfiguring relations enable the navigation of incommensurable worlds by breaking 'communities of identity'.

Managing difference – equality & alterity

How can misrecognition and the presence of difference shape sociability? There are at least three different strategies for dealing with difference in social relations. The first is to artificially suspend difference by imposing a commonality. In *To The Lighthouse* (Woolf, 1927/1977), Mrs Ramsey remembers that when there is disagreement among the company a hostess should insist that everyone speak French – the idea being that this would unite people in the struggle to say anything much at all. Suspending difference is an important strategy with broad applications. Promoting condom-use can be likened to this kind of inclusion – it tries to work with and beyond differences in serostatus, concentrating people's efforts on inclusive practices. But, as Irigaray (1985a) argues, it can also be a form of negation. For example, when Damien told his negative partner that he had recently seroconverted, his partner – probably trying to reassure him – insisted 'this changes nothing'. But at the time, Damien experienced this as sealing the divide between them: becoming positive 'changed everything'. In the context of Damien's struggle to rework his relations with himself and others his partner's reaction was read as an inability to engage with HIV. Inclusiveness always raises a question as to the terms of inclusion.

A second strategy for relating across difference is to insist on the radical alterity of self and other. Foregrounding alterity should not ultimately separate self and other, the other precedes the constitution of the self (Irigaray, 1985a, drawing on Levinas). The concept of alterity posits a radical incommensurability between self and other. Now it is problematic to claim knowledge of the other. The promise here is that insisting on the impenetrability of the other subverts processes of colonization which function through the proliferation of knowledge about the other. The difficulty is that attempts to infuse the concept of alterity into strategies for developing connections *between* people tend to be easily recouped into the affirmation of difference for its own sake. Simply concentrating on the otherness of the other, at the expense of working out *how* to connect, invokes a mystification or celebration of that subject position. It can mean simply substituting passivity in the face of the other for active responsibility for social relations (Gillian Rose, 1996). The risk is that this is a depoliticizing move in which practices of recognition are severed from attempts to intervene in the distribution of inequalities (Santos, 2001).

The excess of sociability – transfiguring relations

In answer to these problems of negating or mystifying difference we want to turn to a third means of connecting across difference – through transfiguring relations which entail an openness to difference and allow for the reworking of self and other. Focusing on the transformative role of sociability in Damien's account allows us to approach change without prejudging its significance, without knowing what Damien did next. But how can we understand the non-linear means of transformation entailed in sociability? How can things which are not 'like' each other, which neither evolve from nor return to each other, relate? Deleuze and Guattari poke fun at the unnecessary difficulties of such questions when they answer: 'It is quite simple; everybody knows it, but it is discussed only in secret. We oppose epidemic to filiation, contagion to hereditary' (1988, p. 241). Social relations entail ingesting the other, embodying aspects of him or her, and in the process transforming the self. Santos (2001) uses this notion of ingestion to talk about the development of cultural relations in Latin America – the cultural practices of the colonizers were neither imposed nor revered, they were taken up and transformed. As with contagion, the metaphor of eating opens the way for thinking about change in self-other relations *without being constrained by notions of similarity*. The connections developed between people can fundamentally alter those involved, without necessarily making each 'more like' the other. Psychoanalysis also offers a means for considering social relations which are not dictated by the logic of similarity. In writing about the difference between mourning and melancholy, Freud (1966) describes two possible modes of ingestion. The melancholic is closed to the ambiguities of the lost relation, living it as a static and refusing to let go of a version of the other which affirms his or her own good. There is no change. Melancholy drags on. It acts as a barrier to reworking the self, undermining engagement with others, and ultimately engagement with socio-political change. In contrast, mourning involves taking in the lost other together with all the paradoxes and ambiguities of the relation, being altered by them, rearranging one's relations with the self and the other. Mourning is a transfiguring relation which changes the self's relation with the world (Gillian Rose, 1996). Like contagion, mourning provides a way of understanding transfiguring relations which fuel transformation and hinge on moments where the self is open to change.

There is a striking absence of a psychological language of intentions and decisions in Damien's account. Damien finds himself embodying the open secret that contagion forges relations between diverse objects: humans and viruses, positive and negative, one man and another, self and self. Without it there is only linear development – mutations of the same. He sees a past partner who may have infected him in a new light, sees the vulnerability of his current partner in an unexpected way, and is struck by his own (current) power and (previous) vulnerability. He is not turning within to identify and harness some previously existing capacity, rather he finds himself moving along a risky and destabilizing trajectory, moving *beyond* himself. Here we have transfiguring relations at work. The trajectory of these connections is expansive, unpredictable, non-linear and often jarring. These forms of engagement are impossible without the 'reconfiguration of that which is given in the sensible' (Rancière, 2000, p. 113).

Transfiguring relations and the social bond

As mentioned earlier, some look to recent changes in sexual practice between men as the grounds for arguing that the social bond is being eroded. More broadly, such concerns are frequently justified on the basis that large scale social shifts – for example, globalization – have resulted in social fragmentation and the absence of shared purposes, making it increasingly difficult to relate to each other in terms of reciprocity or recognition (for example, as discussed by Lash & Featherstone, 2001). From this moralizing perspective it might appear that transfiguring relations are one of the mechanisms through which the social bond is being eroded. We want to suggest a very different connection between this form of sociability and transformations in the socio-political realm.

The demise thesis reflects a partial view, not only of socio-political change, but of social relations. It overemphasizes the role of recognition and ignores both the ambiguity of communication and the productive role of misrecognition in sociability. Sociability always entails an element of *misrecognition*. The unrepresentable is already operating within social relations (de Certeau, 1988), effecting the development of sociabilities, at times throwing us into turmoil, leaving us staggering. So, not only is disease a process of misrecognition and rearrangement of the boundaries of a strategic assemblage called self, but the whole 'immune system discourse is about constraint and the possibility for engaging a world full of "difference", replete with non-self' (Haraway, 1991, p. 214).

The excess to and intrusion of sociability is fundamental to the malleability of social relations. What is present, but unrepresented in social relations with others, is that we are already more than ourselves. Simmel (1950) describes this by invoking the figure of the stranger. There is something of the distance which characterizes interactions between strangers in more familiar relations too. Knowledge of the other is always limited simply because there is more to what they say and how they present than can be fathomed. Instead of apprehending the other as s/he is, people tend to inflate a fragment into a generality by 'imagining the completeness of [the other's] peculiarity' (1910–11). The other is apprehended as a concentrated version of himself or herself, complexities and contradictions are overlooked. However, what remains unknown still plays an important role in social relations. 'This extra-social being, his temperament and the deposit of his experiences, his interests and the worth of his personality … gives the individual still, in every instance, for everyone with whom he is in contact, a definite shading, interpenetrates his social picture with extra social imponderabilities' (Simmel, 1910–11). That is, the excess may be unarticulated but it is not completely excluded.

The unfathomable presence of the excess of social relations explains the humour in a 'comedy of errors' – we all know such comedies, not only have we acted in them, but they have shaped who we have become. Misrecognition can serve as a means for the development of connections between people and transform those involved into something other than themselves or each other. The turn to discourse usefully highlights the dangers of positing human agency as the point from which socio-political change originates: human intentions rarely produce what is intended. However, Simmel's account of social relations explains how sociability, like other parts of an assemblage (social policies, political rationalities, discourses through which subjectivity is constructed) is productive nonetheless. Sociability is more than the mere product of an assemblage; it is part of an assemblage, sometimes driving, sometimes responsive. Transfiguring relations neither develop nor restore order but enable engagement in processes of transgression, transformation, of becoming-other to oneself, of reworking order.

We want to dispute the notion that transfiguring relations are contributing to the destruction of social relations. More specifically, whether it is recognized or not, the social bond between gay men already includes the ambivalences of experiencing infectiousness. Infectivity is present but avoided, included as is excluded. Taking sociability as an object of research allows us to entertain the possibility that infectiousness is not an abstract fact of self or otherness, but an element of relating which can be simultaneously embodied, unknown and productive. In the moment described in Damien's account, an unspeakable excess of sociability is embodied, opening him to the ambivalences of relationships between incommensurable subjects. He is struck by this excess, becomes other to himself and is confronted with the problem and possibility of new forms of connection to himself and to others.

Elaborating sociability, navigating incommensurability

The transitional sociability through which Damien comes to enact his relation with himself and others can only be approached if we resist both the constraints entailed in affirming agency and the paralysis of negating of any productive link between experience and the shifting assemblages through which socio-political transformation occurs. The political effectiveness of the affirmative approach hinges on representing of *already* identifiable practices and forms of subjectification. Here, the role of research is relegated to 'giving voice' to those who have been previously excluded (for example, 'illness stories', Frank, 1995). The risk is that representation replaces questioning, and 'empathy' stands in the way of engagement with alterity. As discussed earlier, this is the problem of identity politics – much criticized on account of the static picture they offer, and because they reify the experiences of oppression they strive to overcome (Butler, 1993). Yet, turning to discourse without an adequate concept of experience limits researchers' capacity to work with emergent, inventive social relations as *part of* the assemblages through which socio-political change is effected. In contrast, turning to the Damien's experience of 'feeling infectious', can facilitate understanding of the crucial role of experience in the development of politically potent sociabilities.

Damien finds himself in a moment of hiatus. The point of interruption occurs as he is confronted with the embodiment of infectiousness. The question arises as to how, in this situation in which communication is already complicated by the chasm between himself and the other man, he can work on the already existing connection between himself and this other man. Damien moves beyond the position of an actor in a 'community of identity', by ingesting the alterity of self-other relations. The trajectory appears virtually unmapped. We can read this as an account of finding oneself in a transitional, baroque sociability. Breaking the respect for form, repose and resolution, this sociability entails a movement beyond the hegemonic discourses through which subjects are positioned. Here, experience is no epiphenomenon. Experience is both the terrain and the trajectory of transition, without it we have only a vacuum and no way of working on the relations between self and other, self and self. The movement of these transfiguring connections is expansive, unpredictable and fractal; it can involve diverse entities and jarring combinations. This is not a relation of similarity; it includes productive symbiotic alliances which test the restrictions of the social bond as it is articulated and known at any one point in time, enabling transformation.

Socio-political change cannot be explained by drawing on the logic of similarity alone. Research can go beyond this logic by considering the productive ambiguities and excesses of social relations – that is, the means which challenge the constraints of clichéd ways of being and which enable the development of new modes of relating to self and others. Transfiguring relations neither develop nor restore order but involve becoming-other to oneself; they are a means of engagement with transformation, of reworking order. Entailing an expansive, active engagement with and reworking of self-other relations, they open possibilities for contesting hegemonic forms of social exclusion. They animate the desire to move beyond the 'cult of the self' (and its long legacy in western thought, for example, Taylor, 1989), to rework relations with the world and to work on the world. The form of political engagement we are describing here entails shared commitments to navigating flux and openness to the inclusion of heterogeneity. Our argument is that suspending fantasies of perfection which destroy political life, and suspending demands for affirmation and recognition as the bases of political action, propels the development of new modes of connecting, and can fuel the reconfiguration of the assemblages which produce the socio-political domain. Importantly, this approach to sociability is not underpinned by a liberal political rationality.

Part III

Experience and Socio-political Transformation

5
Self/Freedom

The politics of subjectification

Maybe the problem of the self is not to discover ... a positive self or the positive foundation for the self. Maybe our problem now is to discover that the self is nothing else than the historical correlation of the technology built in our history. Maybe the problem is to change those technologies, and then, to get rid of the sacrifice which is linked to those technologies. And in this case, one of the main political problems nowadays would be, in the strict sense of the word, the politics of ourselves. (Foucault, 1997, pp. 230–1)

When we consider contemporary attempts to theorize the politics of everyday life, Foucault's work on the aesthetic cultivation of freedom in relations with the self (1984, 1988b, 1990, 1992, 1997) is being widely adopted as particularly promising. This notion of self/freedom appears to disrupt melancholic laments about the impossibility of reworking our current socio-political conditions (discussed in Chapter 3). Importantly, the disruption is instituted *without* re-introducing a self-knowledgeable subject whose political engagement depends on enunciating and gaining recognition of his or her experience. For Foucault, subjectification occurs in the 'the forms within which individuals are able to, are obliged, to recognize themselves as subjects' of a particular discourse or set of practices (1990, p. 4). Although there is something given in relations to the self, Foucault argues, that they are also the site where freedom emerges. In fact, you need freedom in order have the self (Foucault, 1988b). The aesthetics of existence involve refiguring what is given, enabling the creation of new modes of connecting to self and others, new modes of experiencing – the freedom to make life differently (Murray, 2005).

Here we draw on ideas about the aesthetics of existence to explore people's active participation in and reworking of existing modes of HIV subjectification. And, through an analysis of people's accounts of negotiating and refusing the limits of HIV identity, we encounter the risks of working with this account of subjectification. Foucault opposes intervention strategies which entail grappling with the normalizing function of identity with aesthetic strategies which appear to break from the constraining logic of identity politics (the latter being taken up as particularly promising avenues for intervening in our present neoliberal socio-political conditions). However, seen from the perspective of people's everyday struggles with HIV, these two different uses of experience appear as a *situated* response to the constraints of the socio-political conditions in which people find themselves (Gill, 2005). They are not different approaches to the same predicament; they are different approaches to diverse manifestations of connected problems. And HIV is the totality of these connected problems. In other words, these two uses of experience (identity politics and aesthetics of the self) are not really opposed to each other; they are not alternative possibilities but constitutive moments in the problematization of HIV. As with the politics of articulation (see Chapter 2), the limitations of the aesthetics of existence lie in what is excluded: this is a form of experience which is simply incommensurable with and unspeakable within the limits of the particular socio-political terrain in which subjectification processes unfold. In the subsequent three chapters we argue that there is more to experience than the aesthetics of existence can harness.

The tension between obligation and freedom, between being subjected to and refiguring the terms of subjectification, is clearly evident when we consider two very different accounts of HIV subjectification alongside each other:

Rick, (writing in response to the cue) 'social discrimination':
... It was quite a shock to him that his first incident was with a Government Ticket Inspector on a State Rail, local Sydney, suburban train. In front of a crowd of about 20 people the SRA Inspector demanded in a loud voice, (underlying anger) to see the Concession Card and then went on to question him as to why he was on sickness benefits because 'he looked too healthy'. Rick was very indignant to this man's attitude and told him so, in no uncertain terms, to mind his own business. When the man kept harassing for an explanation Rick lost his temper and yelled at the guy that he had AIDS. One of the passengers then said, 'Leave him alone' and the man continued his job. All the other people who had wit-

nessed this were now staring at Rick and he felt so uncomfortable he got off the train at the next station intending to catch another train. It was a reflex reaction just to get away from the whole incident.

A second incident with two Police officers was when Rick was on his way to hospital for treatment. There were NSW Police inspecting tickets and one of them booked him for not having a ticket, even after he explained that the machine was out of order and he was only travelling one station. So a fare of $1.10 was going to cost him $100. One of the constables had asked Rick why he was using a Concession Card and why he was on his way to the hospital and the nature of his illness. He was so angry about this he went to his local Member of Parliament to try to do something about the fine. Seven months later and many letters between the Local Member, State Rail, the Minister for Transport and Rick ended up with the fine being dropped.

Having reported both of these incidents no apology was ever received ...

David, 'Relating Positively'
He remembered two incidents, one happened years before, he'd been sitting around a table chatting with some friends, and both were unwell, seriously unwell. The conversation was getting black but at the same time very hilarious. It revolved around an idea a fourth person had had. To market a series of CDs titled 'Greatest dance/Funeral Hits Volume 1, 2 ... etc'. All of them had been to far too many funerals, far too many. Top of the list was of course 'I will always love you', followed by 'Footsteps on the dance floor'; 'You are the wind beneath my wings' and who could forget the theme to the movie 'Titanic'. They all agreed, if anyone were to play any of these songs again they would be hunted down and killed. They also agreed however there was money to be made in the idea; the CD would go to number one in a flash. ACON* might even consider using the CD as a fundraiser. 'Maybe an emaciated spotty disco queen could be put on the cover?' followed by laughter all around. At the time he was the only negative person in the conversation, he laughed at the jokes but felt on the edge, not really a part of the group.

Years later he found himself in the pub with four slightly tipsy friends ... everybody was having a great time, laughing about their long term prospects, when he started to make a joke about having just bought a house and having decided to only ever pay the minimum repayments necessary on the home loan, he was never going to see the 25 year home loan out, why spend money for someone else to enjoy. Everybody found

---

*ACON is the acronym for the AIDS Council of New South Wales.

this very funny; it was soon followed by a series of jokes about the relevance or lack of relevance of superannuation and then how someone kept buying new puppies based on the theory he had to outlive his dog. As long as he had to take care of his dog he had to stay alive. 'I've got to outlive the dog,' he kept yelling. Rounds of laughter followed, everyone wondered just how long did a dog live for? It was then he realized he was now part of the group, able to make the blackest of black jokes, laugh and not care and really as black as it was, it still at times was very funny.

Being able to circulate humour and the humiliation of being asked to disclose the details of one's HIV status in public – in these written memories David and Rick give radically different accounts of their relations to themselves. What forms of freedom, if any, could emerge from Rick's apparent dogged determinism and disgruntlement over the apology never received, and from David's shared pleasure in being able to make '*the blackest of black jokes*'?

The memory-work groups

These particular accounts of HIV subjectification come from two of three different memory-work groups formed to discuss and analyse experiences of HIV since the introduction of ARV treatment. Each group met between four and six times over a period of several months. In total, there were 15 HIV positive gay men involved, mostly in their 30s and 40s (one man was in his 20s, and three others in their 50s). All had been on treatments at some point, though not all were at the time of the meetings (see Chapter 3 for more details of memory-work).

People in the first group, in which David participated, were all living near the inner city. These men were all professionals working full-time, with the exception of one man who was retired. They were currently or had been previously involved in gay and HIV community organizations, in both paid and volunteer capacities. The other two groups were specifically recruited on the grounds that they did not live near the inner-city gay suburbs. One group met in Sydney's west (and included people living in Western Sydney area as well as those who travelled from outside of Sydney to participate). The other was located in a town a couple of hours outside of Sydney altogether. For purposes of anonymity, we do not distinguish between these two memory-work groups. Rick was involved in one of them. The men in these out-of-town groups were either unemployed, looking for part-time work, or engaged in part-time work – one was retired. The majority of them were living on social security. Some of these men had an (extensive) history of involvement in gay and HIV community organizations, and some were currently involved in volunteer work related to HIV. Many of them had lived in the city in the past.

Unsurprisingly, the groups chose very different cues for triggering their analyses of experiences of HIV. In the city-based group the cues included: Changing medication; Trust/affinity/rapport with doctor; Feeling infectious; and, Relating positively. The men living away from the inner city also wrote about treatment decisions in response to: Making a decision about treatments; Tour guide through the mountain of medication; and Treatment side effects. In addition, they wrote about: Fitting into work; Getting on with life; and Self-limitations. Relating to others was also explicitly problematized in some of the cues they chose: Disclosure; Did that really happen? Discrimination; and, Social discrimination. Although the group which met in the city discussed grappling with how seroconversion positioned them differently in relation to many things, they did not specifically nominate 'discrimination' as a cue for writing and interrogating experiences of HIV.

Entitlement/discrimination

Discrimination

When presented in the memory-work group, Rick's memory was discussed as an example of a fairly common collective experience involving both the threat of being outed as HIV positive to strangers in front of an audience and the sheer injustice of being treated differently. Similar stories were related about bus drivers or ticket inspectors questioning people's entitlement to concession cards, about incidents of discrimination doled out by doctor's receptionists, by state housing officers and by bureaucrats authorized to make decisions about social security and benefits. One man volunteered the fact that, for fear of stigma, he did not use his travel concession card.

What *is* remarkable about this particular account is Rick's persistence in having the fine dropped. For seven months he applied himself to letter writing, to expensive long-distance phone calls, to garnering the support of his member of parliament, and to the awful task of trying to navigate the inner workings of State Rail's bureaucracy. The details are pretty grinding, for example:

Rick: … like a parking infringement [ticket] does state on it that you can contact them and have the case deferred to be heard by a judge. But nowhere on that [train fine] ticket is there an address to write to, anyone. No way of contacting anyone …

Connor: You said that they even wrote the wrong date?

Rick: Well there's no train service between ten and 12 and they wrote 11:18. It was 10:18. And they wrote the previous day's date. Which was a Sunday. Why would I be going to the hospital to see the doctor on a Sunday? You would think if it hadn't been for my local member of parliament actually taking it up on my behalf with the transport minister and then his department referring to State Rail; and all of that nonsense, I mean I would have been arrested. I was quite prepared to go to jail.

Brian: Did they send you a letter saying it was dropped at the end?

Rick: Eventually.

Brian: No apology.

Rick: No, no apology. And there was never any apology from any of the people who had interrogated me. Like the first guy. He never said I'm sorry. And I just felt so conspicuous sitting in that carriage, I got up and got off the train. I should have just walked into another carriage where people hadn't heard. But I didn't think of that. The first thing I thought of was get off the bloody train and get away from there. That's just one style of discrimination that I've heard and read about. Other people have had far more hassles than what I've had.

Seven months of wrangling did not kill his desire for an apology, a desire connected to the idea that discrimination is a shared problem.

Entitlement

'Being entitled' to state support is a precarious, but common, mode of subjectification through which many HIV positive people are obliged to relate to themselves. Most positive people know what it is to be without work for lengthy periods of time. In a recent large scale survey of positive people only 26 per cent were in full-time work, with an additional 17 per cent in part-time work (Grierson, Thorpe, Saunders & Pitts, 2004). Nearly two-thirds of those currently employed had been out of work in the past (for an average period of more than two years) for reasons related to HIV. Of those currently not in paid work most relied on social security. In fact 55 per cent of all respondents were receiving social security.

Negotiating social security emerged as a minefield in the analysis of HIV experience undertaken in the two groups located outside of the city. The past two decades of neoliberal unemployment reform mean that living on social security is an increasingly tenuous affair (Dean, 1995). There is no such thing as an unemployed person in Australian government-speak. Only 'jobseekers' can receive unemployment benefit, and this is regulated through time consuming dole-diaries, interviews with 'Centrelink' (federal state) staff and financial penalties for failing to be active enough in seeking work. For someone who has to stop work (or is fired) due to illness, there is the possibility of getting a 'sickness allowance' as a temporary measure. Once they are well enough to work, they have to either find work or apply for a jobseeker's benefit. For those who can provide sufficient medical evidence of their ill health, another option is to apply for a 'disability support pension' (DSP). If people are ill and unsure what the future holds, the DSP offers relative income stability.

Being on DSP and aspiring to return to work presents a problem. If the job does not last a person will not necessarily be eligible for DSP again. Many of the men in these groups who wanted paid work doubted their chances of getting anything other than casual or temporary work, at least in the first instance. And they had experience of (or worried about) losing significant income, or the prospective job itself, due to periods of illness (or in some cases, discrimination). This meant that they had real questions to consider in giving up access to the DSP and returning to work. But such concerns extended to those who felt that they were *not* well enough to work. This is because the government continually reviews social security benefits. Their close scrutiny of the classification of disability means that doctors are continually asked to re-assess HIV positive people's level of 'disability' (Grierson et al., 2004). The effect of these neoliberal policies is that, whether or not people on DSP want to work, the instability of their situation demands their ongoing investment in the problem of entitlement.

Not only are HIV positive people responsible for their health (as discussed in Chapter 1), but managing social security involves taking on responsibility for poverty and the labour market (Arribas Allyon, 2005). Poverty enjoins positive people to a system of benefits which requires time and the skills for managing: idiosyncrasies in payments (arising from periods of work or income from other sources); glitches in payments; the suspicion (real or imagined) of state administrators; and relations with doctors on whom the government may call at any time to reassess one's entitlement. The administration of social security requires people to simultaneously perform entitlement and to continuously imagine themselves without entitlement. In this process, not only is one's HIV status constantly foregrounded, it becomes a public affair.

Being forced into identity politics

Rick's account of the persistence he exercised in seeking recognition can be read as a trajectory taken by a man who is transposing the skills honed in managing social security to another state bureaucracy. Rick is already bound to a form of recognition of entitlement based on HIV status. But could this form of investment in HIV identity only ever enjoin one to the normative terms of subjectification as a means of entitlement, or can this also be a site for the emergence of freedom? Rick's written memory alone does not suggest a positive answer. Moreover, although there was much trading in techniques for avoiding or managing disclosure in the out-of-town groups' discussions, this was not the case for discrimination. Discrimination was discussed for long hours, but *no* strategies were put forward for dealing with such incidents as and when they occur.

In Chapter 4 we considered how demands for recognition can reify the very experiences they seek to overcome – and the out-of-town groups' discussions of discrimination could be cited as an example of this general problem of recognition as a political strategy. But it does not follow that we can simply discount such strategies: to do so would be to fail to engage with the obligation to seek recognition which many positive people encounter. Positive people living on social security, that is the majority of positive people, are *forced* to seek public recognition of their HIV identity, they have to invest in identity politics. What is crucial for social researchers to understand are the forms of investment made in, and the malleability of, HIV identity.

Investing in collective freedom

To return to the group discussion of Rick's account, the apology figures as important, not only for Rick individually, but for the possibility of addressing a wrong which is felt by many others. This move from individual injury to the need to intervene in a broader field of discrimination was continuously echoed in the group discussion. In place of strategies for dealing with discrimination, people gave numerous accounts of taking on the work of educating the broader population, both in social situations and in purposively sanctioned spaces (such as organized events in schools and workplaces). Here, the promise of recognition is not an individual freedom, but a collective one. When HIV identity is anchored in questions of entitlement, it is cast as an undifferentiated mode of being which pertains to one's HIV status. The men in these groups were involved in reworking these terms of HIV identity. The value of HIV as a collective identity was asserted, not so much on the grounds of similarities between HIV positive (or gay) men, but as a space where one could be accepted by others and as the means for self-acceptance. For example, this value is expressed in the negative by Brian, when he writes about his experience of the push to return to work which started when ARV treatment was heralded as a breakthrough in HIV treatment:

Brian, 'fitting into work'
Life was good, he had a busy lifestyle now. There was volunteer work which had built up to five days a week, though not five solid days. It was a lot of stop start periods which meant he wasn't knocked-out, but a healthy tiredness ... The volunteer work ... combined with the satisfaction gained made for a well rounded life be it very short on cash from subsisting on the pension ...

Attitudes change, a new era was starting. Organisations and social workers were saying 'Re-engage in Life' and 'Go back to work' – you're living now not dying. Well he thought 'how insulting'. What did they think he'd been doing for the past few years? Hibernating!

Well he tried going back to work, finding it isn't that easy. Years ago he was in demand, he was known for being good at his job, but now they would say 'where have you been and what have you been doing for the past few years?' ...

Despite his misgivings he tried to go back to work. He got the chance to do a couple of weeks work. The lure of a more normal life and of a reasonable wage instead of subsisting on the pension convinced him to go for it.

He felt great going off for some regular work, but it didn't last long. After a couple of days the routine became get up go to work, come home to bed then get up again. At the end of two weeks he spent the next week sick, barely able to get out of bed. Not one to give in easily over the next few years he repeated this attempt at a normal working life, unfortunately with the same result each time.

Due to his inability to return to work he discovered a new twist on an old problem, Discrimination. This didn't come from the usual quarters. It came from workers in the HIV field and from other positive people.

Brian does not expect others to be the same as him, but he is disappointed by their inability to engage with his desire to work, a desire which is complicated by the realities of finding and keeping a job. In discussing this account in the group, he expanded:

> Brian: In a sense you're used to [discrimination] coming from other quarters and for other things like being gay or being HIV. But I didn't expect it on that basis. The reason I got it and still get it, I've still had comments recently, is because and when I look at myself in the mirror I look at myself and think 'you look fine'. That's what it is. People look at me and see nothing wrong with him: 'he should be out working'... Rightly or wrongly, whether they intend it or not, when that push [to return to work] and change was happening, that was actually the message they were giving me: 'Okay you've bludged* long enough now you've got to go back to work. *You look fine'.*

In Brian's account the hope invested in HIV identity is that it can and *should* be a means of protection from the ignorance and prejudice of the wider community. Relating to self and others through this notion of HIV identity contributes to forging a secure place of belonging. In the group discussion, the recognition Brian craves was understood as an important means of rejecting the 'subservience' with which people are expected to respond when they find themselves subjected to overly-simplistic notions of HIV status as identity.

Both Rick's and Brian's accounts can be read as attempts to refigure entitlement. The difference between these accounts lies in the ways power is described: a sovereign power appears to be the source of Rick's problems, whereas the difficulties Brian encounters stem from the pastoral power of 'social workers' as well as his encounters with other HIV positive people. But they both contest their positioning as 'bludgers' and in different ways assert that, because they are not who others take them to be, they are entitled. However, the problems remain: the successes of these stories are qualified (Rick's) or absent (Brian's). Rather than explain these ongoing difficulties on the basis of

---

* 'Bludge' is an Australian word meaning to live off someone else. Unemployed people are pejoratively called dole-bludgers.

individuals' capacities (or lack of) to invent or reinvent themselves as properly entitled, we want to consider the double-bind of the predicament being discussed. Being included in the public domain as one who has to be *granted* entitlement is a form of exclusion through inclusion (Rancière, 1998). This illustrates how the successful assertion of identity can be an undermining move. Yet, many positive people are locked into this battle. Although – as Brian's memory suggests – HIV identity *is* being reworked and becoming something more than HIV status, possibilities for challenging the very notion of entitlement itself are hard to realize.

In the city-based memory-work group entitlement was not problematized. Although Australian middle-classes receive many government benefits, in the form of tax breaks or subsidies for purchasing property for example, middle-class welfare has not been subjected to the same public discourse of 'bludging' (Bunker, Gleeson, Holloway & Randolph, 2002). Not surprisingly, some different possibilities for political engagement with HIV identity emerged in these group discussions.

A scope of infinite variations

The only way through a crisis of space is to invent a new space. (Jameson [in an interview with Stephenson], 1988, p. 18)

Refusing normative accounts of the present

A question of sociability, how HIV positive people can relate without invoking the logic of similarity (see Chapter 4), was posed in the city-based memory-work group. For example, Liam discussed giving an invited talk at a conference run by an organization of people living with HIV/AIDS and the subsequent reaction. He was asked to address the (closed) conference as a HIV positive man. Although he was actively involved in community organizations and open about his HIV status in this context, Liam had always avoided 'speaking as a positive man'. At the conference he tried to explain his rationale and his mode of engagement – with some ironic consequences. In a context where 'one of the big questions was why these organizations weren't attracting lots of new members', Liam drew on his own experience to argue that 'one way of coping with [HIV] is to not think about it and it's a perfectly legitimate way and don't problematize people for their lack of engagement, they're just living with HIV'. The audience reaction was unexpected:

Because I was engaging in this personal narrative about my experience of HIV [in the talk] I was then welcomed into the fold by these
people who were like really wary of me for years. And I had a really
ambivalent reaction to that too because in telling a personal narrative about being HIV positive I was allowed into the gang but that
was exactly the sort of dynamic that I was in a way feeling a bit
weird about ... But there's also something about engaging in a confessional sort of mode I think. I don't know. My experience of the
conference was that I felt ... that what made it an occasion to
welcome me to the fold was the fact that I was confessing. Like a
coming out ...

It would be mistaken to suggest that Liam's attempt to eschew 'confession' is an outright negation of HIV identity. Such a reading glosses the
fact that Liam is clearly working on the problem of HIV identity – he is
spending time trying to discuss it with others. Moreover, it overlooks
the possibility for relating to oneself *differently* which is being introduced here. Confession speaks the truth of oneself which, in this
context, amounts to speaking HIV as a fundamental truth of the self.
In rejecting the metaphor of the closet, Liam's account suggests that
integrating HIV into a coherent personal narrative is not the only way
to contest and occupy the terrain of HIV.

The limitations of working HIV experience into a personal narrative
were further elaborated in the group discussion. Anton, for example,
remembered being faced with a myriad of questions and decisions
about HIV treatments for the first time. He signed up to participate in
meetings run by the AIDS Council (ACON):

Anton: ... after the second meeting I already knew this is not for me
... it was sort of okay, [I heard] how other people were
dealing with [treatments] and it was at a time that I really
had to start treatment. And I didn't quite know which way
to go ... So this was ... fact finding ... But very soon it degen-
erated into personal stories and I thought 'hey I don't want
to be here' ... And a couple of people were just so living
their HIV positive life or whatever, and that's not me ...
So it's not that I want to join the flock it's maybe I have no
need for it, I don't know.

Anton is negating neither the centrality of HIV in his life at that time
nor his need for information. Like Liam, he rejects the notion of living

a life centred around HIV as thought by others. By refusing a place in 'the flock' (the flock, and Liam's 'fold', evoke a form of passive belonging) Anton insists on the possibility of relating to himself as other than a subject of pastoral power in need of guidance. Pastoral power functions through individuals' internalization of a normative notion of what constitutes a 'good life' (Foucault, 1984). Historically, the insertion of a Christian notion of pastoral power into the government and administration of populations marks the point at which the state starts to govern through people's aspirations to health and well-being (Bevir, 1999). In rejecting the coherent alignment of HIV, experience and subjectivity which occurs in 'HIV identity' both Anton and Liam can be understood as defending the possibility of cultivating their own ideas about how to live a good life.

It was in these discussions – about the difficulties of identifying with other HIV positive people without internalizing normative notions of HIV identity – that 'relating positively' was suggested as a cue. David's memory (above) describes joking about death with positive friends at two different points in time. In the first, when he is HIV negative, he *laugh[s] at the jokes but feel[s] on the edge'*. Years later, after he has seroconverted, David makes fun about his *'long term prospects'* and *'realis[es] he [is] now part of the group'*. As the memory-work group tried to understand the sense of belonging to which being *'part of a group'* alludes, they grappled with the logic of similarity assumed in the notion of identification. For example, David explained that the men with whom he was joking about mortgages and dogs were a group of positive friends:

David: ... I knew all of them before they seroconverted. But that reflects, I haven't sought out new friends as such, specifically because, I would never do that because friendship is based on a range of things. That's not to say that I wouldn't make friends with a positive person. But they all either seroconverted or came out [as positive] soon after [I got to know them] ... But coming together with them at times is a nice experience sometimes ...

Andrew: Do you identify with them when you do?

David: No.

Andrew: So it's not an identification?

David: No it's just ... to be able to talk openly with somebody, to share your paranoia, and laugh it off and tell them a worse story ... So it's just to be with somebody in the same position yeah. It can be really useful at times. I find it hard to say identify because I don't like, I mean obviously there's part of your identity it's kind of who we are, but it's not as well.

Liam: ... I don't think I identify with people who are positive when we come together but we definitely do something with being in common together or something and that's important and has often been positive for me. But it's not, I don't know why I have this resistance to say that I'm identifying with them

Niamh: Because it's not based on likeness?

Liam: Well it is based on some sort of likeness but being in a similar sort of a situation.

David: It's not an identity, it's part of what shapes your identity but it's not an identity. Not for me anyway.

Anton: I almost see it more like for instance if I hear someone speak Spanish [his native language, de-identified], and maybe you talk and for that instant you have something in common and then you go your different ways ...

Liam: That's a really interesting analogy actually to think of it like a language where you've got a scope of infinite variations. Something shared, some in-commonness.

Whilst connections based on a shared identity are eschewed as cramping one's style, the 'scope of infinite variations' made possible by HIV as a 'shared language' is valued. Before we discuss the potential for freedom entailed in these kinds of relations, we want to consider the mode of connecting with others which is being invoked here.

The differential terms of occupation

It is possible to distinguish between relations with others which function through crude empathy and those where openness to the unknown makes connection possible. Crude empathy (which, as we discussed in Chapter 3, memory-workers are advised to avoid), involves translating the other's experience back into what we already know, and failing to encounter the experience of the other *in its own terms*. Because it frequently produces sentimentality in place of the effort to explore experiences which challenge the world as we know it, crude empathy works to shore up normative modes of subjectification (Bennett, 2003). This is both the problem with which Liam is presented when he is interpellated as confessing and coming out, and the

seduction to which he alludes when he notes that, despite his reluctance, 'there's also something about engaging in a confessional sort of
mode I think'. However, crude empathy is not the only form of shared
experience. Social relations can be forged by *experiencing with* the other rather
than *engaging in* their experience (Foucault, 1997). This means trying to
stand in the shoes of the other without making the colonizing assumption that such a step is possible, it is a partial and necessarily mistake-
ridden step. Being open to the alterity of the other is disorientating and
destabilizing. A very different notion of experience is being invoked
here. To experience with the other is not an invitation to try to grasp a
truth of the other, or even to know what it was like to be another.
It demands more than attempting to understand the *meaning* of past
events in people's present lives – it demands that we inhabit the world
differently (Bennett, 2003). Experience is of interest here, not for what it
indicates about interiority, but as a process of out-folding, of occupying
intersubjective, transitional space, and of remaking that space. Hence,
experiences of displacement or confusion in the face of the other may
not signal a lack of connectedness, but the possibility of inquiring and
of collaborating in *developing* relations which actualize and rework the
socio-political conditions in which people find themselves.

For example, in discussing attempts to grapple with the experience
of the Holocaust in post-WWII Europe, Jean Améry (1964/1980) rages
against accepted psychological explanations of 'healthy' survival as the
result of individuals' proper incorporation of historical events into
personal narratives. He totally renounces any idea that his persecutors
should rework their guilt through a process of internalization. He does
not purport to be an example of psychological health: Améry is
patently aware of the damage done to him through torture, loss and a
lifetime of displacement. He yearns for a life unplagued by his past, but
he does not think that, realistically, his efforts will contribute to the
development of a new trajectory in his own life. Améry insists that
there is an excess to normative accounts of history. He rejects any idea
that the past could be refigured 'in the process of internalisation ... but
on the contrary, [only] through actualisation, or, more strongly stated,
by actively settling the unresolved conflict in the field of historical
practice' (1964/1980, p. 69). It is, not by articulating experience, but
only by externalizing experience that we can begin to work with the
irresolvable, enduring problematic presence of the Holocaust.

Améry attunes us to the *depoliticizing* risk of identifying history at
work in narrative accounts of experience. On the one hand, he refutes

the notion that the personal is necessarily political; on the other, he uses his own experience to intervene in the political landscape of post-war reconstruction in Europe. He recognizes his own resentment as an instance of Nietzsche's slave morality, the motivation of a loser. But he painfully realizes that to mask it, or to try to transform it into a noble movement into the future, would be to negate the facts that he *is* one of history's losers, that the future will never belong to him.

We do not want to suggest that the inner-city group's discussions of HIV identity are motivated by a sense of resentment in any way similar to Améry's, or by experiences of analogous injustice or loss. Moreover, the simultaneous strength and hopelessness of Améry's critique of historical accounts of the Holocaust is incomparable with the attempts to rework HIV identity under discussion here. (Below, we will consider in more detail the points of divergence between Améry's insistence on the excess of experience and Foucauldian accounts of work of investing in relations with the self.) However, Améry's condemnation of strategies which hinge on the interiorization of experience does help to illuminate the refusal to take up HIV identity as a personal narrative. Instead of thinking of (or aspiring to) experiences of HIV as moments in a coherent, normative narrative of HIV identity (and being disappointed by its failure to develop), what emerged in the city-based group's discussions was a notion of experience as the site in which a transformative ethics of discomfort (Foucault, 1997) is practiced. Here, experience is 'a locus of placement and displacement, and of differential terms of occupation' (Bennett, 2003, p. 187).

Two sides to the shared language of HIV are evoked in these men's questioning of identity. There is the sheer pleasure of connecting over speaking death in David's account. As the joke flows between friends, being augmented at every point, death becomes funnier and funnier, and the seeming effortlessness of this connection brings people's everyday struggles with HIV into high relief. It seems that, only when David can joke about his own death in the same way, can he share in the full ease of this mode of subjectification. Yet, avoiding crude empathy and risking the incomplete attempt to experience with others can be a fraught and contested step. Such a move can be easily stymied (for example, Anton decides to avoid hearing people who 'were just so living their HIV positive life' and stops going to the meetings about treatments). Or it may be the initial point on an open trajectory moving further and further from normative modes of HIV identity (as could be the case with Liam's attempt to question the assumption that positive people should be identifying with HIV community). But in what sense could this trajectory bring us any closer to a 'politics of ourselves'?

The politics of aesthetics

Researching subjectification opens a way of considering how resistance is materialized in relations with the self which – through questioning the connection between central and marginal versions of self – produce new forms of life. In *The Use of Pleasure* (1992) and *The Care of the Self* (1990), Foucault undertakes a genealogical analysis of sexual practices and relations between men. His objective is to find the means to challenge the deployment of sexual desire and sexual liberation as speaking a fundamental truth of the self. He differentiates between modes of relating to the self which offer more or less possibilities for resisting an understanding of subjectification as expression of the truth of sexual desire. Normalizing relations act as a means for 'internalising, justifying or formalising general interdictions imposed on everyone' (1992, pp. 252–3). These are distinguished from relations with the self that entail the aesthetic cultivation of 'active freedom' (1992, p. 92).

The aesthetics of existence are elucidated through analysis of the subjectification of a minority of Greek men (privileged citizens, not slaves, not women) who were positioned as 'free to select, adapt, develop and – above all – innovate' in their relations with themselves (1992, p. 252). This mode of subjectification can be contrasted with the contemporary everyday understanding of sexuality as speaking the truth of the self – a decipherable, textual truth of the subject. The ancient Greeks did consider the self and truth to be connected, but in a different way. the self is 'constituted through the force of truth' (Foucault, 1997, p. 197). This meant that reflecting on sexual practice was valued, not for what it revealed of one's interiority, but for how it contributed to constituting a person in relations with others and the world:

> [R]eflection on sexual behaviour as a moral domain ... was a means of developing – for the smallest minority of the population made up of free, adult males – aesthetics of existence, the purposeful art of freedom perceived as a power game. Their sexual ethics ... rested on a very harsh system of inequalities and constraints (particularly in connection with women and slaves); but it was problematised in thought as the relationship, for a free man, between the exercise of his freedom, the forms of his power, and his access to truth. (1992, pp. 252–3)

For free citizens, the aesthetics of existence involved working on sexuality as a site of creative transformation. From a present-day perspective, what is interesting about this particular connection between the self and freedom is that (rather than targeting a unitary sovereign power) it interrupts the *normalizing function* of subjectification; it challenges any 'indirect exaltation of the normal, rational, conscientious, and well-adjusting individual' (Foucault, 1977, p. 226). Hence the promise of this 'act of freedom par excellence ... [is that it] opens the door to the unheard of, the unforeseeable', it offers a means of repoliticizing experience (Eribon, 2004, p. 7).

Although the emphasis in this account of aesthetic modes of subjectification is on the relation with oneself (for example, in the quote above), there is more to the 'politics of ourselves' being described here (for example, Foucault, 1997). The very possibility of freedom 'rests on' and is realized in the exercise of power in relations with others – in the case of the Greeks, a citizen's relations with other citizens, with women, with slaves. Self/freedom may be problematized in relations with the self, but it is actualized in relations with others. And in Foucault's example, people's differential positioning in relation to each other is hierarchical and hinges on their relations with the sovereign state. How does the political promise of the aesthetics of existence shape and work in relations of power which emerge as diffused flows within and between networks of acentrically organized actors? We want to consider this question by returning to the differences between the moments described in Rick's and David's accounts of HIV subjectification.

Beyond identity politics?

Rick's and David's memories seem to evoke different possibilities for intervention in the normalizing functions of subjectification. In response to the obligation to represent oneself as entitled, the strategy which emerged in discussions of experiences like Rick's was to contest and rework normative notions of collective HIV identity. But this strategy does not question the way in which the entitlement granted to positive people functions to constrain and curtail people as it includes them in the public sphere (Rancière, 1998). Despite this, it has been a productive strategy. For example, in the late 80s and early 90s, gay community demands for recognition of HIV identity effectively forced government and researchers to acknowledge and respond to a new social group – People Living with HIV/AIDS or PLWHA (Ariss, 1997).

The reverberations were broadly felt: recognition of HIV identity became the first step of the insertion of a discourse of 'patient empowerment' into Australian health regulation and policy (in the following chapter we give further consideration to the deployment of HIV identity). It is always possible to invoke the critique of identity politics – that they reify the terms of identity they seek to challenge – in the attempt to understand the limitations of this strategy. However, as discussed above, such a critique fails to take account of how the material conditions of people's lives necessitate the public visibility of HIV identity. This is why any attempt to argue that, in place of identity politics, Rick might consider cultivating an aesthetic subversion of entitlement is problematic. It masks the privilege granted to those who *can* be understood as pursuing an aesthetics of HIV existence. If, instead, we consider Rick's identity politics as a situated response to the imperative to demonstrate entitlement we start to challenge any assumption that there is a unified experience of HIV, that there is one HIV identity which positive people are involved in contesting in different ways. Rather than oppose identity politics with an aesthetics of the self, we can see them as different ways of harnessing experience – both of which contribute to the loose assemblage which is the problem of HIV. We are not simply suggesting an eclectic approach in which these two strategies are cast as different but equal. They each offer different political possibilities – the limitations of identity politics have been much discussed, but what of self/freedom?

In interrogating the politics of self/freedom Foucault makes an important break. Politics is no longer understood as action directed towards a sovereign power and – in addition to the state – social and cultural life can now be understood as important sites of change (see Chapter 6 for further discussion of this). Does turning to the aesthetics of existence to understand socio-political change in the terrain of social and cultural life, give researchers any purchase on the ongoing and ever-changing activity of the state in the regulation of everyday life? For example, simply approaching HIV identity as the product of the activities and connections between a diffuse network of actors does not, in itself, equip social researchers with any tools for understanding how the state functions in that network. One of the difficulties here (which we will discuss in Chapter 7) is that, as the state increasingly moves away from the role of central organizer and adopts disseminated strategies for governing, it is becoming harder to identify exactly how and where the state functions (Sassen, 1999). Familiar notions of the state as a hierarchical and sovereign power no longer suffice. Yet, the state is no less active in the government of everyday life. Now the efficacy of the state hinges (in part) on the fact that its dispersal in everyday life makes the means through which it operates harder to identify, challenge and rework (Papadopoulos & Tsianos, 2006). So, although Foucault theorizes action outside of sovereign power, the socio-political landscape has changed such that he is in fact theorizing a new configuration of state power. His anti-étatisme is serious and decisive but, because the state is so thoroughly present in the social and cultural terrains in which aesthetic freedoms function, this break is not enough to think social and political action from the outside. (In the last three chapters of this book we will develop the idea of outside politics.) Foucault's thinking remains driven by the logic of state power, either in its presence (sovereign power) or in its apparent absence (aesthetics of the self). Foucault is the theoretician of the social state par excellence. This is the value of his work and this is also its limitation.

In the written accounts and discussions of HIV identity, which we have been examining in this chapter, the state appears to simultaneously occupy this double function. Sometimes it is cast as a sovereign power (as in Rick's account). At others its functions are dispersed. For example, when Brian's difficulties are described as stemming from '*workers in the HIV field and from other positive people*' the pastoral care of social workers is explicitly nominated as part of the problem. The role of the state is more implicit in the experiences discussed in the city-based group. The meetings about HIV treatments which Anton attends are organized by a community run, state-funded AIDS Council. Yet, in this account the other positive people who 'were just so living their HIV positive li[ves]' appear as the problematic figures, less so the organization itself. And, although there is no explicit mention of it, the organization which is hosting Liam's conference is also state-funded. Hence, we could read his argument (that people's disengagement with HIV organizations needs to be valued) as an aesthetic resistance to the way the state functions through pastoral regulation of HIV identity. Yet, could this strategy unintentionally reify the very mechanism through which techniques of the self are brought into alignment with the neoliberal state? Or, could we assert that the aesthetics of the self is the cultural logic of neoliberalism? In other words, the question which remains is if the cultivation of active freedom – a strategy which is commonly understood as a critique of identity politics – can actually take us *beyond* identity politics. Or is it just a different but complementary form of social action which extends, without challenging, the state's function? In the following chapters we argue that any attempt to harness the aesthetics of existence which returns us to an individual, autonomous, self-mastering agent cannot intervene in the new configuration of state-power. But rather than discount the connection between subjectification and freedom Foucault offers, we extend it to take account of the role continuous, collective experience plays in the emerging 'politics of ourselves'.

There is a hint of the argument we are going to advance in David's memory. On first reading it appears to stand out for two reasons. Firstly, it is the only account where the unspeakable – death – is mentioned. Death is the matter which flows and forges alliances between people. And secondly, the jokes are shared between existing friends in the private realm (in contrast to the experiences discussed above, all of which take place in public). Yet, there *is* implicit recognition of the state, and it is more than a part of the scenery in the background. The state-funded AIDS Council is to be the vehicle for generating income out of marketing death. Perhaps the force of this joke does not stem from its potential role in the development of any new ability to accept death on the jokers' part, or from its role in the rearrangement of their relations with themselves or each other. Rather, this joke is funny because it is ludicrous. It externalizes the 'unresolved conflict' (Améry, 1964/1980, p. 69) of the state's role in managing the lives and deaths of HIV positive gay men; a conflict which is keenly felt by these men, not only because they are gay and HIV positive, but because they are invested in and constituted through this biopolitics. They are constituted in relation to their serostatus, their sexuality *and* in relation to the AIDS Council. This reading of David's memory suggests that an aesthetic account of self/freedom can certainly foreground the state's involvement in the proliferation of biopolitical forces, explaining just how deeply funny this joke really is. But it does not illuminate the full force of the joke, nor the trajectory it might be moving on. If there is any excess to the biopolitical regulation of life being introduced here, it cannot be harnessed through an analysis of the aesthetics of existence. To begin to elucidate this position, we want to turn to an alternative approach to politicizing experience than that offered by Foucault.

In the face of the ever-present risk that the aesthetics of freedom not only overlooks, but reproduces, the privileged positioning of those who cultivate it (Spivak, 1999), the particular way in which Améry politicizes experience is vital. Regarding his own mode of subjectification, although he refuses to accept his fate, his hopelessness is enduring. There is no noble sacrifice here, only anger and the energy to continue to do battle with history. Refusal, resistance simply do not translate into hope, freedom. Self/freedom is not Améry's point of departure. The political promise of experience lies in its excess, that which resists incorporation into any relation with the self and which demands externalization in 'the field of historical practice' (Améry, 1964/1980, p. 69).

This will be the starting point for the following chapters, where we will sketch an account of socio-political action and an understanding of experience which might rid us 'of the sacrifice which is linked to ... technologies' of internalization (Foucault, 1997, p. 231).

6
Rethinking Collectivity

The concept of collectivity

> [I]n a historical moment in which individual personal identity has been unmasked as a decentred locus of multiple subject positions, surely it is not too much to ask that something analogous be conceptualised on the collective level. (Jameson, 2000, p. 68)

The concept of collectivity is a cornerstone of much politically engaged social research. Yet, its political relevance is now virtually invisible to some, hence Jameson's (2000) call for a new conceptualization of collectivity. Here, we consider the tension between critiques of collectivity as a politically potent tool for social research and emerging ways of understanding what collectivity and collaborative action are now becoming. Like that of other concepts, the value of the concept of collectivity hinges, not on the degree to which it reflects universal truths of existence, but on its capacity to make 'the future different from the past by affording new forms of description, thought and action' (Patton, 2000, p. 133).

Collectivity as a means of resistance to liberal individualism

The importance of collectivity stems, in part, from a Marxist decentring of individual consciousness: '[i]t is not the consciousness of men that determines their existence, but their social existence that determines their consciousness' (Marx, 1970, p. 21). Social existence is collective, and 'collectivity' is a particular mode of social cooperation.

119

In contrast to the relations of production in which subjects find themselves – relations which constrain the material conditions of social, political and intellectual life – 'collectivity' denotes specific forms of cooperative, rational action which hold the key to freedom.

This explains why collectivity has been valued as a means of resistance to liberal individualism (that is, resistance to an ideology which restricts people's capacity to effect political change, through isolating them from each other and narcissistically redirecting energy towards oneself). Whilst research which takes the individual subject as its focus of study is active in producing liberal ideology (Parker, 1999), focusing on collectivity has the potential to redress this problem. As we discussed in Chapter 3, in devising the method of memory-work Haug and others argue that the emergence of collectivity in the memory-work group brings researchers towards their 'aim to live collectively and thus to escape individual isolation' (1987, p. 282). This suggests the promise of collectivity, indicating the future possible worlds it conjures up and those being negated. Collectivity figures as the antidote to liberal processes of individualization and ideologies.

Limitations of collectivity

There has been extensive debate over how to distinguish better or worse practices and concepts of collective cooperation. Moreover, the value of collectivity as an intervention into current socio-political problems has been questioned. Individuals can be blind to the workings of ideology, but groups which are specifically formed as collectives are not immune to this problem. The capacity for collective cooperation can be regulated and redirected against freedom (Osterkamp, 1999). Cooperation can be a means of resistance, but it can also be productively harnessed and used to promote individualistic modes of being (for example, Sennett [1998] identifies the proliferation of individualism in the practices which pertain to 'team-work' in contemporary workplaces). This then, presents the problem of how to distinguish between collectives that might actually intervene in the materialization of individualistic social relations and those which only claim a radical political agenda (for example, see the debates between Parker [2000] and Newman & Holzman (2000]). But disagreements over more or less, effective modes of collectivity cannot be resolved without attending to a more serious criticism of the concept.

The notion of ideology underpinning Marxist concepts of collectivity has been intensely criticized on the grounds that it suggests the possibility of accessing some truth lying behind false-consciousness (Althusser,

1971; Foucault, 1986). A collective, in Marxist thought, is a group of subjects who work towards realizing new forms of social existence by identifying and responding to what is hidden by false-consciousness. But if subjects are already produced through discursive construction and regulation (rather than oppression), and subject-positions are afforded by discourses, there is no reason that well-planned, well-intended cooperation between subjects should be enlightening or transforming. For example, speaking about the events of May 1968, Foucault argues that political action is not inhibited because the truth of collective existence is being stifled. People are neither blinded nor deluded about the effects of power: 'the masses know perfectly well ... and they are certainly capable of expressing themselves' (1977, p. 207). The difficulty lies in the operation of a 'system of power which blocks, prohibits, and invalidates' some discourses and knowledges by 'subtly penetrat[ing] an entire societal network' (p. 207). Affirming the authenticity of one's experience through the adoption of an 'I' speaking position ('the author function') is simply not effective in the face of such a network (Foucault, 1977; Hook, 2001). By the same analysis, speaking or acting as 'we' is also highly likely to serve to solidify rather than rework the discourse it seeks to contest (Eribon, 2004).

Any attempt to theorize the freedoms pertaining to collectivity needs to take account of a collective's ever-present potential to become a means of oppression (Frow, 1999; Jameson, 2000). This point is sometimes expressed as a misreading of a Marxist notion of collectivity as essentially homogenizing (Jameson, 1993). Yet, in practise the problem is real: collectives can always lapse into policing normalizing modes of existence. Hence, any attempt to shore up the universal value of collectivity as a mode of resistance by identifying formal structures or transcendental qualities of 'good' collectivity is bound to fail. It can only reify particular strategies of resistance, abstracting them from the diverse material conditions in which subjects are differently produced, isolated and regulated. In such cases, theory functions to inhibit the multiplication of a given concept, leaving the concept more vulnerable to the totalizing workings of power (Deleuze & Foucault, 1977).

There is an alternative to judging concepts according to notions of universal value. What is demanded instead is an approach to collectivity which can intensify the momentum of efforts to counter processes of normalization. Recognizing the shifting and contingent powers and constraints of collectivity could contribute to opening pathways for refusing what we think, do and who we are (Foucault, 1986). However, the possibility of rethinking collectivity has not been extensively explored by social researchers. There are particular difficulties entailed in theorizing collective resistance and collaborative action in the face of our contemporary conditions of social regulation and social control.

Biopower and the problem of collective resistance

The powers of resistance attributed to collectivity appear to be rapidly dissolving. The promise of collectivity may be evident if we are contesting a (sovereign) hierarchical power which constrains subjects through isolating and individualizing them. However, when we consider the productive regulation of subjects through fragmented administrative apparatuses which take populations as their object of control (biopower) the role of collectivity in power relations is deeply ambiguous. Here regulation entails acting on the stuff of collectivity, the avenues of social cooperation, in enabling and constraining ways. Foucault's identification of biopower posits the social as the very terrain on which exploitation occurs. This tension is illustrated in the emergence and capture of 'HIV identity' as a collective strategy for intervening in the regulatory practices of both government and pharmaceutical companies.

In his ethnographic study of Sydney gay community mobilization through the 80s and into the early 90s, Ariss (1997) offers an insightful analysis of the ambiguous achievement involved in the constitution of 'HIV identity' or 'PLWHA'. He traces the constitutive relationship between institutional and political recognition of HIV identity on the one hand (as discussed in the previous chapter), and the proliferation of regulation and constraint on the other. For example, pharmaceutical researchers were compelled to reconsider the requirements of 'good science'. Two moves – threats of non-compliance with experimental drug regimens (practices which would render the results of clinical trials meaningless) and the work of HIV activists – forced pharmaceutical researchers to consider the *treatment* benefits of participation in experimental trials. The significance of such changes in scientific practice cannot be underestimated. Yet, this success was measured. Ariss argues that the newly emerging scientific practices simultaneously brought about the capture of gay community's potential. A direct consequence of pharmaceutical researchers' reconsideration of scientific methods was that gay community was reconstituted as a source of acquiescent, docile bodies readily available for experimentation. This double-edged trajectory of freedom and capture illustrates the workings of biopower. Ariss does not make grand claims about the total pacification of gay men's bodies. Nor is he hugely optimistic about future possibilities for harnessing or redoubling biopower. Rather, his close analysis of the unfolding of events opens possibilities for approaching collective political engagement as a continual movement between regulation and 'modes of being in the world ... that are creative, subversive, and ... transformative of the received world order' (1997, p. 201). The point is, not to lament the capture of HIV identity, but to elucidate the challenges for future political engagement.

This analysis of the unfolding and refolding of collective resistance can be contrasted with collectivity as it is thought in social research which (implicitly or explicitly) invokes power as sovereign power. However, if power no longer resides in the body of the sovereign or within an institution, but is productive and diffuse, what exactly is a collective to resist? Any attempt to rethink collectivity needs to address the workings of biopower.

Working with human potential

For millennia, man remained what he was for Aristotle: a living animal with the additional capacity for a political existence; modern man is an animal whose politics places his existence as a living being in question. (Foucault, 1984, p. 143)

Foucault (1984) identified disciplinary-biopower as emerging over the course of the late 18th to early 19th centuries and continuing to proliferate in the 20th century. It entails two distinct forms of the exercise of power over life. These two techniques of power are never united in a general theory of government or power, but come together in concrete practices of organization. The first pole is individualizing: disciplinary power focuses on regulating the potentials and docility of the body. This gives rise to the paradox discussed in Chapter 1, that is, how to challenge a form of power through which subjects are both constituted as self-regulating and constrained by their very efforts to realize freedom (Rose, 1996b). The second pole is *collectivizing*. It operates through and is constitutive of a particular form of collective subject: the population, constructed as a social object and agent (Bevir, 1999). Disciplinary-biopower encompasses both poles, but it is the latter which is particularly important for discussions of collectivity; its focus is on 'processes of life' thought in terms of the social body (Foucault, 1984, p. 139).

The emergence of 'the population' as an object of governance can be traced to the late 18th century use of particular techniques of government. New forms of description meant that it was not only subjects who needed to be governed, but '"a population" with its specific phenomena and peculiar variables: birth and death rates, life expectancy, fertility, state of health, frequency of illness, patterns of diet and habitation' (Foucault, 1984, p. 25; Donzelot, 1984). Thus the state's interest in and control of sex became an important tool of government (and a productive one, leading to the modern interest in *both* regulating and liberating sexuality).

The object of biopower is life itself. The mechanisms of biopower regulate the emergence of any specific subjectivity or form of collectivity. That is, through the operation of biopower both the individual and the social body are always, already politicized. Here, 'life' does not simply refer to biological existence, but to *human potential*. Biopower incorporates life in the form of:

> the basic needs, man's concrete essence, the realization of his potential, a plenitude of the possible ... [t]he 'right' to life, to one's body, to health, to happiness, to the satisfaction of needs, and beyond all the oppressions or 'alienations', the right to rediscover what one is and all that one can be, this 'right' – which the classical juridical system was utterly incapable of comprehending – was the political response to all these new procedures of power which did not derive, either from the traditional right of sovereignty. (Foucault, 1984, p. 145)

Efforts to realize, increase and augment human potential are the mechanisms through which biopower operates. Consider how people's capacities for creativity, for communication, sharing and cooperation are increasingly incorporated into the workplace. The mechanisms through which human potential is harnessed are at work, for example, in the construction of 'flexible workers' and 'affective workers', in the regulation of relations between workers and in the discursive shift towards a 'knowledge economy' and an 'economy of services' (Virno, 1996; Sennett, 1998; Boudry, Kuster & Lorenz, 2000; Gorz, 2004).

The biopolitics of social existence

As discussed above, collectivity is valued as a strategy which counters individualization by cultivating and opening the social domain as an object of inquiry. But this overlooks the fact that biopower cannot be contested by opposing the proliferation of liberal individualism with 'the social'. Where Marx identified work as the formative site of exploitation, Foucault's genealogical analyses consider the formation of the social domain as an intrinsically regulative space (Foucault, 1988a; Henriques, Hollway, Urwin, Venn & Walkerdine, 1984/1998). Like HIV identity, the terrain of the social has been colonized as it has been constructed. If we think Marx and Foucault together (they deliver, even if very differently, an approach to the same terrain: state power) then we can conclude that society is not outside of labour. Labour and society are intermingled, control is exercised simultaneously on both levels, work becomes living labour, life and society become productive.

Biopower harnesses the capacity to relate to oneself as part of a collective, community or society and uses it to enjoin the population to systems of governance (Larsen, 2003). For democratic systems of governance to be distinguishable from totalitarian systems, they rely on the active engagement of the population as citizens. Observing the emerging US democracy in 1830s, de Tocqueville (1961) argued that in order to ensure stability without force, people had to be convinced to willingly link their own interests with those of society. This link was made through technologies of the self which encouraged social participation, enabling the powers of government to be transferred to the general will of the people: 'Every man allows himself to be put in leading-strings, because he sees that it is not a person or a class of persons, but the people at large that holds the end of his chain' (Tocqueville, 1961, p. 383). The regulative function of collectivity is also evident in analyses of the state-society relationship which emerged in 19th century European states (Eisenstadt, 2000). No longer figuring in the body of the king, sovereignty was located in the collective figure of citizens who are prepared to sacrifice their idiosyncratic desires and prioritize working towards the common good (McDonald, 2004). A moral imperative for individuals to appropriate collective identities is being introduced here. When active collective participation is the key to the regulation of populations, collectivity becomes the means through which biopower operates.

Notably, the mechanisms of biopower are colonized by neither governments nor any particular knowledge base (scientific, medical or otherwise) (Rabinow & Rose, 2003). There are a host of actors involved. For example, in the field of HIV medicine described by Ariss there are government departments and agencies, biomedical sciences, pharmaceutical companies, HIV specialist doctors, social researchers, PLWHA, gay community, activists, community organizations and carers. Both the realm out of which collectivities are forged and the actors involved are produced in and through relations of power. This returns us to the imperative for any concept of collectivity to take account of how collective practices are *already* organized to produce and constrain possibilities for thought and action.

Normalization

> A normalising society is the historical outcome of a technology of power centred on life ... we should not be deceived by ... a whole continual and clamorous legislative activity: these were the forms that made an essentially normalising power acceptable. (Foucault, 1984, p. 144)

Together the two poles of disciplinary-biopower operate through the *inclusion*, optimization and generation of life. Biopower controls through normalization, as opposed to exclusion. Normalization works, not through decree, but through the active appropriation of micro-practices; that is, incessant, imperceptible practices of control which shore up particular forms of power relations in everyday interactions (Dreyfus, 1996). Biopower is unfounded (Foucault, 1997). It is not inherent in the micro-practices of everyday life, rather through its coordinating and organizing function biopower seizes and orders the everyday, normalizing some ways of being and marginalizing others (Lazzarato, 2004a, 2004b). Hence, normalization proliferates through policing and *inclusion*.

This raises two immediate problems for any attempt to think resistance, collective or otherwise. Firstly, like disciplinary power, biopower is productive and the notion that it *should* be resisted is not immediately evident. For example, Ariss (1997) describes how the very real gains achieved by gay activists arose from working *with* biopower. Similarly, Foucault understood the techniques of the welfare state as effective tools coordinated by biopower, whilst simultaneously recognizing their real value. The point is not to take a stand against biopower – or against the welfare state or the department of health – *per se*. Secondly, having identified a specific reason for resisting biopower (such as the reconstitution of PLWHA as a docile population of experimental subjects) because it is diffuse and operates through micro-practices, there is no concrete target for direct resistance. Historically, demanding legal rights or recognition gave rise to, and now works with biopower, rendering: 'an essentially normalising power acceptable' (Foucault, 1984, p. 144). That is, because calls for inclusion and recognition *enhance* biopower's normalizing function, direct resistance is impossible:

... [W]hat ultimately needs to be resisted is not particular technologies nor particular strategies but rather a tendency in the practices towards *ever greater order and flexibility* that produces and sustains them. Thus the current understanding can only be resisted by first showing that it is not inevitable but is an interpretation of what it is to be, second by connecting our current style with our current discomfort and then by taking up marginal practices which have escaped or successfully resisted the spread of techno/bio-power. (Dreyfus, 1996, p. 12)

Resistance to modes of understanding can take the form of forging counter-discourses (for example, Macleod, forthcoming) or the resignification of existing ones (for example, Butler, 1993). But the discourses through which biopower operates are not merely textual, they are material (Papadopoulos, 2005). Hence, both strategies require that people subvert processes of normalization by cultivating marginal practices and embodying alternative social relations (for example, as discussed in relation to Damien's memory, in Chapter 4).

Aesthetic resistance?

It is true that the number of objects that become objects of governmentality reflected inside political frameworks, even liberal ones, has increased a great deal. But I still do not think that one should consider that this governmentality necessarily takes on the tone of containment, surveillance and control. (Foucault, 1997, p. 157)

Foucault's work can be approached as a sustained interrogation of resistance through the analysis of historical, collective and social experiences, an analysis which is opposed to phenomenological descriptions of interiority. He negates analyses of power relations which conclude 'that finally we are imprisoned in our own system' or that '[t]he chords which bind us are numerous and the knots history has tied around us are oh so difficult to untie' and claims that his own work does 'just the opposite' (1997, p. 160). What has emerged historically can be destroyed politically. Foucault's analysis of aesthetic resistance to the capture of human potential can be read as an attempt to grasp the inner workings of such political mechanisms. As discussed in Chapter 5, the analytic objective in tracing the emergence, mutation and foreclosure of specific freedoms is to open possibilities for becoming other. Theorizing marginal practices which disrupt the normalizing function of sexuality can contest subtle, virtually imperceptible forms of power. For example, *The History of Sexuality* can be read, not as a book about the past, but as an attempt to anticipate and promote 'the materialisation of specific conditions ... and the psychological conditions we are "before"' (Parker, Papadopoulos & Schraube, 2004). Written in the 70s, it promotes and provides the concepts which are necessary to understand the subsequent shift from gay liberation to queer activism in the 90s.

Resistance to biopower is resistance from within: it takes the form of cultivating the human potential to resist its own capture. This is the main political promise of the aesthetics of the self. However, this later project of Foucault (1990, 1992) seems to be problematic from a number of angles. Some argue that the mode of resistance he describes appears to entail a deeper investment in a liberal, disembodied and masculine subject (for example, McNay, 1994). We cannot ignore that the historical possibilities for freedom Foucault identifies in *The History of Sexuality* are firmly located in the lives of the ruling class (as discussed in the previous chapter). Emphasizing the capacity to cultivate an aesthetics of existence seems to affirm (rather than challenge) the 'indirect exaltation of the normal, rational, conscientious, and well-adjusting individual' (1977, p. 226). What is being questioned is the form of politics emerging from an aesthetics of the self which seems to return us to an individual's work on himself. In the face of these critiques, we want to argue that it is possible to think the cultivation of active freedom *without* returning to an individual, autonomous, self-mastering agent as a foundation point. This possibility hinges on the distinction between individualizing practices and practices of individuation. And, in examining this distinction, the importance of actively rethinking collectivity, as opposed to allowing it to drop from view, becomes evident.

The role of collectivity in socio-political transformation

How might collectivity be a potent force in the subversion of normalizing powers and the cultivation of active freedom? Jameson's point of departure – imagining collectivity as a decentred site of multiplicity – is not entirely new; historically it has appeared as promising vision to some, and a nightmare to others. First the nightmare. What this vision threatens is the alignment – common in both liberal and conservative political theory from the 17th century onwards – between the collective subject and the state (Calhoun, 2002). If the powers of social regulation and integration are thought to ultimately reside in government, effective collective action must work through these powers. Other forms of collective action either appear to be ineffective, or to derail the proper processes through which governments regulate public spheres.

Corrupted collectivity

Hobbes (1983), in the 17th century, foregrounded the importance of a specific form of collectivity – the state aligned 'people': 'The *People* is somewhat that is *one*, having *one will*, and to whom one action may be attributed' (p. 151). 'The people' signifies a homogenous entity, manifest in the collective adoption of shared practices and a shared ethos. Subjects relinquish their authority to a sovereign state and become the people through entering into a social contract. The social contract mutes the dangerous multiplicity of singular wills, trajectories and powers, and unifies them into a set of agreed responses to social problems. The promise of the social contract is participation in a community which protects against the unpredictability of life. In this context, Jameson's point of departure is to be abhorred: multiplicity, difference and differentiation threaten chaos and instability.

Hobbes recognizes both the productive aspect of power and the possibility that the exercise of power over others is not a bad thing in and of itself. Yet, here power is essentially reactive: it is focused on control and regulation of *existing* forces and directions (as opposed to active power, in the Nietzschean sense, a form of power which fuels new configurations in social relations). Hobbes' people are akin to Nietzsche's slaves who hand to another both the powers to regulate their own actions and to punish their transgression. Lacking trust in their own capacities for the ongoing development and maintenance of social relations, the social contract functions to channel the people's individual powers and capacities into the service of the state. Ultimately, socio-political change is regulated by and captured by (a now disembodied) sovereign power.

There are gaps in Hobbes' account of how collectivities – in the form of the people – are involved in social and political change. These gaps are not simply oversights, they are intended. Collectivity is purposively theorized in such a way as to privilege forms of political action which are exclusively tied to the state. Other forms are to be discouraged. Now the likelihood of politically effective collective action in other realms (for example, civil society, the private sphere) is only evident when such action is channelled through and accepted by the state in the first instance. Collectivity becomes corrupted by the state. The political relevance of collective action on culture, for example, is completely foreclosed, and with it the possibility 'that through the exercise of social imagination and the forming of social relationships the public sphere could constitute a form of social solidarity' (Calhoun, 2002, p. 159). However, Hobbes fully acknowledges (as he discourages) the possibility that collective action may not bring subjects into alignment with the state. Not only does the state regulate the people, but it plays a productive role in *constituting* collectives as the people. What is being guarded against is the emergence of other forms of collectivity – in particular, collectivity as a centrifugal movement towards multiplicity. For Hobbes, the unruly potential of collectivity constitutes a basic threat to the state. He casts the people as essentially orderly: they forgo their dangerously multiple, singular wills and ascribe to one common will.

The centrifugal movement of collectivity

Collectivity entails both specific forms of unity and heterogeneity. For instance, Spinoza was interested in conceptualizing collectivity as a move along a trajectory of increasing differentiation, a move which avoids lapsing into the one of the people. Here, plurality is an enduring and workable feature of social and political existence, and collectivity is cast as a network of individuals in which singularity emerges (Virno, 2004). The potence of Spinoza's notion of collectivity stems from its role in the production of singularity. Singularity is neither universal nor particular, but occupies the terrain between these two poles. The concept of collectivity becomes part of the attempt to understand how the irreducible differences of singularities 'can be extended close to another, so as to obtain a connection' (Deleuze, 1991, p. 94). This marks a radical shift from collectivity thought as individuals aggregated in the form of the people. Unlike individuality, which enjoins subjects to representing some notion or aspect of themselves, singularity exceeds representation and interrupts self-coincidence (Patton, 2000). Singular connections are not based on shared identities, but on shifting (and sometimes temporary) relations of affinity between concrete others (McDonald, 2004). Singularity emerges from collectivity rather than acting as its foundation.

But a collective entailing irreducible differences is comprised of more than singularities. It has something in common which stems, not from any social contract, but from shared experiences. The contemporary pervasiveness of experiences of displacement – when we increasingly live as strangers to ourselves and to each other – partly explains the current interest in rethinking collectivity through Spinoza's work (for example, Hardt & Negri, 2000). Experiences of non-belonging do not necessarily render collectivity impossible. Whereas the familiarity associated with belonging means that interaction with others can be facilitated by a shared ethos, to be a stranger means that experiencing with others demands effort. Here, the unity of a collective is akin to a meeting of strangers. What remains invisible in interactions between those who can assume a shared ethos becomes evident as strangers struggle to communicate and connect. The most basic elements of common discourse are made public, for example, capacities for communication and thought, the basic 'life of the mind' – or the general intellect. Although ordinarily thought is understood as private and solitary, the increasingly evident materialization of the general intellect in everyday encounters foregrounds the collective, exterior dimension of thought.

There are both positive and negative sides to the lived experience of exterior thought. On the one hand, when 'the fundamental abilities of the human being (thought, language, self-reflection, the capacity for learning) come to the forefront, the situation can take on a disquieting oppressive appearance' (Virno, 2004, p. 40). For example, the contemporary working conditions of post-Fordist employment emphasize the constitutive roles of language, of shared thought processes and of self-reflection both in the organization of work and in appraisals of workers' utility and value. In such instances, the unity of the general intellect can bring actors into stifling and totalizing alignment with each other, resulting in submission to groundless hierarchies. On the other hand, the general intellect is the foundation of a social cooperation. And because shared, collective existence is *not* intrinsically tied to the state, as it is rendered more visible so too is 'a non-public sphere ... a non-governmental public sphere, far from the myths and rituals of sovereignty' (Virno, 2004, p. 40).

Laid bare, the collective dimension of thought can intensify the multiplicity of political-social existence and spawn increasing differentiation. This suggests that the cultivation of singularity, which underpins Foucault's aesthetic relations with the self, does not only pertain to privileged, self-reflexive individuals who differentiate themselves from the normalized masses. Our current conditions of biopolitical regulation open their own possibilities for active freedom – they subvert the foreclosure of collective action in non-state realms. The people, as a collective actor, is always already captured and corrupted by the state. But the collective of those who do not belong anywhere is beyond capture when it escapes aggregation and acts as a performative orchestration of minorities who refuse transformation into a majority, normalizing force. Its unity is neither derived from nor aspires to alignment with the state. Neither the state nor state politics are its direct target.

Individuation

Although biopower works on and through subjective existence, the subject is conceived, not as an entity, but a process, a multiplicity of immanent, connective practices which evade self-introspection (Bove & Empson, 2002; Papadopoulos, 2005). The reflexive turn inward cannot illuminate this process (as discussed in Chapter 4). Connections between individual actors do not emerge through shared revelations of interiority, but through processes of *non-personal* modes of individuation – not through self-recognition, but through moving beyond the self (this process is further described in Chapter 8). Functioning as an assemblage of singularities, rather than subjects or individuals, collectives can interrupt the neoliberal turn to individuality as a source of difference and transformation.

Evidently, this approach to collectivity troubles the individual-collective opposition frequently invoked in social research. As discussed above, in this opposition, the collective is cast as the antidote to the depoliticizing isolation of individuals. In contrast, here the collective is the space where *individuation occurs*. In place of individual subjects, there are processes of individuation, processes which are always ongoing, never finished. Now, the political potential of collective experience is that it acts as the site of individuation, cultivating singularities, enabling new desires and giving rise to increasing differentiation. The common experience of the people weakens individuation (for example, through the unifying force of the social contract), but that of the multitude can amplify and radicalize individuation. As in liberal and neoliberal thinking, autonomous action is valued, but for very different reasons. In liberal discourse, autonomy promotes (and constrains) individual freedoms and the cultivation of 'individuality' (Rose, 1996). In contrast, the autonomy of individuation promotes singularity, enriching what is already common – that is, the non-governmental public sphere of the many.

The idea that individuation occurs through collective experience is not completely unfamiliar. For example, social constructionist thinking holds that without collective experience there would be no individual to speak of. This is illustrated in accounts of development which foreground the intersubjective ascription and appropriation of psychological intentions, feelings and characteristics. Such approaches power-fully decentre any concept of the autonomous individual, revealing the construction of what is commonly assumed to be a pre-given entity (for example, Shotter, 1984; Bradley, 1989). However there is an important tension between social constructionist notions of the individual and the process of individuation being described here. In invoking collectivity as a centrifugal movement beyond subjectivity, the status of the subject – even as a socially constituted entity – is being contested. 'The subject' entails both individuated singularities and pre-individual elements of life. Pre-individual aspects of the subject (including shared language, but also biological matter and sensations which escape subjective representation) continually contest individuation. The result is that:

> Not infrequently do pre-individual characteristics seem to call into question the act of individuation: the latter reveals itself to be a precarious, always reversible, result. At other times, on the other hand, it is the precise and exact 'I' which appears to endeavour to reduce for itself, with feverish voracity, all of the pre-individual aspects of our experience. ... Either an 'I' that no longer has a world or a world that no longer has an 'I': these are the two extremes of an oscillation which, though appearing in more contained forms, is never totally absent. This oscillation is prominently signalled, according to Simondon, by feelings and passions. The relation between pre-individual and individuated is, in fact, mediated by feelings. (Virno, 2004, p. 79)

Whilst social constructionism explains how feelings and thoughts *become* subjective, in this account they never do become fully subjective. The reason for this is not simply that – because social contexts are always changing – the social construction of individuals is an unfinished, ongoing process. Rather, the social construction of individuals is only one process, continually interrupted by pre-individual and social forces. Vygotsky elucidates this process in his later work with such concepts as sense and meaning, drama, and inner speech (Vygotsky, 1934, 1989; Papadopoulos, 1999).

This shift from subjectification to individuation has important implications. Critical theorists (Adorno & Horkheimer, 1979; Arendt, 1970) hold that the separation of individuals from the processes of their construction gives rise to alienation and inhibits people's capacity to act. But the account of alienation given here stems from the opposite difficulty. When the subject is too closely aligned with the social conditions of existence (unable to think outside of them) negative, oppressive feelings result. Interiorizing experience causes human anxiety and discontent, locking the individual into his or her private oscillation between individual and pre-individual realms. Although there is movement in this relation with the self, the process of interiorization ensures that it is along a fixed path governed by an imperative to reveal the truth of the self. Experience is constrained by the ontological crisis of subjectivity. The form of political engagement arising from this alignment is familiar: recognition and identity politics.

In contrast, the singularity cultivated by collectives fuels experience with the world beyond the subject. The (reassuring or terrifying) containment of self-reflection – thought as an 'I' reflecting on a 'me' or even a 'we' – is shattered and replaced. The collective of those who do not belong anywhere experiences the same internal incommensurability of being a subject, and the sheer impossibility of being an 'I' in any kind of stable, predictable relation with oneself, others or the world. But there are alternate ways of living this crisis, of working with rather than against what is being revealed. Non-personal modes of individuation – involving experience exterior to the subject – enable new forms of participation in social and political change. They disrupt the current neoliberal, biopolitical production of subjective experience by opening ways of working on the specific connections between singularities – that is, connections which intensify and embellish singularities through their relation with what is common – so that what is created is common, non-personal and between.

Repoliticizing collectivity

Collectivity can work in the self-same terrain as biopower, where regulation is no longer a hierarchical affair engaging individuals through a social contract with the state but occurs in micro-practices of subjectification. Collectivities are likewise regulated through their biopolitical existence. But this existence is not static; it incorporates the potentials housed in living bodies, including potentials to contest the capture of dynamic processes, to contest their transformation into unified, static collectivities. These potentials are realized neither through representational politics nor through the implementation of state policy and legislation, but through the disruption of identities and the exposure of what is being excluded in representation. Practising this mode of relating strains and disrupts the empty 'tyranny of the subjective' (Deleuze & Guattari, 1988) – it is liberating.

In taking the unpredictable, immanent, lived experience of non-personal modes of individuation as its point of departure, this approach challenges the common notion of collectivity as an 'old-world' concept with little relevance for contemporary socio-political change. What is revealed is the political importance of transformations in social relations which are neither directed by nor channelled through the sovereign power of the state or the contained powers of individual subjects. If, in fuelling singularity, collectives are not enticed by promises of subjectification (for example, recognition, inclusion or individual freedoms) they can deploy alternative modes of being which go beyond the organizing function of biopower. Importantly, there is no utopian political promise here. Firstly, this attempt to rethink collectivity is not a claim about the empirical reality of collectives. There is an inherent risk of submission and defeat in any attempt to work in and on the terrain of collective, exterior experience. And, of course, the fact that it is political does not mean that it is 'good', its non-identitarian invisibility is the risky 'dark side' of collectivity (Bove & Empson, 2002). Equally collectives can fail to develop political action, or can be captured and transformed into the homogeneous people. Secondly, this conceptualization does not offer the means to identify the right strategies or programs for collective action. The purpose of this concept is to disrupt the current neoliberal exclusion of the potential of collectivities, and to render visible what we are before and what we are becoming. This is a re-politicization of collectivity in the sense that it subverts the perceptible demarcations of identity and allocations of proper place which perpetuate the normalizing social order (Rancière, 1998).

Outside Politics

Of course, rethinking collectivity as a decentred site of multiplicity does not take us far enough. To strengthen the way concepts of collectivity can contribute to new modalities of thinking and acting, and new forms of political experience, another step is required. That is, to locate this attempt to conceptualize collectivity as one strand of thinking about a broader problem of the contemporary meaning and function of the political.

If life itself is already politicized, if the personal is political, if the micro-practices of life are thoroughly infused with relations of power, perhaps there is little to be gained by explicit discussion of 'the political'? For instance, analyses of subjectification, ethical relations, or the micro-practices of everyday life can uncover the political dimensions of life (for example, Connolly, 2002). However, as we argued in the previous chapter, they do not seem to be providing effective avenues for understanding socio-political changes which are already occurring, or might take us, beyond the constraints of neoliberal regulation. Thus, analyses of the inner-workings of subjectification seem to have an inherent political use, but what remains unquestioned in this move is politics itself.

An interest in aesthetic or ethical relations is frequently aligned with criticism of the attempt to explicitly focus on the political dimensions of life. From one perspective this is understandable: if 'politics' is understood to denote activity designed to target sovereign power (at the expense of acknowledging the ubiquitous pervasiveness of governance in *all* aspects of life), to take politics as an object of analysis appears naïve. It then seems possible to contrast the analysis of ethics or subjectification with the analysis of politics: the former is a site of regulation and creativity, whilst the latter is cast as an essentially moral and normalizing space. But this is a misreading of the Foucauldian distinction between ethical freedom and moral injunctions in which politics is assumed to equate with ethics (and policing with morality). Certainly, our existence is always already politicized, but this is not to say that we are already *doing* politics through our very existence. 'If everything is political then nothing is. So while it is important to show, as Michel Foucault has done magnificently', that subjects are regulated through the micro-practices of everyday life 'it is equally important to say that nothing is political in itself merely because power relationships are at work in it' (Rancière, 1998, p. 32). Is it possible now to explicitly think the political *without* reverting to state targeted politics? This returns us to questions about what politics actually is, how it arises, and about the role of collectivity in doing politics.

Politics is not the sheer exercise of power over – simply exerting one's power over others is domination. Politics arises when the principle of equality reveals any social order to be utterly contingent (Rancière, 2001). This entails a very specific challenge to the social order, in the form of the emergence of those who have no place in the normalizing organization of the social realm. There is no such thing as a completely egalitarian society. Any social order is based on a demarcation between different parts of the community or groups of people – the particular form of demarcation may differ, but the fact that all social orders are made up different parts remains. Moreover, groups are perceived to have different properties of value to the community – for example, the financial capital and know how to provide employment, reproductive capacities, the ability to create, to labour, etc. The degree to which a person is involved in the organization and governance of that community is granted on the basis of who he or she is perceived to be – for example, a wealthy financier, a mother, a worker. The egalitarian principle demands that all have an equal role, but of course equality is a principle, an assumption, not an empirical fact. Problems inevitably arise when, as is frequently the case, the capacities of a mother or a worker are simply imperceptible to those involved in ruling.

This was Plato's argument against democracy: *demos* denote people who appear to have nothing to offer – no wealth, no experience pertinent to government. Theirs is a paradoxical, empty freedom: being included on the basis of an egalitarian principle actually indicates that some parts of the society really have no role to play in governance – if they did they wouldn't need to be incorporated as the *demos*. Democracy involves the inclusion of people who otherwise have no part. Rather than directly contest Plato's critique, it is possible to draw out the insight being offered here in relation to our socio-political current conditions. Plato illuminates how, at the same time as egalitarian principles and practices are being put forward, the possibility of partaking is being effectively foreclosed (Rancière, 1998). Beyond ideological blindness, the problem lies at the level of perception, of sensory experience. This kind of miscounting of the different parts of the community, of exclusion through inclusion, gives rise to politics. The community is political, not because it is the site of disputes over rights, but through the existence of those who have no part.

Those who are miscounted, invisible cannot partake in or even contest the ordinary organization and governance of the social order unless they accept their paradoxical part of having no part. The realm ordinarily thought to pertain to politics, is in fact the site where the policing, normalizing functions of inclusion and exclusion are enacted. For Rancière (2000), policing produces a sensibility that can identify neither excess nor absence (see Chapter 7 and Chapter 8 for further discussion of how state politics occlude imperceptible experience). The result is that society appears to be comprised of completely identifiable, self-evident groups or parts – of people who occupy the space that has been allocated to them and no other.

This is important for the debate over the politics of micro-practices. Ethical relations with the self play a role in the emergence of subjectivities, they involve relations of power and the regulation of conduct.

But unless the modes of subjectification being developed effectively challenge the orderly distribution and perception of parts of the community by introducing the incommensurable logic of equality, they can only fail to fracture normalizing, police logic. Unless subjectification interrupts policing, it is not politics. To do politics necessitates *dis*identification, refusing who one is supposed to be. Doing politics refigures the perceptible, not so others can finally recognize one's proper place in the social order, but to make evident the incommensurability of worlds, the incommensurability of inegalitarian distribution of bodies with the principle of equality. Politics, in this strict sense, is a refusal of representation. Politics happens outside of representation. Rethinking collectivity provides a way of pursuing this refusal, of introducing the part which is outside, which is not a part of community. Outside politics entail working with imperceptible experience.

Thinking collectivity as the radical proliferation of singularity can act as a point of departure for engaging with non-representational politics. This form of collectivity evades both the multiplication of difference and its recapture through strategies employed to produce consensus. What is foregrounded, instead, are the shifting and momentary meeting points between incommensurable differences. Rather than lamenting experiences of non-belonging, thinking collectivity as centrifugal trajectories of singularity offers the possibility of rendering visible what is imperceptible to state-targeted politics. That is, the specific forms of connection and cooperation which are undertaken beyond 'the community', outside of policing and of normalizing modes of subjectification. The concept of collectivity can contribute to subverting the foreclosure of political action in non-state realms. Instead of focusing on the subject positions produced through subjectification, rethinking collectivity allows us to reconsider those who are excluded, not as victims of exclusion, but as the invisible and imperceptible engine of socio-political transformation. This leads to the final question of the book: what is imperceptible experience and how can we grasp it, that is, what particular form of experience pertains to the collective action of outside politics?

Part IV
Continuous Experience

7
Three Paradigms of Experience

Experience as universal, situated and continuous

In this chapter we consider the relationship between experience and socio-political change from a historical perspective. Hence, our purpose is to situate a series of broad concepts and critiques of experience in relation to historical transformations in modes of thinking and doing politics (rather than to give an in-depth account of the complexities and debates within each of the positions we are discussing). We start with a discussion of what is considered to be the dominant paradigm in contemporary understandings of politics: this paradigm privileges forms of political engagement which target the state and draw on a notion of experience as universal. The limitations of state politics have led to a second paradigm, micropolitics, which entails a radical questioning of foundational notions of experience. Instead, experience is understood as situated. Yet the efficacy of micropolitics is open to question: as this position has developed so too have the reach and the strengths of neoliberal state powers. Seen historically, micropolitics and neoliberalism can be understood, not only as related movements, but as constitutive of each other. Is it possible now to rupture this connection, to think politics beyond our current socio-political conditions? In Chapter 6 we introduced the notion of outside politics. Here, we locate the move to outside politics as an attempt to harness tools for political intervention (tools which micropolitics have offered) and to move towards an alternative, third, paradigm of experience: continuous experience. The final step in our argument is to elaborate the concept of continuous experience, which we do in Chapter 8.

Universal experience

There is a particularly modern understanding of experience (common in both everyday and philosophical approaches) which – firstly – takes the distinction between perception and experience as its point of departure, and – secondly – tries to explain the relation between them. In answer to the question 'how do we experience the world?' the Kantian position proposes that a subject perceives objects in the world in the form of sensations. These sensations are the raw data of experience; they are subjected to the same procedures in each and every subject's mind. That is, each subject applies a set of predefined categories to the raw data of the senses, categories which are inherent in the subject's mind – time, space, causality, unity, limitation, etc. These categories, and the procedures through which they work, are universal. Whilst subjects have different encounters with the world, different sensations and perceptions, each and every subject processes the raw data of experience in identical ways. For example, different people may witness very different events of 'causality', but because they apply the universal category of causality to their perceptions (a category which is simply given in their minds), these different events are communicable and comparable. It seems that experience is produced in a universal way, as if there was a universal abstract machine located in the mind of each individual subject. The capacity for reflexivity is central to this understanding of experience. Here, reflexivity is the application of universal categories to subjective sensory perceptions: it generates everyday lived experience of the world.

The power of this account of the universal production of experience is that it does not deny the fact that lived experience is subjective. In one sense it even embraces the subjective dimension of experience. Consider Chomsky's explanation of an individual's everyday use of language: there are infinite possibilities for speech, but they are all generated by an innate universal linguistic device, a device which is located in every subject. Similarly, this account of universal experience proposes a productive relation between universal and subjective experience, but its explanatory power rests on the notion that experience is constituted by a universal abstract machine.

The subject entailed in this account of experience is both subjective and universal. Each subject has different experiences (that is, experience is subjective). Yet, at the same time, all these different experiences are structured along universal principles. Individual subjects are monads – they are simultaneously unique and identical. Because the universal abstract machine is at work in each individual mind, there is the potential to grasp experience by studying the functioning of the mind of one subject alone. The concept of universal experience gives rise to the much disputed logic which still dictates the design of most experimental studies in psychology or cognitive science (Holzkamp, 1991). Experimental situations are designed to minimize the possibility of the intrusion of extraneous variables. Once the world has been excluded, experimental subjects' reactions are assumed (in principle) to be universal. This is a genuinely individualistic account of experience because it is alleged that, ultimately, each subject's experience can be understood by recourse to universal principles. There is no imperative to approach experience as situated, intersubjective, or social.

The politics of universal experience

If universal experience is constitutive of the subject of modernity, then citizenship defines the coordinates of his or her political activity. Nation states grant rights to their citizens. And the political involvement of citizens revolves around the nation state, principally in the form of demands made on its institutions. In this sense, the political engagement of citizens is channelled though the state institutions of a particular nation. We said earlier that universal experience shores up the notion of an individual subject, contributing to the political strength of individualistic ideologies. With the birth of nation states (in the late 18th century and mainly in the 19th century) a new form of political regulation appears: national citizenship (Anderson, 1991; Balibar & Wallerstein, 1991; Hobsbawm, 1990). The nation state grants equal rights to all individual subjects who are considered to belong within the national territory.

The political activity of citizens assumes that the state can, in principle, represent its subjects universally. Hence, the corollary of the subject of universal experience is the state which unifies and universalizes the common interests of its citizens. There is a mirroring-process at work here. Citizens address a paramount regime of power. The role of the state then becomes one of regulating the expression of its citizens' demands through the imposition of a set of principles common to all (as discussed in the previous chapter). The state is here cast as the sole power which acts to contain and pacify society (Elias, 1981).

Rights formalize the interaction between the individual citizen and the nation state. In this constellation, state institutions are cast as universal entities which can accommodate the subjective experience of each individual citizen. This is important for the question being addressed in this chapter, namely the relationship between particular concepts of experience and particular historical forms of political engagement. It means that the individualistic tenet of universal experience corresponds with a form of politics which is solely focused on the state. Throughout the 19th and into the beginning of the 20th century, political engagement was predominantly understood to involve attempts to intervene in, to modify, or even to seize state power. Universal experience privileges state politics as *the* way to do politics. That is, citizens' efforts to initiate and participate in socio-political change principally target state policy and legislation as sites for transformation.

The limitations of universal experience

The uneven distribution of universality within nation states

Although the promise of state politics is that the state will ensure equality for all, clearly it has not delivered. Since the end of the 19th century, it has become increasingly apparent that national citizenship and the concomitant rights granted to citizens cannot accommodate the needs of many different and disparate social groups. National citizenship is being constantly revealed as a form of citizenship which reflects and responds to the experience of certain social groups, actively occluding the experience of others. This problem constitutes the most serious challenge to modes of political engagement which are founded on the notion of universal experience.

Consider, for example, the struggles for universal suffrage in the late 19th century, Indigenous Australians' attempts to gain citizenship (finally achieved only in 1967), and contemporary debates over the human rights of people who have infectious diseases – all of these examples reveal that national citizenship has always been unevenly distributed and can only be conceived as imperfect (Gunsteren, 1998). There are limitless examples which demonstrate that the state functions by granting and withholding citizenship, and by codifying and channelling the claims citizens make. Some claims are upheld as rights whilst a myriad of others are expelled, many before they have even been articulated. It has become obvious that the state's adjudication can never be impartial.

Geopolitical exclusion

The limits of state politics founded on universal experience come to the fore when we consider the uneven distribution of rights between the citizens of a nation state. But it is not only citizens who reside within the borders of nation states, there are also those without citizenship – irregular arrivals and people claiming asylum. By definition, the fact that these people do not belong within the nation's territory means that they have no rights; they are excluded from claiming national citizenship and from participating in state politics.

Turning to the relationships between states, and to the roles states play in geopolitical regulation, reveals how the partiality of national citizenship arises as a problem both within a nation's borders and beyond. In their efforts to actively promote their own interests beyond their borders, nation states neglect the rights of others. For example, colonization entails ignoring indigenous rights and actively imposing the means of social, cultural and political regulation on colonized societies. And, on the geopolitical level, the impossibility of national citizenship means that the rights of many social and cultural groups outside the nation state are excluded.

The cracks in the concept of universal experience are apparent when we think about the exclusion of certain groups' experience from both national politics and geopolitics. Moreover, it seems that state politics (which, as we described earlier, hinge on the idea of universal experience) produce new forms of exclusion in the realm of the nation as well on a global plane, even when they strive to create equality. Participation in a political field infused with universal experience takes a particular form: that is, political activity is founded on strong, self-confident articulations and elaborations of the subject's experience. Yet, post-colonial critiques of euro-centrist positions have powerfully exposed how a subject attributed with universal experience amounts to a subject who pursues the universalization of its own experience (Chakrabarty, 2000). The subject's belief that his experience is universal hides the fact that his experience is partial and only reflects a specific viewpoint (Spivak, 1999).

Co-option and reductionist accounts of social transformation

Casting the state as the final judge of the legitimacy of people's claims restricts political activity to state politics (as discussed in Chapter 6). In this situation, subjects are always under pressure to articulate their experience in terms which are readily understandable to existing state institutions. Of course, when experience is mobilized in political activity which primarily targets the nation state, it can be a potent means for effecting change. But in the process of translation much is lost; for example, the possibility of developing alternative modes of everyday life, ways of being which are not easily translated into prevalent policies. The enunciation of experiences which seem irrelevant to the actual needs of state institutions becomes redundant to efforts to bring about political change. Hence, when experience is mobilized in state politics it is always already co-opted by the state. In its strong form co-option entails adopting the state's agenda, but perhaps in its most lethal form it simply involves losing one's own.

What the concept of state politics fails to grasp is that the active role people take in transforming society is played out in social spaces which are only partly regulated by the official policies of the nation state. This means, as we will discuss below, that the political significance of different social subjectivities (for example, as constituted in local community groups temporarily aligned around a specific issue such as an environmental concern, or a town-planning dispute) is neglected in favour of a universally codified and regulated subject. The result is that the concept of state politics offers a limited account of the actual processes involved in socio-political change.

For example, if we consider the gains made by feminists in Western societies in the post-war period, it is only partially true that they resulted from successful claims made to the relevant state authorities. There was a dramatic shift in the everyday lives of women prior to entering into this mode of state directed political activity. And this shift in lived experience was not driven by the state. In fact, the state was not actively involved in contesting gender hierarchies; it had expelled the multiplicity and complexity of equality claims pertaining to gender-relations from its central concerns. Instead, state policies maintained long-standing gender-inequalities. The fracture in this configuration occurred at the point when struggles over gender hierarchies (familiar, ongoing struggles which were being played out in social life) generated new everyday forms of social and personal relationships, and new spaces for organizing and self-empowerment. Women were afforded new modes of participating in economic and public life as well as cultural politics. State politics were the *result* of these shifts, and people's everyday struggles in social and cultural spheres were their origin.

Reifying experience

Drawing on a conception of socio-political change as driven by the interaction between the universal subject and state government seems to foreclose and suppress the operation of a crucial process of transformation. That is, this approach cannot grasp how society exists and continues to develop *beyond* state regulated spaces, how it develops through unruly, informal, and unsystematic exchanges and practices between subjects and collectives. In addition to blocking any understanding of the function of social movements, the notion of universal experience cannot account for the role of subjective participation in political engagement. If, as we described above, the actors involved in state politics are confident about the universal nature of their experience, then rethinking experience is hazardous, those who do it risk undermining the basis of their own political legitimacy.

From the perspective of the universal subject, rethinking the universality of one's experience – its validity for and generalizability to others – threatens one's political effectiveness. Hence, state politics constitute social actors as permanently reproducing their own position and experience. Because the universal subject is not thought to reinterpret his experience, he is eternally locked into a reified relation to himself and to other political actors. Adorno (1983) describes this situation as the fabrication of 'ever-the-same'. State-directed political activity solidifies self-coincident and ever-the-same historical actors.

Interpretation and the everyday

Over the past three decades there has been an ever-strengthening response to the aporias of universal experience and to the constraints it places on attempts to think political activity: micropolitics. Now, experience is thought to be differentially constructed through a subject's positioning in the world. Experience is always a matter of interpretation, and the universal capacity to interpret the sensory world is no longer fixed or given (Vattimo, 1997). Interpretation is a battle, and the meaning of subjective experience becomes a matter of doubt (Foucault, 1977). In place of the universal subject, a new subject occupies the political scene in the post-war period, one whose confidence and consciousness are always questionable, and whose self-understanding is simultaneously enabled and limited by the immediacy of his or her contact with others.

Post-structuralist theory has contributed to this turn from universal experience, and from the foundational role of universal experience in socio-political change (Scott, 1991/1993). That individuals have subjective experience is not disputed, but the possibility that it can be elucidated by a universal abstract machine is. Subjective experience is understood as a process which is constituted in discursive formations – a process which unfolds differently in specific social and historical contexts. In situated accounts, the connection between experience and possibilities for political activity is mediated by the contingencies of positioning (Haraway, 1991). This is in sharp contrast to notions which hold that the authenticity and universality of experience act as grounds for political engagement.

Now experience is always a matter of interpretation, but no one interpretation can lead back to an understanding of the processes through which experience has been constituted (Taylor, 1971). In its most radical conception, interpretation is no longer the 'the slow exposure' of hidden meaning but 'the violent or surreptitious appropriation of a system of rules, which in itself has no essential meaning, in order to impose a direction, to bend [humanity] to a new will, to force its participation in a different game' (Foucault, 1997, p. 151). Questioning the universality of one's experience can open the subject to the possibility of perceiving and relating to the others' difference (Butler, 2001). The rejection of universal experience dismantles and scatters the universal abstract machine into a distributed network of disparate, but interconnected, relations between various actors. Experience is situated and socialized in this move. And because of this, experience as an object in itself becomes problematic (as we discussed in Chapter 1). The analytic focus shifts, instead, to the means through which experience is constituted. Discourses, social processes, networks, assemblages, all frequently replace experience.

Why is it that particular ways of working with experience (for example, as universal, or as situated) come to the fore or retreat at different points in history? Above, we alluded to the fact that there is a continuum between ontological and political debates over experience. Some authors are principally concerned with how experience is constituted (for example, Middleton & Brown, 2005; Mos, 2005; in relation to existentialism, Stenner, 1998). Others may enter debates about the ontology of experience whilst their central concern is to identify a politically useful concept of experience (for example, Henriques, Hollway, Urwin, Venn & Walkerdine, 1984/1998; Wilkinson & Kitzinger, 1996). We argue that the emergence and solidification (in the 1970s) of a new field of study, cultural studies, has to be understood as a response to the intensification of the role of lived experience in social transformation. Cultural studies connects this turn to lived experience with a political project. And this happens when it has become obvious that state politics are not an effective means to address the differences and inequalities proliferating in the immediate, everyday lives of different communities (Hall & Jefferson, 1975; Hall, Critcher, Jefferson, Clarke & Roberts, 1978).

Entering into state politics always involves a degree of co-option. State politics neglect situated experience and its concomitant politics of everyday life, on the grounds that they are inappropriate means for political intervention. But this rationale is self-supporting – this account of politics contributes to generating the limited practices of political engagement it claims to describe. The exclusions of state politics only makes sense if political activity is already constrained to targeting the nation state; that is, if the point of intervention is conceived as state apparatuses which are concerned with the allocation of rights and resources to different social groups, broadly conceived (for example, social classes, big interest groups such as trade unions, business or professional associations). In response, cultural studies rejects all-encompassing notions of social groups or classes as objects of analysis and inserts new syntheses of social life using the components of ethnicity, gender, race and lineage. The forms of social analysis and social activity developed in cultural studies can be understood as tools for intervening in the local everyday problems of communities.

Cultural studies research is informed by an understanding of political engagement as taking place in the realm of everyday life. This shift from state politics to, what is commonly known as, micropolitics is illustrated in contemporary debates around citizenship. As mentioned earlier, one of the main terrains on which state politics are played out is that of citizenship. Citizenship, in this case, denotes a genuine identity which links universal experience with the right to live within a nation's borders. In response to this preoccupation with nationalist ideology, cultural studies posits notions of cultural citizenship (Rosaldo, 1993) and flexible citizenship (Ong, 1999). The claim being made here is that the right to participate in national politics and social life does not arise from the capacity to be a universal subject, but from the situatededness of those who belong to a cultural community or to specific migrational routes traversing the national space.

The cultural studies' project reinstates the micropolitical as both a legitimate object of analysis and a productive tool for changing the conditions of everyday existence. The micropolitics of existence are understood as fuelling socio-political transformation. At the same time, any notion of state government as the universal and solitary domain of politics is rejected. Instead, the unruliness of haphazard discursive formations is introduced as the productive site of alternative politics. Working with the concept of micropolitics opens possibilities to encounter and to understand the formation of emerging social and cultural spaces. It enables the development of strategies of intervention which stem from specific communities' needs and problems as they are lived in everyday life.

Micropolitics at work

The dissolution of the universal subject of modern state politics, affected in cultural studies, enables political analyses of previously neglected fissures and terrains of everyday life (for example, Connolly, 2002). For instance, the analysis of micro-practices through which HIV positive gay men forge a relation to ARV treatment illustrates how people adjust to the immediate necessities posed by the treatment regimens by organizing a myriad of social interactions beyond institutionalized regulation. Although, as discussed in Chapter 1, there may be a common desire to respond to the expectation that people 'take charge' of treatments, the finely differentiated practices entailed in people's responses can open starkly different modes of relating to the self and to others. A focus on micro-practices reveals how all these different modes of subjectification unfold in realms which are not hierarchically driven by health policies, by clinical management agendas or by psychological discourses of 'control'. The embodiment of personal control is related to, but not determined by these sites. For example, 'being in charge' can act as a vehicle for a new trajectory into employment and work. In other moments, it can require the renegotiation of one's relation to biomedical authority. (For instance, advances in treatments can enjoin people who have previously constructed themselves in opposition to biomedicine to finally finding themselves submitting to doctor's advice; or people subjected to a new push to follow doctors orders may 'take charge' by refusing medication). Alternatively (as discussed in Chapter 1), there are modes of relating to the imperative to take charge which question the very possibility of that goal.

The real possibilities being opened by biomedical advances in HIV treatments (for example, that it is possible to relate to HIV as a chronic illness rather than a death sentence) force a move beyond any blanket criticism of biomedicine, beyond the separation of medical and social domains of life (Rosengarten, forthcoming). In this move, people reconstitute themselves in relation to biomedicine, realizing possibilities for socio-political change – not through resistance to institutional or biomedical authority – but through actively organizing and reorganizing their relation to all the various actors in the social field (as discussed in Part III). In the power relations of the post-ARV chronotope, there is no one privileged subject imposing a dominant mode of sociality. There is a network consisting of different actants – for example, pills, doctors, patients, tests, pharmaceutical companies, state institutions, community organizations and activists. The ongoing transformations in the connections between nodes in this network open new possibilities for living with HIV and close others. Thus, the process through which change occurs cannot be understood as principally driven by state legislation and policy.

The lines of inclusion and participation which emerge between different actors in the field of HIV are constantly shifting. These changes occur in the absence of any centrally dictated logic of participation – there is no institutional demand for the reconstitution of alignments and relations between gay men. Instead, it is in the contingent configuration of gay men's social and sexual relations that the politics of exclusion and inclusion are renegotiated and reconstituted. What this means, is that for positive men the post-ARV moment of unprotected anal intercourse is now a very different moment (Rosengarten, forthcoming). Caring for the other is still a question. But ways of doing this have been transformed through, for example, the ongoing individualization of risk and the emergence of subjectivities regulated by their differential relationship to risk (Rosengarten, Race & Kippax, 2000; Flowers, 2001; Race, 2001).

Drawing on the related concepts of universal experience and state politics, as discussed above, fails to elucidate informal configurations which – although they may include institutions – are not themselves institutionalized. Hence, the micropolitics of everyday life demand different analytic tools. Micropolitics purposively work against the logic that posits the state as the genesis of socio-political change. What is being broken here is the link between state policies and sociality. For example, analyses of the micro-practices entailed in people's ongoing struggles in the field of health question any assumption that these practices originate in response to the enunciation of policies pertaining to patient empowerment/responsibility. Many political struggles do not address state institutions, neither are they premised on a common project. Rather they entail acting on the multiple actants involved in informal networks to perform and pursue different interests and political agendas: interests ranging, for example, from pharmaceutical companies efforts to constitute and expand into lucrative markets through to the efforts of activists to contest unequal access to drugs. Now, instead of a universal subject in a mirror-like relation with the state we have a multiplicity of actants re-weighting the power of different nodes in the network.

Contesting representation

The move away from notions of universal experience as the bedrock of state directed rights-based claims opens up the space of the social to polyvocality. The interpretive battle over experience is multi-voiced (Bakhtin, 1986). Interpretation touches on all the small movements, positions, interactions and skirmishes unfolding in the course of everyday life. When experience is no longer understood as universal, the process of representing experience is problematized. The necessity to name and contest given representations of experience arises when the subject's capacity to represent his or her experience as universal is questioned. Micropolitics employ representational strategies in order to materialize interpretations as active transformations of the world. Like an actor who renders a character real for the play through a singular interpretation of her lines, this form of political engagement constitutes experience through interpretive representation.

The problem of naming experience spawned new forms of politics in the post-war period, politics which had previously been discounted as ineffective: identity-politics, politics of difference, and politics of recognition. It became more apparent that state politics were co-opting political agendas by forcing people into standardized representations of their interests (that is, representations drawing on language and terms which privileged existing concerns of the state and the national imagination). Social movements, grassroots mobilization and alternative forms of cultural politics have responded by implementing new strategies of representation. Queer movements for example refuse the categories of gender and sexuality which order the public and private domains, a move which contests the logic underpinning state regulation (Rubin, 1984). As Michael Warner argues, although lesbian and gay politics continue to successfully conduct state politics – for example, targeting military policy, partnership legislation, health policy – 'most of the imaginative energies of queer culture have come to be focused on a rigorously anti-assimilationist rhetoric invoked only in non-state public-sphere contexts' (2002, p. 212). The transformative powers of queer movements lie in their capacity to insert possibilities for new modes of being into people's everyday lived experience. That is, queer is effective to the extent – not that it seeks its power through appeals for institutional recognition – but that it materializes. Where the identitarian politics of gay liberation left the everyday organization of heterosexuality relatively intact, queer seeks out alternative means to infiltrate heterosexual privilege and to undermine the heteronormative order of social relations.

The importance of representational practices for micropolitics goes beyond the eternal creation of new interpretations. Representation is more than interpretation. Representation also involves the process of connecting these interpretations to a social group, that is, speaking-in-the-name-of (Spivak, 1999). Micropolitics work, not only by fabricating new interpretations of experience, but by producing connections within and between communities of social actors. This is where the political efficacy of micropolitics lies; they generate new capacities to affect others and to participate in re-weighting the relations of power in a network. As situated experience flows between the nodes of the network, it intensifies alliances in some junctions, erodes nerve centres of concentrated power in others, and is caught by and sweeps away blockages in the process. Here, to exercise power by harnessing experience means acting upon present or coming actions in order to cultivate or to nullify possible relationships within and between social groups or communities of actors. This is action in a truly Foucauldian universe (Foucault, 1994). A universe whose horizon is not dominated by the centralized power of a paramount symbolic order (to which all actors dutifully refer), but is a polycentric system of power in an acentrically organized world (Luhmann, 1995, p. li).

Micropolitics and the problem of neoliberalism

Can we take it that micropolitics do as they intend, that they avoid the problem of co-option entailed in state politics? Or, does the form and function of the state mutate; that is, could it be that the neoliberal state does not retreat from the social and cultural realms, rather its occupation of these terrains is constantly expanding, and taking new forms? The power of micropolitics is thought to lie in the fact that they bypass the reproduction of the state as an intact and paramount entity of power. Micropolitics harness everyday lived experience as a vital matter of political struggles which aim to reinvigorate civil society, that is, the struggles of associations of people who exist beyond and outside of state institutions. It would be an oversimplification to say that micropolitics do not address state institutions or that they do not attempt to intervene in state legislation or policies. Micropolitics do not completely supplant state politics – they can work together, and in fact they do (Warner, 2002). Their particular strength is that they acknowledge and work with the multiplicity of actants in a social field – including actants which are part of state institutions. Moreover, as discussed in Chapter 5, by fracturing the ongoing process of capture entailed in state politics, they create spaces of freedom. Micropolitics not only respond to but fuel socio-political change. There is an important aspect of micropolitics which we have not yet discussed. Seen historically, micropolitics have gradually become integral to the effective realization of neoliberal governance. This has come about since the 1980s, occurring both in functions of the state and in modes of social regulation. The neoliberal state is not a silo: it works through distributed networks of power, networks which thoroughly permeate the banalities of everyday experience. Over the past three decades, the domination of post-Fordism and the dismantling of welfare systems have accelerated, and finally consolidated, the state's withdrawal from the traditional role of centralized organizer of society. But the state is no less present. Instead, it has disseminated into the finest fissures of society. In this process situated experience and micropolitics have become necessary elements for the functioning of the neoliberal state. The state needs more than self-regulating individuals; it needs networked subjects who, by assuming responsibility for creating connections between disparate actants, actively forge the assemblages neoliberal governance requires in order to make the shift from centralized to disseminated modes of regulation.

Micropolitics were introduced as an answer to the limitations of state politics. The intention was to counter everyday normalization, to counter the effacement of subjectivities, the codification of otherness and Fordist immobility. But, as we will argue in the next chapter, in situations where the neoliberal, post-Fordist state recuperates the production of experience into a crucial moment of its own reproduction, there is still an excess of experience which infringes on and ruptures the new logic of control. The political relevance of this excess, we will call it continuous experience, does not hinge on an opposition between state politics and micropolitics – both have merged into a new aggregate of governance and continuous experience works with and contests this elision.

Continuous experience & outside politics

We have argued against the notion that micropolitics offer an effective means for intervening in neoliberal governmentalities. Yet, the concept of micropolitics is no less useful because of this. If micropolitics are understood to denote, not 'good politics', but a set of processes through which socio-political change (for better and for worse) is achieved, they are a potent tool for participating in current forms of politics. In fact, micropolitical techniques are being effectively employed across the political spectrum: from right-wing infusions of fear as a tool for regulating populations, through green efforts to pervade everyday life with concerns about the environment, to the HIV/AIDS activist organization ACTUP's use of anger as a basis for political engagement. In all of these examples, subjects are constituted, not only as having experience, but as compelled to work on it in everyday life. Evidently, experience is being employed to further a wide array of interests. Micropolitics work on the terrain of experience – in fact, they cannot function without experience.

But to what extent does researching micro-practices elucidate the role of experience in socio-political change? As discussed previously, research on micropolitics involves turning away from explicit analysis of the problem of experience and instead the focus has been on the connections between actants and the situatedness of social relations. The rationale is that because experience is thought to invoke an individualistic and universal subject, it is an unlikely tool for intervening in the proliferation of the individualism we have witnessed in recent decades. This has been the micropolitical answer to the apotheosis of universal experience; a response which has powerfully dissected the concept of universal subjectivity and exposed its political implications.

Although the efficacy of micropolitics hinges on the mobilization of experience, in the effort to repudiate individualism analyses of micropolitics neglect both the concept of experience and its role in everyday life and socio-political change. This arises as problem, not because the concept of experience is important in itself, but simply because individualistic notions of experience have continued to proliferate in recent decades. As we indicated at the outset of this book, the public appetite for experience is insatiable. Consider, for example, the proliferation of reality TV, autobiography, psychotherapy, psychoactive drugs, new-age advice, life stories, personal narratives or 'the gap year'. This appetite is being both invoked and fed by micropolitical strategies which work on the level of experience. Considered historically, it has become increasingly clear that political interventions which move away from experience have not made substantial inroads into everyday cultural life: they have failed to establish a viable entry point into the ways in which experience proliferates and its role in the conduct of micropolitics. The growing interest in affect and neuroscience on the part of cultural analysts – that is, an interest which involves entering into terrain previously thought to be colonized by individualistic concerns – can be understood as a response to this problem, and an attempt to elaborate new means of intervention (for example, Connolly, 2002; Massumi, 2005; Murphie, 2005).

What micropolitics have inserted into the agenda of political movements in recent decades is the idea that socio-political transformation can only be conceived as an immanent process of change. Recent social movements (for example, no border campaigns, counter- and anti-globalization movements, cyberactivism, and precarious work mobilizations) have taken up, expanded and transformed these ideas in the attempt to develop ways of intervening in the present configurations of power. The concept of immanence constitutes the common ground for the elaboration of a new form of politics, beyond state politics and micropolitics as we described them earlier.

Clearly, working with immanence entails a radical rejection of both transcendent accounts of socio-political change and the universal subject invoked in such accounts. But there is a more specific way in which the concept of immanence offers a means of intervening in the present. In a context where regulation and systems of control are so pervasive, to speak of resistance makes little sense because there simply is no position which can be adopted outside of control. Immanent politics cut through the feelings which arise when attempts at resistance are condemned as naïve or dissolve into mourning (Brown, 1995). Immanent politics offer a means to work with the possibilities of the present and to develop modes of participation which question the very foundation of neoliberal governmentalities – and they do this *without* making recourse to a transcendental vision.

Approaching politics as an immanent process opens possibilities for challenging the familiar grounds on which politics are most frequently enunciated – those of state- and micropolitics. The focus of state politics constrains political interventions to the given realm of institutional change, undercutting possibilities for formulating questions which are not already considered legitimate by the state. Although they arose as an attempt to redress the overly-narrow focus on the state, micropolitics have played a vital role in the historical transformation of the state from a centralized institution into a disseminated network which operates effectively in the terrain of social and cultural life. In this sense, both state- and micropolitics articulate their political agendas inside the terrain of the state. Immanent politics question this restriction, invigorating political agendas and interests which remain outside – outside politics.

Outside politics, as discussed in the previous chapter, are an attempt to interrupt the normalizing policing which stands in for politics. The focus of policing is on inclusion, and the policing mentality is blind to excess and absence. Outside politics arise when the constraints (in the form of demands for particular forms of articulation, legitimization or self-representation) placed on those attempting to engage in socio-political transformation are revealed as artefacts which occlude the pursuit of equality. That is, when these constraints are understood as contingent on a particular social order (a social order in which equality is elided with representation) they can be subject to questioning on the grounds that social orders are never static. But such revelations can only occur when questions which have remained unformulated, when those who have been granted no place in policing, are inserted into political disputes *in their own terms*. The purchase of outside politics is not that they occur and remain outside of ordinary regulation. Firstly, actors and objects are outside in the sense that they are neglected and – in the nation state's imaginary – their very existence is paradoxically foreclosed. And secondly, these actors do not spurn the importance of directly targeting the state, rather they are engaged in projects of inserting themselves within, but as the un-representable and impercep-tible entities that they are. This is why, as we discussed in Chapter 6, doing outside politics involves refusing who one is supposed to be, it is a matter of dis-identification.

For example, much political activity around migration attempts to control (and to intervene in the control of) border-crossing, detention and the legislation of residency and visas. In state politics and micro-politics migrants are interpellated as either threats to a nation state's integrity, victims of the state's punitive policies, or as forces of resis-tance with the potential to reveal both the oppressive reach and the limits of state policies. But all of these positions approach migration from the outside. The focus of these observer perspectives is always on people's points of departure and arrival: the journey only matters to the extent that it reveals the machinations of irregular border-crossing, or the suffering of those on the move. What becomes impossible to grasp is the journey itself, the inside story of movement and migration, the dynamic fluidity of the experience of migration, the contradictory trajectories being opened, crisscrossed and closed again and again as people travel in their lives. In response, theories about the 'autonomy of migration' conceive of migration as an unruly, constitutive, trans-formative force which unfolds outside of state regulation and which exists within, but remains imperceptible in, everyday social and cultural life (Bojadzijev, Karakayali, & Tsianos, 2004; Karakayali, & Tsianos, 2005; Mezzadra, 2001). Instead of starting with how to rep-resent migrants in order to subsequently expose them to the pressure of assimilation and integration, theories about the 'autonomy of migration' take a radically different perspective. They no longer focus on how migrants become integrated into the societies in which they reside, but on how people move and change these societies by *de facto* – by integrating the given restrictions and conditions into their mobility. The French riots of November 2005, the permeability of the highly patrolled US-Mexican border, the proliferation of autonomous communities in almost every city of our societies, the Ceuta and Melilla crisis of September 2005 – these are just a few recent examples showing that the primary concern of migrants is, not if and how they are represented in the pubic imagination and in institutional policies, but how they can establish pathways which give them possibilities for living as part of the societies in which they find themselves or to which they are moving. Outside politics are concerned with how migrants themselves organize their mobility, their informal social networks, their employment opportunities, their participation in the institutional policies of a certain country. That is, outside politics are the means through which migrants finally engage in processes of de-representation and dis-identification in order, not simply to enter into the game of policing, but to break the rules of representation and integration, transforming the game into a political dispute over their 'right to be' (Papadopoulos & Tsianos, 2006).

Whilst the possibility of politically effective dis-identification may seem inconceivable to some (on the grounds that there is no outside of power) we want to insist again that, although power is pervasive in every moment of experience, there is always an excess. And this experiential excess is always produced anew because current state or micropolitical regulation cannot accommodate and insert the totality of social actors and of their experiences into the processes of regulation. As power seizes on experience, ordering experience, reifying some experiences and simply overlooking others, there is a supplement to its functioning. Whilst experience which has already been seized has been subjected to considerable scrutiny, outside politics reopen questions as to: *what* is being seized in the first place; what imperceptibility might actually entail (that is, if it is to mean anything more than a glorified account of non-paradoxical non-existence); and what it might enable. The matter of outside politics, the means through which imperceptibility can be politically effective, we will argue in the next chapter, is continuous experience. The excess of experience to which we have alluded throughout this book takes the form of continuous experience. Working with continuous experience challenges our conventions of visualization and refigures the perceptible, the already represented and regulated.

8
Experience after Representation

Opening Night

Myrtle Gordon is a star. And she has been for some time now. Manny Victor is glad to have cast her. This is not the first time they have worked together, nor is it her first encounter on stage with the lead actor Maurice Adams (John Cassavetes), a past lover. John Cassavetes' film, *Opening Night* (1978), observes the play in the week leading up to the Broadway premiere. They are using a short run in New Haven to fine-tune the production. But it would help if the director, playwrite, cast and crew first shared a common vision of exactly what they will be producing. Myrtle (Gena Rowlands) seems to be disturbing the cooperation required to get there. Manny (Ben Gazzara) and Myrtle both know that the power of Myrtle's work stems from her capacity – not just to represent a role – but to be *in* the play, to move with the part in a way that pushes, strains and opens new possibilities in the script. This is what makes her the star she is. But now Myrtle's capacity is being tested: she fears that it may not be possible to enter into this particular role without playing it as the straight-jacket the playwrite, Sarah Goode (Joan Blondell), has written her into.

   Is it possible to realize for an audience a woman's experience of ageing without succumbing to the idea that ageing (and especially the ageing of a childless woman whose relationship is on the brink) necessarily involves the gradual loss of one's ability to have an effect on the world, on others? The script of the play offers a representation of anxious passivity – of ageing as a loss of feminine powers – but the actress designated to play the role is a woman who continuously rejects and shatters this way of being in her own work and in her life. It is not that Myrtle is untouched by such fears, certainly she has had to negotiate them in the past. And now she is being re-subjected to a specific version of this anxiety. Myrtle fears that by convincingly playing the older woman Sarah, the playwrite has written, she will initiate a transition in her own career: once marked as an actress who can be cast as a despairing, ageing woman, she will never be offered other roles. There is an added twist to Myrtle's situation. It is not so much that ageing threatens her own sense of her femininity, rather the threat comes from her professional success. Myrtle is repeatedly told – admiringly, lovingly, jokingly or with the intention to hurt – that because she is a professional who puts her work before all else, she is not a real woman.

Manny is forced to accept that in order to realize her part, to make the play a success, the star needs the licence to tarry with the material. But he needs to keep the ever-present playwrite on side, as well as the investors, the cast and crew all of who are being suspended in uncertainty about *what* play they are involved in. Manny and Myrtle work together in such a way that each tries to shape the vision of the play, and these efforts both bring them into tension with each other and form the basis of their close relation. The leading actress knows her task is not just to play her own role, but to put her vision into motion in the connections between actors, to allow it to emerge in the performances of others even in the scenes in which she herself is absent. Her goal is not to do a star performance. Rather she tries to realize a play that breaks with the misunderstanding that the script is a vehicle for the amplified representation of her own personal experience of ageing. Myrtle strives to interrupt the overall logic of staging a play in which each actor is confined to taking responsibility for their part alone: she wants to bring to life not only what the script demands but what the play could be. And she tries to do this by going beyond the script itself and by injecting her own sense of what the play *should* be into the production. This necessitates involving and connecting with the rest of the cast over the truth of the play as she sees it.

Cassavetes' films were made as attempts to understand ordinary, everyday life. The films ask questions about Cassavetes' experiences, as well as demanding that viewers explore their own experiences. This is not unusual across the arts: it is what poems, novels, and paintings commonly do. But exploring your own personal experience was something American directors did not do. They told stories. They made 'entertainment' that distracted people from their problems. Cassavetes was not interested in running a circus. And, of course, the result was incomprehension from studio heads, producers, distributors, viewers and critics – all fighting to hold on to an idea of films as an escape from life.

Myrtle's attempt to shape the play appears to all those involved in the production as a mere reaction, as an expression of her personal anguish prompted by having to confront ageing. *Opening Night* is about the tensions which arise in working with experience. Cassavetes contests the illusion that experience can be represented in a linear cinematic narrative. Instead of telling a story of this or that experience, he explores the mechanics of experience in ordinary life (Carney, 2001). It is no coincidence that Cassavetes' films were improvised, emphasizing the weight of the actors' role (Cassavetes, 1976; Charity, 2001). His films are anti-narratives which attempt to reveal how our familiar narratives of everyday life are nothing more than clichés – ready to break down any moment, to become incommensurable, to move in unexpected directions, or simply to disappear. Cassavetes moves from representation to improvization, from narrative to experience. *Opening Night* considers the suffocating treatment of experience as something reified and readily representable. Into this, Cassavetes introduces the attempt to render experience continuous. The film focuses on a character subjected to a familiar anxiety in which ageing figures as a loss of power. This rendering of experience is not mistaken – the playwrite offers something insightful about a woman's experience of being subjected to this hegemonic discourse. What is awry is the perspective from which the experience is taken up by the playwrite. The play presents only what can be said about experience when we look from outside of the lived moment; that is, it is stuck in the perspective of a self-reflexive, over-arching 'I'. It works only with experience which has been folded onto the subject. It does not offer any sense of a person being in the midst of the immanent unfolding of experience. But Myrtle tries to refuse the imperative to interiorize the character and then to struggle with the experience of ageing in a reflexive way. Instead, she tries to perform this experience as a shared and continuous mode of relating to the others involved in the production.

When experience is approached from within, from the perspective of its immanent unfolding, clichéd discourses dissolve and the indivisibility of experience emerges. Ageing, for Myrtle, is not lived separately from her experience of success. Both simultaneously involve an augmentation of her powers to affect people as well as a threat to those same powers. An immanent experience of ageing may certainly contain but is not limited to the anxieties portrayed in the play. For example, it could also contain a movement towards the future – a movement made with anticipation, or with anticipation and concurrent dread. Myrtle refuses to represent *the* experience of ageing, she does the experience of ageing as something which drifts through indivisible terrain, allows new connections with others, new forms of intimate relations, a new feeling of one's own position in the world.

The politics of continuous experience

In what sense can Myrtle be read as intervening in the functions and mechanics of experience? What are the politics of Myrtle's engagement with experience? As with *Tristana* (see Chapter 2), it is a mistake to read Myrtle as trying to resist a normative mode of subjectification to ageing by just proposing and articulating an alternative. Such a reading imposes an overly-narrow understanding of everyday politics as the result of acts of resistance. Myrtle is not in the game of articulation and resistance, her intervention consists of the attempt to introduce the players to another game altogether. She does politics by introducing what is outside of politics, by bringing the fundamental indivisibility of experience into play. The interruption she imposes on the production, her attempt to move the play, is not an individual's effort to affirm the complexity of her own unique experience of ageing. It is an act of individuation. Myrtle neither preaches nor lectures the cast on the complexity of ageing, she does not try to bring them into her personal experience. Rather, she emits signals which might fire shared experiences of the continuous and contradictory nature of ageing: she tries to invoke a common space in which, together, they can perform the immanent unfolding of experience. It is only in such a space that the singular threads of experience running between them can be activated and connected with each other, that a new play can be rendered. Such a play will be successful to the extent that it pushes its audience away from the familiar shorthand and back to the ambiguity of everyday experience, offering a point from which alternative modes of ageing can be harnessed.

By creating a space for interaction, continuous experience contests the normative and normalizing understanding of experience. If the classic understanding of experience is that each individual owns his or her experience, reflects on it and negotiates its meaning, then the idea of continuous experience asserts that there are only common experiences on which different actors work, taking different points of entrance. And this is individuation (see also Chapter 6). It is not about trying to induce convergence between different people's experiences by enunciating the unique properties of one's own experience. Rather, starting from fluid, fragmented, common experiences, individuation involves working with them by tracing singular paths, paths which often collapse again into each other, sometimes diverge from each other, sometimes develop in parallel, and sometimes connect up with other unexpected paths. The stuff of individuation is singular experiences, which move through individuals rather than belonging to them. Working with experience in its continuity illuminates how it is only *after* the work of demarcation that we can speak of 'an experience' or 'my experience'. That is, experience is rendered representable by *ad hoc* impositions made from the transcendent perspective of normative discourses of social life. There is a difference between living according to a super-imposed norm and according to the situated logic of action. The insertion of a normalizing, external form of regulation secures a viewpoint from above, a transcendental viewpoint of the continuous experience flowing between the actors in a certain context. It is only from this transcendent perspective that you can cut into the continuity of experience and make it divisible (Barad, 2003). The cut scatters continuous experience into pieces, pieces which are then distributed across and allocated to individuals. An additional step, the constitution of individuals as having reflexive interiority and the capacity to exchange, sustains the picture of experience as essentially private – 'my experience'.

Myrtle is subjected to all this: as an ageing star she is expected, not only to represent the normative understanding of ageing, but to do it by amplifying 'her' experience of ageing. Not only is this normative vision alien to Myrtle's everyday struggles, it is also hostile to her attempts to involve others in the continuous nature of experience and to work with experience as imperceptible and dispersed. How then does Myrtle put continuous experience to work under these aversive conditions?

Materialization of experience

The potence of working with continuous experience lays in its materialization, not in its narration, in its performative power to change things, not its capacity to represent them. 'I don't want to argue about this, we'll rehearse it' Manny says when Myrtle rings at 4.30 in the morning and insists that the play does not work for her, highlighting the point where her character is slapped, the moment where a couple realize that their relationship is over. The following day the rehearsal falls apart. Manny first tries to introduce another slap: Myrtle's character hits back at Maurice's character (and, perhaps, because the female actress has not been trained in the art of 'stage-slapping' Maurice is surprised and stung by her acting). Manny mistakenly reduces Myrtle's aversion to the scene to her struggle with oppressive heteronormativity. But Myrtle is not trying to realize gender equality on-stage. Rather, she is challenging the despair she is being asked to represent. Why should despair be the overwhelming feeling as her character's relationship ends?

As Myrtle struggles with the scene all the others involved become increasingly assured that her resistance to the play stems from the fact that she is an ageing female star who is being forced to confront her own personal problems with ageing. That is, her attempts to respond to these normalizing discourses only serve to intensify their imposition. The possibilities for exchanging with the others are totally saturated. The situation cannot absorb new attempts to put experience to work. The rehearsal has come to a point where it can only allow endless negotiations, negotiations which are constrained by the eternal reproduction of discourses which simply have no purchase on Myrtle's concerns. Because the situation is over-determined, those involved have lost the capacity to access the continuous nature of the experiences they are trying to work with.

Myrtle has to act. There is no possibility for her to intervene in the discourse, the discourse is now faking a life of its own. She simply has to redo the situation. When Manny asks her to perform the slap scene again and again she does not refuse to do it nor does she argue against it, but she simply does not go with it. She falls to the ground and starts shouting. She stays there. Maurice is forced out of his role; he cannot say his lines to a body on the ground. Myrtle refuses to participate in the normative modes of relating to others which shore up the discourse she is trying to circumvent. Without negotiation, she inserts a new fact. She breaks the blockade. At this point the others cannot bypass the facticity of her act, they cannot close this act with a reading that seals Myrtle into her personal dilemma. Of course, they try – some of them think that she might be sick. But once a rupture has been made evident, this hegemonic reading can only be introduced in *reaction* to a new fact, a new possibility. Myrtle's doing continuous experience has affected the situation. It can no longer continue as it was. In order to keep the rehearsal moving, Manny is forced to retreat to act 1, scene 1 – and Myrtle and Maurice leave the stage.

The politics of materialization

Continuous experience materializes. The concept of materialization has two meanings, and both are important here. Firstly, although experience is bound to the symbolic and constituted through interpretation, this is not all there is to experience. Materialization means to act both on the inside and outside of existing discourses, to make world, to open world, to affect others (Brown & Stenner, 2001). Materialization is beyond discourse, it is the objective making and remaking of the world in ways that are simply un-representable in given discourses. That is what Myrtle does, for example, when she stops the 'normal' flow of the rehearsal.

Secondly, continuous experience materializes in things, flowing not only through people but also through objects. Elements of the material world become artefacts of experience (Schraube, 1998, 2005). Experience is – literally – the objective making of world. There is more than the subject or 'I' of experience. In various ways, other people, things, material spaces, situations – all these actants – actively carry and participate in the unfolding of experience. Alcohol is one of the leading actants in *Opening Night*. Everyone drinks a lot. Alcohol flows between and mediates the interactions between people and opens possibilities for relating to oneself. There are many scenes where Myrtle's excessive drinking is observed by others. But she is not a compulsive drinker, she chooses and refuses her drinks. Alcohol is more than a bad habit, or a tool to release the pressure leading up to Broadway. In *Opening Night's* universe alcohol is a substance which is just as plausible, banal and legitimate as the make-up of the actors, the props on the set or the script of the play. All these objects and many others are there invisible and yet actively involved in the experience circulating amongst the actants. They organize and produce the aesthetics and sociability of the situation. And there are of course many occasions when they emerge out of the background of everyday activity and become major players. A broken prop – a cigarette lighter – forces a response: Myrtle breaks from the script and sulkily refuses to pick up the telephone when it rings. In this moment the telephone is not a regular, invisible prop but transforms the drama into a comedy. The unlit cigarette, the broken lighter, the neglectful stage manager and Myrtle's gestures of frustration bring the play beyond the script and allow the audience a laugh which was not intended. And now that the play seems to have taken on an unpredictable life of its own, the curtains and Manny interrupt the show.

But objects do not only emerge as active on exceptional occasions – for example, when they fail to work or emerge in unexpected places forcing new responses. Objects are mainly invisible as they participate in the materialization of experience. The climax of the film is the opening night on Broadway. This is the moment where experience materializes in the first sense: Myrtle affects the others. Maurice cooperates as she breaks from the script. Finally the normative discourses of relationship breakdown and ageing are shattered. What emerges as the couple parts are the generosity, warmth and play of imagination that they have shared, and still share. Instead of the anguish and despair of the script, we find an immanent interrogation of ageing and hope as undertaken by Myrtle and Maurice's characters and the audience. There is an additional generosity in this performance – Myrtle pushes Maurice out of his sense of himself as her off-sider, and into a star performance. He excels in a way he had previously resisted by breaking with his own obedience to the script. Now Maurice knows that the best performances are rule-breaking.

How does Myrtle trigger this cooperation? Alcohol. Myrtle appears drastically late for the premiere and completely drunk, she can barely stand. When she goes on stage her performance is a relay – between herself, the booze and the cast. This is the moment where experience materializes in the second sense. Like her own body, alcohol is a material object through which her continuous experience is realized, becomes facticity. Alcohol does not act as a disinhibitor allowing her to say the previously unsayable. Rather, it is an object which carries experience between actants and contributes to a new rendering of the play. The rest of the cast know of its presence, after waiting long hours for Myrtle's arrival they have all seen her staggering around backstage. However, Maurice's character is not responding to a drunken woman, but a woman with whom he shares a life and an understanding, and the audience are brought into their relation. Unlike the faulty props, alcohol is invisible in this materialization of continuous experience.

Experience is not primarily a matter of thought, it is always matter. Things and spaces are carriers of experience which becomes ours. When, in Chapter 6, we distinguished between individuation and individualistic modes of being, we suggested that experience is a common space of existence, the site from which individuation arises. But this common space is not just an intellectual representation, not just a symbolic construction, it is matter: structured through objects, artefacts, landscapes, buildings. Individuation harnesses the experience things carry with them as it passes from things to people to things to situations and so on.

The materialization of experience reverberates in the politics of everyday life, in how it is undertaken and manifest. When experience materializes it transforms our conditions of visibility and action in a certain field of action. And it does that by bypassing the very basic legitimizing foundations of that field's hegemonic discourses. That which had previously been dismissed, or simply invisible, is inserted into a new matrix of legitimacy. Myrtle acts from outside of the normalizing discourses at work in the script and in people's misinterpretation of her resistance to it. She is forced to do politics from beyond, outside politics. She does not try to make her position comprehensible. Myrtle already knows that her attempts to gain others' understanding will necessarily be captured, tamed and reinserted into the framework of the situation. She has to affect the situation in a different way. And she does this by seducing new participants into the relay between her and the alcohol – Maurice and most importantly the audience. The audience is connected with the stage, brought into the flow of experience. The performance moves people. Her politics are effective.

Tarrying with the event

We have been describing how continuous experience unfolds through people and things. But experience is not only an immediate process which takes place in space. Immanent experience evokes a particular relation to time, it departs from the logic that experiences are discrete points on the timeline of an individual's life story. *Opening Night* has a linear time frame, the highly pressured week leading up to the premier on Broadway. The expectation is that each day will bring the production closer to the dazzling success they all want to perform in New York. But, Myrtle retreats from this chronology. Instead of becoming increasingly tight over the course of the week, the production becomes progressively looser, open and more unpredictable. Likewise with Myrtle – she does not have a clear intention, nor is there any linear depiction of the development of her efforts to work outside of the constraints of the production. There is no move through progressive increments to ever closer understanding or deeper sharing with the others. The rule-breaking, moving performance is not a result of the play's progressive refinement. It is idiosyncratic and contingent, and could just as easily have failed. Despite this, Myrtle anticipates and invests in a shift which may or may not occur. She does this by tarrying with time (Theunissen, 1991). She enters into a different relation with time, being distant from the imperative of linear time, in this case the imperative to engage in the progressive refinement of the show. To follow the structured order of the successive events leading to the premiere would be to constrain herself to the logic of the discourses being imposed on the situation. Normalization occurs in time, structuring time and controlling the flow of everyday activities. Myrtle realizes this and her efforts to go against the discourses in play include a move against the regulation of time.

An early indication we have of tarrying with time occurs when Myrtle interrupts an intimate moment between Manny and Dorothy (his wife) by calling Manny at 4.30 in the morning (this is the scene referred to earlier, where she tells Manny that she does not want to be slapped). They have just done the first performance of the play in New Haven and Myrtle is not happy with it. She wants to discuss playing the scene differently. At first Manny ignores Dorothy's instructions to deal with the issue in the morning. Myrtle's call is not simply about conveying her anxiety, it signals her refusal of the already regulated flow of time. It is an act which induces a new order of time necessary to the attempt to render the play differently. To realize the facticity of continuous experience she needs to change the rhythm of time. By being distant from the immediate flow of proceedings, Myrtle engages in a more intimate sense of the present and the different possibilities which it holds. She stops the given schedule of events and takes the time to explore a different way of realizing continuous experience. Manny is released from any obligation to find a solution for the scene there and then when he engages with the problem, not as an anxiety on Myrtle's part, but as an active effort to intervene in the performance by tarrying with time. This is not something to be discussed but rehearsed, he says, and that can only happen in the morning.

Tarrying is unintentional. Before she intervenes, Myrtle does not know what she wants Manny to do, how she thinks the others should respond, or what the outcome of her efforts should look like. Intentionality is relatively unproblematic for those working within the constraints of the discourses at play: they want to bring Sarah's script to life in the most effective way possible. But positioned outside, Myrtle cannot articulate an intention – even to herself – because what she is trying to evoke is already outside, illegitimate. Tarrying occurs before intentionality. What her tarrying does is to expand the present, to create a moment of slowness, a moment where she can start realizing her desire to move beyond the pre-defined course of the script. Tarrying precedes agency. Suspending the pace of linear time enables continuous experience to erupt into the situation.

Perhaps we are over-interpreting some vague confusion on Myrtle's part? How can Myrtle be consumed by her own active efforts to change the situation on the one hand, yet acting without intention on the

other? Immanent experience unfolds in space and time without constituting a coherent subject. Continuous experience does not produce
intentionality; it produces action as part of a social field in which it
unfolds. Hence, tarrying entails the dissolution of the reflexive subject.
Tarrying involves a mode of being which is inextricable from others,
from the situation – a move beyond the self. The dissolution of the
subject releases experience, enabling the permeation of experience
with the world. Tarrying is intentionless and targetless: it has no
object.

The immanent politics of tarrying

We are suggesting that tarrying plays a vital role in engagement in
socio-political change. But what kind of role can an objectless mode of
being really play in doing effective politics? Maybe talk of tarrying is
just a glorified account of purposeless waiting in the hope of deliver-
ance. Perhaps tarrying is passivity masquerading as activity. Certainly,
what we are describing involves a move away from familiar forms of
political engagement. That is, effective politics is commonly thought
to be underpinned by the capacity to adopt a God's eye view of the
situation, work out what is happening and – from this transcendent
perspective – figure out the most promising strategies for intervening.
Of course, such an account has been roundly criticized on the basis
that it cannot take account of situatedness (Haraway, 1991). But there
is an additional problem with accounts of political action which hinge
on transcendence. Political action involves working – not with what is
already present and in existence – but what is unfolding, with possibilities which may or may not be realized. And, in overlooking this, transcendent accounts of politics exclude what is not yet there. In this
sense, tarrying is not political activity as such; but it is a precondition
for everyday political action. It affords the means to break with prevailing forms of political engagement which reproduce the already given,
normative mechanics of experience.

Myrtle is subjected to the foreclosure affected through a God's eye
perspective. Captured in the incessant circulation of discourses about
ageing, femininity, relationship breakdown and success, there is little
possibility for working on something which exceeds these discourses.
The terms of the exchanges between the cast and crew are defined and
any attempt which seems to introduce a different mode of being is
recuperated into the transcendent viewpoint. Myrtle retreats from any
transcendent entry point into doing politics and occupies a place

which lies outside the existing discourses. In so doing, she inhabits a space without guarantees. Outside politics are contingent, unpredictable, and unintentional.

Myrtle works with unrealized trajectories, possibilities which do not yet exist (not even in the symbolic, nor the imagination), potentials which may never manifest. And yet, she is driven by these non-existent possibilities. Not because she has had a vision of an alternate future, but because this expanded, slowed-down present fuels new relations with other actants and new forms of action, possibilities she is compelled to explore, but which only later and unexpectedly will materialize in a new version of the play on the opening night. Myrtle could never have intended this event, but at the same time, she engages in a process of change which is orientated towards this event (Badiou, 2001). And the non-existent event of the new play could not have come into existence without this unfolding of her continuous experience.

Continuous experience is necessary to outside politics in a double sense. On the one hand, it reconstitutes a situation as a space which affords drifting and movement, a space which is transformable through the recombination of actants. This first dimension is connected to the immanent materialization of experience. On the other hand (through tarrying), continuous experience breaks with the regulated time and order of a situation opening it to non-present possibilities. Continuous experience is both immanent and full of potentiality. It is incorrigibly present. It is mesmerized by suddenness (Bohrer, 1998). This is political action from within, an active mode of being in the present which prepares and evokes a change in the unfurling present.

Sociability in the making

It might be argued that the change which occurs in *Opening Night* is not effected through the flow of continuous experience between actants – as we are suggesting – but is really the result of Myrtle's personal success in contesting the normative meanings of ageing, success and femininity being imposed on her. We have already countered the psychological individualism of such a reading in discussing individuation: experience is not the property of an individual. But there is another question to be addressed. Whilst continuous experience may not necessarily be denied in such a reading, it is cast as exceptional, something only a minority have the opportunity to tap into (stars like

Myrtle) or which only exists at special points of rupture. In contrast, we argue that it is simply there. It is particular neither to special actors nor to extraordinary moments. And it is through the 'recalcitrant ordinariness' of continuous experience that 'bureaucratized and technocratic worlds and discourses are put in question and transformed. "Ordinariness" becomes a generic index of hitherto uninvestigated processes through which people make sense of their lives given the material and cultural resources available to them' (Sandywell, 2004, pp. 175–6). Although what we are describing is an ongoing, largely overlooked aspect of being, the reasons for its neglect extend beyond its ordinariness. Whereas already captured modes of connecting may be easily identifiable, it is harder to see sociability in the making.

In the first section of this book we considered how social and cultural researchers have been deeply involved in both the turn towards experience as an object of research and in contesting this broad shift. On the one hand, experience is valued as the source of articulations which evidence subjection or resistance to hegemonic discourses. On the other, such promises are contested when experience is recast as the end-product (or by-product) of discursive assemblages. At the extreme ends of these debates, experience is either irrelevant to or identical with socio-political regulation and change. Continuous experience is grasped by neither of these poles. It operates at the level of sociability; it is a mode of doing everyday politics which interferes with hegemonic politics by creating connections between actants which circumvent the normative terms or relating. Unlike current dominant forms of sociability which are already captured by neoliberal governmental rationalities, the political importance of these emergent modes of relating lies in the fact that they are sociability in the making. The successful premiere is not the result of Myrtle's stardom, but of the contingent event in which various actants are involved in emergent sociability.

Dispersal

Sebald's *Die Ausgewanderten* (1993/1997) evokes the experience of being pushed out of history; of people who, because of the passage of history, have limited possibilities for representing their experience in the present. Yet they can still act in accordance with their experience and work through it. They can forge a different understanding of history without representation. Hegemonic discourses – of survival or loss, for example – cannot be avoided, but the migrants circumvent the reinstallation of such discourses as central principles which order the trajectories of their lives. Sebald's migrants travel with history without ever making it their point of departure or arrival. History is constituted as continuous experience. It is never far away, neither does it determine life trajectories. It is dispersed, unevenly distributed in the times and spaces of people's lives.

Max Ferber's life is not given meaning by the Holocaust. When he is 15, his parents arrange for him to leave Munich and to go into his uncle's care in England. Their plan is to follow. He lives in, what he describes as, an anarchic boarding school populated by boys who wear brightly coloured school uniforms – at times Ferber feels like he has become one of a flock of parrots. He receives fortnightly letters from home. After two years, in 1941, the letters stop. Only later he learns the reason: his parents had been deported to Riga. One might think here, that his parents' disappearance will steer Ferber's course in life, an experience which will become memory, a memory which will become the most crucial principle endowing meaning in Ferber's life. But as Ferber ashamedly says, he was relieved to stop receiving the letters. Only later did he gradually grasp the fact of what happened, but he never grasped the meaning. There is no meaning. The moments when the Holocaust enters Ferber's experience are black holes in his life. The Holocaust is unspeakable, beyond meaning, and beyond representation. It is dispersed in Ferber's ever-present: 'There is neither a past nor a future' (Sebald, 1993/1997, p. 181). There is only a present. The Holocaust is dispersed in situations, encounters, things, people, Ferber's artwork, the way he lives as a hermit artist. History disseminates in the most unexpected corners of one's existence. It is not possible to collect dispersed moments of continuous experience into *the* experience, the one crucial, divisible, overarching experience of the Holocaust.

Sebald evokes this dispersal of experience in Ferber's life and beyond. The account we read is written by a raconteur who, after a period of close friendship, has lost touch with Ferber. Twenty-five years later, the raconteur chances upon a story in the magazine supplement of a Sunday paper about a now famous artist, Ferber. He reads about the disappearance of Ferber's parents, and wonders why, when they were so close, he had never asked about his friend's early life. He goes to rekindle their relation and is warmly welcomed. Now the raconteur takes up Ferber's experience of the Holocaust. Ferber gives him the diaries his mother wrote between 1939 and 1941, a period during which she grew to understand her fate. But the diaries are not about

the Holocaust. Luisa writes, in precious detail, about her early child-
hood in the small village of Steinach, the years she spent living in the
Bad Kissingen, her love affairs with two men both of whom died, her
arranged marriage and developing love for the man who later became
Ferber's father. This is how Luisa experiences the Holocaust; she knows
her fate and actively moves towards it as a woman who is deeply
engaged in the life she is living, in the community of which she is a
part. The trajectories of Luisa's everyday life run through her son, to
his friend, who is entrusted to write about Ferber's life, and does. The
friend writes what we read. But before this he writes, deletes, rewrites,
deletes and writes again. He is not confident about giving his account
back to Ferber, concerned not only about doing justice to Ferber, but
about 'the entire questionable business of writing' (Sebald, 1993/1997,
p. 230). When Ferber gets emphysema the friend goes to see him in
hospital, a space where he is surrounded by death. Although Ferber is
now beyond speech, his friend knows that the sick man has decided to
'put his condition behind him one way or another' (Sebald, 1993/
1997, p. 231). He never gives him what he has written. The text makes
up the fictive biographical account that we read. Sebald works with dispersed experience, not by giving it a coherent return to a person to
whom it might be thought to belong, but as it circulates, by tracing its
course through bodies, time and place.

In *Die Ausgewanderten* continuous experience is dispersed in a
twofold way: in the way it is felt (Ferber), but also in the way it is
grasped (Sebald). Experience is a unified whole, without a centre of
gravity, without a central historical reference point, yet held together
by innumerable scattered pieces of historical events. As Luisa writes in
1941, 'when I think back to those days', the winter days of ice-skating
in the Englischen Garten of her hometown between the wars, 'I see
shades of blue everywhere – a single empty space, stretching out in the
twilight of late afternoon, crisscrossed by the tracks of ice-skaters long
vanished' (Sebald, 1993/1997, pp. 217–8).

When the friend returns to Kissingen to search for traces of Luisa's
family, the elderly Germans he encounters appear as George Grosz
caricatures living out their lives against the stage-set of a spa town. The
city officials with whom he deals in trying to track down the Jewish
cemetery cannot fathom him. He is given instructions to take 1000
paces south from the town centre and keys to the cemetery, keys
which do not fit the locks on the gate. Clambering over the high walls
he finds a neglected wilderness, 'a stone placed on top of a grave witnessed that someone must have visited the dead – who could say how

long ago' (Sebald, 1993/1997, p. 224), and finally the gravestone of Luisa's mother. In one sense, this grave is what he has come for, but now before it he does not know what to think. He marks his presence with a stone and leaves.

The trip to Kissingen, this encounter with a past which has been sealed and neutralized, leaves the friend reeling. Although the cemetery has not been completely destroyed, the space it is allocated in the town's life is a suffocating one, history never moves beyond the walls of the cemetery, never seeps into the streets, the restaurants, the hotels of Kissingen. The Holocaust is divided and contained in one single experience, as such it can be dealt with, but it is not allowed to flow and contaminate everyday life. The friend breaks the sealed, discrete, mummified, consumable experience of the Holocaust which dominates post-war Germany. He does this by identifying the dispersal of the Holocaust, its manifestations in seeds which have fallen and grown outside of the cemetery's walls, outside of the standardized story of the Holocaust. But also in seeds which have never really grown, but which just appear as bearers of the passage of historical time.

Sebald conveys this dispersal of continuous experience by refusing the imperative to present 'the Holocaust experience' in the form of a coherent and cogent story. He deals with (fictive) biographical material, but without allowing it to be captured by the logic of narrative. There is no climax, no resolution, no dawning realizations about the meaning of experience. The point when the friend stands in front of the Ferber family grave is not illuminating. He simply says he does not know what to think, and leaves.

Dispersal is more than an attribute or quality of continuous experience. It is the process through which experience escapes capture and travels, destabilizing clichéd renditions of events, crisscrossing space, realizing details of existence from their neutralized designation. The dispersal of experience is the means through which continuous experience flourishes and opposes any attempt to allocate a proper place to history's leftovers. The friend leaves Kissingen deeply disturbed by the efficiency with which a generation of Germans have cleaned-up history. It is not that they have extinguished all evidence of the past, they have just tidied everything up and now they no longer need to actively remember it. They have made the move against which Jean Améry (1964/1980) rails: you cannot relegate the past to memory, it is always active everyday experience, even when it is elusive (Middleton & Brown, 2005). Dispersed experience is anti-memory: 'And the last remnants memory destroys' (Sebald, 1993/1997, p. 1).

Fluidity and imperceptibility

Die Ausgewanderten is populated by imperceptible characters. There are neither heroes nor anti-heroes in the four separate and fictive biographies Sebald writes. The migrants, whose everyday existence is touched by the Holocaust, do not live as Holocaust survivors. Their lives are not dominated by the trauma of survival, or by their exclusion in the cleaned-up version of history. Of course this exclusion does mark their lives, but they are not driven by the felt necessity to live their lives as a response to exclusion. In fact, living the Holocaust as a dispersed continuous experience is their response to this exclusion. They live lives which are no more and no less exceptional than the lives of most. The composition of their life trajectories is not dominated by the meaning of this historical event. They live arbitrary lives, they live in imperceptibility. But in doing that, they let history emerge and flow through many different unconnected, small incidents of life.

Sebald evokes this proximity to life through a series of unrelated figures who, as they age, forsake exceptionality, enter into ordinary life and embrace a mode of being unmediated by the clean-up of history. Their intimate relation to the Holocaust is not placed outside of their lived everyday existences; nor is it super-imposed on them, condemning them to permanent states of loss and anxiety. *Die Ausgewanderten* is not a book about loss, or about potentials unrealized. It deals with the individuation of the experience of the Holocaust. It is not a book about survival, but about the making of worlds. Each of the figures develops the most intimate and fluid relation to life, engaging with it in disparate ways. They have a single commonality: their proximity to death. But this proximity is individuated in different ways; each follows a trajectory faithful to the details of their own lives. Their proximity to death is realized on the immanent plane of their lives. Sebald enters the terrain of death without invoking tragedy. Death is just another element of the migrants' singular, fluid relations to life.

Continuous experience is fluid (Irigaray, 1985a). It is most closely connected to the surroundings, the vicinities, to the habitats of everyday life. After assimilating into his new country, Dr Henry Selwyn pursues a career as a doctor in England and in his later years devotes himself to his garden. In the last decade of his life, Paul Bereyter lives with a French woman and still retains a connection to his home town in Germany, where he had worked as a primary school teacher. Ambros Adelwarth leaves Austria and becomes an exclusive butler; he travels throughout the world accompanying the extravagant American,

Cosmo Solomon. Max Ferber pursues his art in a corner of Manchester's abandoned docks, completely retreating from the normal business of the art world. In the crisscrossing paths of their migrations, Sebald's figures encounter death by making life. The Holocaust is carried with them, in them, in their lives. They dive into the realm of imperceptibility (Deleuze & Guattari, 1988).

The migrants retreat from the world without spurning it; they slip into the fissures between clichéd modes of everyday exchange, opening new ways of connecting. They are not hostile to others, they forge singular connections with those crossing their paths. The relations Sebald evokes are striking for their warmth, the openness of the curiosity which flows between people, the quality of the affections which emerge, the care taken – not out of a sense of obligation, but because people appreciate, are implicated and interested in the possibilities being cultivated in each others' trajectories of individuation.

Doing imperceptibility means retreating from the invitation to connect to others along terms dictated by the need for recognition of an individualized, divisible experience. For example, it involves refusing the interpellation of oneself as a 'survivor', an identity which always risks constraining experience. Imperceptible experience is a force which interrupts the representation of selves and the affirmation of identity. Instead of relating to others on the basis of a common interest, connections emerge from a shared search for a viable way to change the very conditions of existence. It is only through such connections that people can work against the constraints of hegemonic identities, expanding the terrain on which the experience of the Holocaust can be lived out in radically different ways.

But here, possibilities for relating are not structured by the imperative to bring difference into play, nor does doing imperceptibility necessitate denying difference. Imperceptibility starts from difference but involves a continuous drift away from the identities which are related to different subject positions. Hence, imperceptibility is a process of dis-identification; it works with singular, continuous experience. In this sense, outside politics do not aim to amplify either pole of the identity-difference axis: the migrants are liberated from the terms of this axis. This allows for new forms of inclusiveness in political disputes. By becoming imperceptible, actants without legitimacy can insert themselves into the political field, changing the architecture of the discourses in play.

Although the mode of engagement we are describing here does not involve a final, unified goal, it is not purposeless. By contesting the policing Rancière (1998) identifies as standing in for politics it generates alternative means for doing politics (as discussed in Chapter 6). That is, in our current socio-political conditions both state politics and micropolitics provide the necessary terrain for the proliferation of neoliberalism. In Chapter 7, we argued that neither of these modes of activity manages to establish a break from the neoliberal machine. This is because state politics are, by definition, oriented towards the totality of the neoliberal state, and micropolitics fail to mount a serious challenge to the emerging formations and operations of the neoliberal state. From the perspective of micropolitics, working with totalities of power is understood as a means of being absorbed, or re-absorbed, back into state politics – hence micropolitics direct their concerns to localized practices of difference. (This is why Foucault's aesthetics of the self are so appealing to micropolitics, as discussed in Chapter 5.) Yet, although micropolitics offer powerful critiques of state politics, they fail to develop the means to challenge the neoliberal state. Instead they avoid it and, in so doing, they fold into themselves. In Chapter 7, we argued that this folding and self-referentiality is neither a failure nor an intentional strategy but a symptom of the new functioning of neoliberalism. In contrast, as outside politics start from positions which have been effaced from the neoliberal state, they do not baulk at addressing the totality of the neoliberal state. The difference between micropolitics and outside politics is that the latter do not fear corruption. This is because outside politics is, in the current historical moment, outside of the logics of representation – or better, this mode of doing politics is *outside and against* the logics of representation. Whilst state politics play the game of representation and micropolitics are concerned to contest the conditions through which existing representations are produced, outside politics refuse representation. Outside politics achieve this to the extent that they create the conditions for connections which generate common projects of changing the world – connections which are not predefined by the forms of policing in force in the fields to which they pertain. We are not proposing that continuous experience is inherently subversive of dominant neoliberal rationalities. Rather, we are suggesting that if there is one form of politics which *can* be subversive it is this. The potential of outside politics stems from the insistence that – through the making of sociability – a world which is neglected or silenced by the dominant discourses of neoliberal power becomes apparent in everyday activity, political engagement and in social research. Continuous experience insists that another world is here.

The subjectlessness of continuous experience

In discussing *Opening Night*, we described how the week leading to the Broadway premiere fractures the clichéd rendition of ageing, femininity and relationship-breakdown on offer in Sarah's script. By tarrying with time Myrtle manages to distance the production from the predefined outcome of the script and to engage others in the performance of a new version of the play yet to come. Continuous experience materializes in the production – not through the resolution of tensions between all those involved – but as a fact with which all have to contend. The cast and crew are actively involved in a performance in which the facticity of continuous experience materializes. A new play is there.

The film depicts the struggle over a move from recognition and identity politics to the politics of imperceptibility. Myrtle's attempt to rupture the script is read by others in the production in terms of her personal difficulties with ageing; this reading is mistaken. Myrtle does have a deep subjective interest in the play. Yet, she is not interested in getting others to understand this interest, nor does its existence prevent her from retreating from herself. There is another barrier to the move to imperceptibility in Cassavetes' film. Myrtle is already 'someone', her fame and prestige mean that all eyes are on her – there is a public appetite for *Myrtle's* skill, *Myrtle's* capacities. The situation does not assist in dis-identification. By turning up for the premiere completely drunk (forcing others to question her capacity), she finally manages to break this star positioning and to affect the others through different means. The paradox of Myrtle's stardom is that she achieves it by working at the level of imperceptibility, by harnessing continuous experience.

Unburdened by others expectations of their success, or even failure, Sebald's migrants are free to move imperceptibility without Myrtle's struggle. As *Die Ausgewanderten* traces the scattered paths of four migrants, the book conveys continuous experience as both unified and dispersed. The Holocaust experience is dispersed across continents, centuries and bodies. Sebald's characters take up this dispersal and in so doing they reveal the social relations which are being forged in the neglected spaces between hegemonic discourses of tragedy and loss – modes of sociability which rework our sense of the everyday lived experience of the Holocaust and the futures such experience makes possible. Henry Selwyn, Paul Bereyter, Ambros Adelwarth, Max and Luisa Ferber dwell in their ordinary lives, rather than in any abstract crystallization of a history which relegates them to the position of victims or survivors. All of them are deeply connected to the immediate incidents of their lives.

There is no standard story of survival and death, pain and defeat. The migrants' lives consist of fluid, continuous experience as it flows through their encounters with innumerable contingencies. Their everyday experience is the place where history unfolds. As social researchers might with memory-work, Sebald simultaneously plays with the familiar genres of biography and memoir and breaks with the notion that biographical material is best understood in terms of linear, causal representations of the chronology of one's life. He adopts these genres' intimate relation with the details of everyday experience. But, instead of personalities whose futures are determined by their pasts, he brings forth imperceptible figures. Navigating without ever puncturing the 'mist that no eye can dispel' (Sebald, 1993/1997, p. 25), the migrants remake the historical facticity of the Holocaust by putting continuous experience to work in the present, as they engage with others and with their everyday worlds. Moving deeper into the immanence of the present necessitates a refusal of clichéd subject positions, a retreat from the self. This is the subjectlessness of continuous experience.

References

Adorno, T. W. (1983). *Negative dialectics*. New York: Continuum.

Adorno, T. W. & Horkheimer, M. (1979). *Dialectic of enlightenment*: London: Verso.

Althusser, L. (1971). *Lenin and philosophy, and other essays*. London: New Left Books.

Améry, J. (1980). *At the mind's limits: Contemplations by a survivor on Auschwitz and its realities*. Bloomington, Ind: Indiana University Press. (Original work published 1964)

Anderson, B. (1991). *Imagined communities: Reflections on the origin and spread of nationalism*. London: Verso.

Ang, I. (1997). Comments on Felski's The Doxa of Difference: The uses of incommensurability. *Signs: Journal of Women in Culture and Society*, *23*(1), 57–64.

Aranda, F. J. (1976). *Luis Buñuel: A critical biography*. New York: Da Capo Press.

Arendt, H. (1970). *The human condition*. Chicago: University of Chicago Press.

Ariss, R. (1997). *Against death: The practice of living with AIDS*. Amsterdam: Gordon & Breach Publishers.

Arribas Ayllon, M. (2005). *On the medicalisation of welfare: Towards a genealogy of dependency*. Unpublished PhD thesis, Cardiff University, UK.

Badiou, A. (2001). *Ethics: An essay on the understanding of evil* (P. Hallward, Trans.). London/New York: Verso.

Bakhtin, M. M. (1986). *Speech genres and other late essays*. Austin: University of Texas Press.

Balibar, E. & Wallerstein, I. (1991). *Race, nation, class: Ambiguous identities*. London: Verso.

Barad, K. (2003). Posthumanist performativity: Toward an understanding of how matter comes to matter. *Signs: Journal of Women in Culture and Society*, *28*(3), 801–831.

Beck, U. (1992). *Risk society: towards a new modernity*. London: Sage.

Bennett, J. (2003). Tenebrae after September 11. In J. Bennett & R. Kennedy (eds), *World memory: Personal trajectories in a global time* (pp. 177–194). London: Palgrave.

Bevir, M. (1999). Foucault, power, and institutions. *Political Studies*, *47*(2), 345–359.

Bhabha, H. K. (1994). *The location of culture*. London: Routledge.

Bohrer, K. H. (1998). *Plötzlichkeit: zum Augenblick des ästhetischen Scheins: Mit einem Nachwort von 1998*. Frankfurt: Suhrkamp.

Bojadzijev, M., Karakayali, S. & Tsianos, V. (2004). Le mystère de l'arrivée. Des camps et des specters. *Multitudes*, *19*, 41–52.

Boudry, P., Kuster, B. & Lorenz, R. (eds). (2000). *Reproduktionskonten fälschen!: Heterosexualität, Arbeit & Zuhause*. Berlin: b_books.

Bove, A. & Empson, E. (2002, October). *The dark side of the multitude*. Paper presented at the Dark Markets conference in Vienna, Austria.

Bradley, B. (1989). *Visions of infancy: A critical introduction to child psychology.* Cambridge: Polity Press.

Brown, S. & Stenner, P. (2001). Being affected: Spinoza and the psychology of emotion. *International Journal of Group Tensions, 30*(1), 81–105.

Brown, W. (1995). *States of injury: Power and freedom in late modernity.* Princeton, NJ: Princeton University Press.

Buache, F. (1973). *The cinema of Luis Buñuel.* London/New York: Tantivy Press/A. S. Barnes.

Bunker, R., Gleeson, B. J., Holloway, D. & Randolph, B. (2002). The local impacts of urban consolidation policy in Sydney. *Urban Policy & Research, 20*(2), 143–167.

Buñuel, L. (1983). *My last sigh.* New York: Knopf.

Buñuel, L. & Alejandro, J. (1971). *Tristana: A film.* New York: Simon & Schuster.

Burchell, G., Gordon, C. & Miller, P. (1991). *The Foucault effect: Studies in governmentality.* Chicago: University of Chicago Press.

Burman, E. (1994). Experience, identities and alliances: Jewish feminism and feminist psychology. In K. K. Bhavani & A. Phoenix (eds), *Shifting identities-shifting racisms: A Feminism & psychology reader* (pp. 155–178). London: Sage.

Butler, J. (1990). *Gender trouble: Feminism and the subversion of identity.* New York/London: Routledge.

Butler, J. (1992). Contingent foundations: Feminism and the question of 'Postmodernism'. In J. Butler & J. Scott (eds), *Feminists theorize the political.* New York/London: Routledge.

Butler, J. (1993). *Bodies that matter: On the discursive limits of 'sex'.* New York/London: Routledge.

Butler, J. (1994). Against proper objects. *differences: A Journal of Feminist Cultural Studies, 6*, 1–26.

Butler, J. (1997). Against proper objects. In E. Weed & N. Schor (eds), *Feminism meets queer theory* (pp. 1–30). Bloomington, Ind: Indiana University Press.

Butler, J. (2001). Giving an account of oneself. *Diactritics, 31*(4), 22–40.

Calhoun, C. (2002). Imagining solidarity: Cosmopolitanism, constitutional patriotism and the public sphere. *Public Culture, 14*(1), 147–171.

Carney, R. (2001). *Cassavetes on Cassavetes.* London: Faber.

Cassavetes, J. (1976). Interview. *Positif, 180,* 11–24.

Chakrabarty, D. (2000). *Provincializing Europe: Postcolonial thought and historical difference.* Princeton, NJ: Princeton University Press.

Charity, T. (2001). *John Cassavetes: Lifeworks.* London: Omnibus.

Clandinin, J. & Connelly, M. (2000). *Narrative inquiry: Experience and story in qualitative research.* San Francisco, CA: Jossey Bass Publishers.

Clifford, J. (1997). *Routes: Travel and translation in the late twentieth century.* Cambridge, MA: Harvard University Press.

Clifford, J. (2000). Taking identity politics seriously: 'The contradictory, stony ground ....' In P. Gilroy, L. Grossberg & A. McRobbie (eds), *Without guarantees: In honor of Stuart Hall* (pp. 94–112). London/New York: Verso.

Clifford, J. (2001). Indigenous articulations. *The Contemporary Pacific, 13*(2), 468–490.

Cole, M. (1996). *Cultural psychology: A once and future discipline.* Cambridge, MA: Belknap Press.

Collier, S. & Ong, A. (2004). *Global assemblages: Technology, politics, and ethics as anthropological problems*. Oxford: Blackwell.

Connery, C. L. (1999). Actually existing left conservatism. *boundary 2, 26*(3), 3–11.

Connolly, W. (2002). *Neuropolitics: Thinking, culture, speed*. Minneapolis, MN: University of Minnesota Press.

Crawford, J., Kippax, S., Onyx, J., Gault, U. & Benton, P. (1992). *Emotion and gender: Constructing meaning from memory*. London: Sage.

Crossley, M. L. (1999). Stories of illness and trauma survival: Liberation or repression? *Social Science & Medicine, 48*(11), 1685–1695.

Cruikshank, B. (1993). Revolutions within: Self-government and self-esteem. *Economy & Society, 22*(3), 327–344.

Danziger, K. (1990). *Constructing the subject: Historical origins of psychological research*. Cambridge: Cambridge University Press.

Davies, B. & Harré, R. (1990). Positioning: The discursive production of selves. *Journal for the Theory of Social Behaviour, 20*, 43–63.

Dean, M. (1994). 'A social structure of many souls': Moral regulation, government and self-formation. *Canadian Journal of Sociology, 19*, 145–168.

Dean, M. (1995). Governing the unemployed self in an active society. *Economy & Society, 24*(4), 559–583.

Dean, M. (1999). *Governmentality: Power and rule in modern society*. London: Sage.

Debord, G. (1981). Perspectives for conscious alterations in everyday life. In K. Knabb (ed.), *Situationist International anthology* (pp. 68–75). Berkeley, CA: Bureau of Public Secrets.

de Certeau, M. (1988). *The practice of everyday life* (S. Rendall, Trans.). Berkeley/Los Angeles: University of California Press.

de Certeau, M. (1997). *Culture in the plural* (T. Conley, Trans.). Minneapolis, MN: University of Minnesota Press.

de Lauretis, T. (1984). *Alice doesn't: Feminism, semiotics, cinema*. Bloomington, Ind: Indiana University Press.

de Lauretis, T. (1987). *Technologies of gender: Essays on theory, film, and fiction*. Bloomington, Ind: Indiana University Press.

de Lauretis, T. (1988). Displacing hegemonic discourses: Reflections on feminist theory in the 1980s. In D. Gordon (ed.), *Inscriptions. Vol. 3/4: Feminism and the critique of colonial discourse* (pp. 127–144). Santa Cruz, CA: Center for Cultural Studies.

Deleuze, G. (1991). A philosophical concept … In E. Cadava, P. Connor & J. L. Nancy (eds), *Who comes after the subject?* (pp. 94–95). London: Routledge.

Deleuze, G. (1994). *Difference and repetition* (P. Patton, Trans.). London: Athlone Press.

Deleuze, G. & Foucault, M. (1977). Intellectuals and power: A conversation between Michel Foucault and Gilles Deleuze. In M. Foucault, *Language, counter-memory, practice* (pp. 205–217). Oxford: Basil Blackwell.

Deleuze, G. & Guattarri, F. (1988). *A thousand plateaus: Capitalism and schizophrenia* (B. Massumi, Trans.). London/New York: Continuum.

de Tocqueville, A. (1961). *Democracy in America, Vol. 2* (H. Reeve, Trans.). New York: Schocken Books.

Deutscher, M. (1983). *Subjecting and objecting*. St Lucia: University of Queensland Press.

Diprose, R. (2003). The hand that writes the community in blood. *Cultural Studies Review*, *9*, 35–50.

Donzelot, J. (1984). Die Förderung des Sozialen. In J. Donzelot, D. Meuret, P. Miller & N. Rose (eds), *Zur Genealogie der Regulation. Anschlüsse an Michel Foucault* (pp. 109–160). Mainz: Decaton.

Dreyfus, H. (1996). Being and power: Heidegger and Foucault. *International Journal of Philosophical Studies*, *4*, 1–16.

Eagleton, T. (2005). Lend me a fiver. London Review of Books, 23 June, 23–24.

Edwards, G. (1995). *Indecent exposures: Buñuel, Saura, Erice & Almodóvar*. London: M. Boyars.

Eisenstadt, S. (2000). *Fundamentalism, sectarianism and revolution*. Cambridge: Cambridge University Press.

Elias, N. (1981). Zivilisation und Gewalt. Über das Staatsmonopol der körperlichen Gewalt und seine Durchbrechungen. In J. Matthes (ed.), *Lebenswelt und soziale Probleme. Verhandlungen des 20. Deutschen Soziologentages zu Bremen 1980* (pp. 98–122). Frankfurt: Campus.

Eribon, D. (2004). *Insult and the making of the gay self* (M. Lucey, Trans.). Durham, NC/London: Duke University Press.

Fanon, F. (1967). *Black skin, white masks*. New York: Grove Press.

Flowers, P. (2001). Gay men and HIV/AIDS risk management. *Health*, *5*(1), 50–75.

Foucault, M. (1977). *Language, counter-memory, practice: Selected interviews and essays*. D. F. Bouchard (ed.). Oxford: Basil Blackwell.

Foucault, M. (1981). The order of discourse. In R. Young (ed.), *Untying the text: A post-structuralist reader* (pp. 48–77). London: Routledge/Kegan Paul.

Foucault, M. (1984). *The history of sexuality: Volume one, an introduction* (R. Hurley, Trans.). Harmondsworth: Penguin Books.

Foucault, M. (1986). *The Foucault reader*. P. Rabinow (ed.). Harmondsworth: Penguin Books.

Foucault, M. (1988a). Technologies of the self. In L. Martin, H. Gutman & P. Hutton (eds), *Technologies of the self: A seminar with Michel Foucault* (pp. 16–49). Amherst, MA: The University of Massachusetts Press.

Foucault, M. (1988b). The ethic of care for the self as a practice of freedom. An interview with Michel Foucault on January 20, 1984. In J. W. Bernauer & D. M. Rasmussen (eds), *The final Foucault* (pp. 1–20). Cambridge, MA: MIT Press.

Foucault, M. (1990). *The care of the self: The history of sexuality, volume three* (R. Hurley, Trans.). New York: Vintage.

Foucault, M. (1992). *The use of pleasure: The history of sexuality, volume two* (R. Hurley, Trans.). New York: Vintage.

Foucault, M. (1994). Wie wird Macht ausgeübt? In H. L. Dreyfus & P. Rabinow (eds), *Michel Foucault: Jenseits von Strukturalismus und Hermeneutik* (pp. 251–261). Weinheim: Beltz Athenäum.

Foucault, M. (1997). *The politics of truth*. S. Lotringer (ed.). New York: Semiotext(e).

Frank, A. (1995). *The wounded storyteller: Body, illness, and ethics*. Chicago: Chicago University Press.

Freud, S. (1966). Mourning and melancholia. In J. Strachey (ed.), *The standard edition of the complete psychological works of Sigmund Freud* (Vol. XXIV, pp. 239–258). London: Hogarth Press.

Frow, J. (1999). Cultural studies and the neo-liberal imagination. *The Yale Journal of Criticism, 12*(2), 424–430.

Gallop, J. (1988). *Thinking through the body.* New York: Columbia University Press.

Gallop, J. (1997). *Feminist accused of sexual harassment.* Durham, NC: Duke University Press.

Gill, R. (2005, May). *Psychosocial studies and cultural analysis: a critical dialogue.* Paper presented at the International Society for Theoretical Psychology Conference, Cape Town, South Africa.

Gillies, V., Harden, A., Johnson, K., Reavey, P., Strange, V. & Willig, C. (2004). Women's collective constructions of embodied practices through memory work: Cartesian dualism in memories of sweating and pain. *British Journal of Social Psychology, 43*(1), 99–112.

Gillies, V., Harden, A., Johnson, K., Reavey, P., Strange, V. & Willig, C. (2005). Painting pictures of embodied experience: The use of non-linguistic data in the study of embodiment. *Qualitative Research in Psychology, 2*, 199–213.

Gilroy, P. (1993). *The black Atlantic: Modernity and double consciousness.* Cambridge, MA: Harvard University Press.

Gorz, A. (2004). *Wissen, Wert und Kapital: zur Kritik der Wissensökonomie.* Zürich: Rotpunktverlag.

Greco, M. (1998). *Illness as a work of thought: A Foucauldian perspective on psychosomatics.* London: Routledge.

Grierson, J., Thorpe, R., Saunders, M. & Pitts, M. (2004). *HIV futures 4: State of the (positive) nation* (Monograph Series No. 48). Melbourne: LaTrobe University, The Australian Research Centre in Sex, Health & Society.

Grosz, E. (1994). *Volatile bodies: Towards a corporeal feminism.* Sydney: Allen & Unwin.

Gunsteren, H. V. (1998). *A theory of citizenship: Organizing plurality in contemporary democracies.* Boulder, CO: Westview Press.

Hall, S. (1981). Cultural studies: Two paradigms. In T. Bennett, G. Martin, C. Mercer & J. Woollacott (eds), *Culture, ideology and social process* (pp. 19–37). London: Open University Press.

Hall, S. (1986a). On postmodernism and articulation. An interview with Stuart Hall. *Journal of Communication Inquiry, 10*(2), 45–60.

Hall, S. (1986b). Gramsci's relevance for the study of race and ethnicity. *Journal of Communication Inquiry, 10*(2), 5–27.

Hall, S., Critcher, C., Jefferson, T., Clarke, J. & Roberts, B. (1978). *Policing the crisis: Mugging, the state and law and order.* London: Macmillan.

Hall, S. & Jefferson, T. (1975). *Resistance through rituals: Youth subcultures in postwar Britain.* London: Hutchinson & Co.

Haraway, D. (1991). *Simians, cyborgs and women.* New York: Routledge.

Haraway, D. (1994). A game of cat's cradle. Science studies, feminist theory, cultural studies. *Configurations, 1*, 59–72.

Haraway, D. (1995). Ein Manifest für Cyborgs. Feminismus im Streit mit den Technowissenschaften. In D. Haraway (ed.), *Die Neuerfindung der Natur: Primaten, Cyborgs und Frauen* (pp. 33–72). Frankfurt: Campus.

Hardt, M. & Dunn, T. (2000). Sovereignty, multitudes, absolute democracy: A discussion between Michael Hardt and Thomas Dumm about Hardt and Negri's Empire. *Theory & Event, 4.* Retrieved October 12, 2005, from http://muse.jhu.edu/journals/theory and event/

Hardt, M. & Negri, A. (2000). *Empire*. Cambridge, MA: Harvard University Press.

Harré, R. (1983). *Personal being: A theory for individual psychology*. Oxford: Basil Blackwell.

Haug, F. (ed.). (1987). *Female sexualization: A collective work of memory* (E. Carter, Trans.). London/New York: Verso.

Haug, F. (1992). *Beyond female masochism: Memory-work and politics*. London/New York: Verso.

Henriques, J., Hollway, W., Urwin, C., Venn, C. & Walkerdine, V. (1998). *Changing the subject: Psychology, social regulation and subjectivity*. London: Routledge. (Original work published 1984)

Higginbotham, V. (1979). *Luis Buñuel*. Boston: Twayne Publishers.

Higginbotham, V. (1988). *Spanish film under Franco*. Austin: University of Texas Press.

Hobbes, T. (1983). *De Cive*. Oxford: Oxford University Press.

Hobsbawm, E. J. (1990). *Nations and nationalism since 1780: Programme, myth, reality*. Cambridge: Cambridge University Press.

Hoggart, R. (1957). *The uses of literacy*. London: Chatto & Windus.

Holzkamp, K. (1980). Zu Wundts Kritik an der experimentellen Erforschung des Denkens. *Forum Kritische Psychologie, 6*, 156–165.

Holzkamp, K. (1984). Zum Verhältnis zwischen gesamtgesellschaftlichen Prozeß und individuellem Lebensprozeß. *Konsequent Sonderband, 6*, 29–40.

Holzkamp, K. (1991). Experience of self and scientific objectivity. In C. Tolman & W. Maiers (eds), *Critical psychology: Contributions to an historical science of the subject* (pp. 65–80). Cambridge: Cambridge University Press.

Hones, D. (1998). Known in part: The transformational power of narrative inquiry. *Qualitative Inquiry, 4*(2), 225–248.

Hook, D. (2001). Discourse, knowledge, materiality, history: Foucault and discourse analysis. *Theory & Psychology, 11*(4), 521–547.

Hurley, M. (2003). *Then and now: Gay men and HIV* (Monograph Series No. 46). Melbourne: LaTrobe University, The Australian Research Centre in Sex, Health & Society.

Irigaray, L. (1985a). *This sex which is not one* (C. Porter & C. Burke, Trans.). Ithaca: Cornell University Press.

Irigaray, L. (1985b). *Speculum of the other woman* (G. Gill, Trans.). Ithaca: Cornell University Press.

James, W. (1996). *Essays in radical empiricism*. Lincoln: University of Nebraska Press.

Jameson, F. (1993). On 'cultural studies'. *Social Text, 34*, 17–52.

Jameson, F. (2000). Globalisation and political strategy. *New Left Review, 4*, 49–68.

Jameson, F. & Stephenson, A. (1988). Regarding postmodernism – A conversation with Fredric Jameson. In A. Ross (ed.), *Universal abandon? The politics of postmodernism* (pp. 3–30). Minneapolis, MN: University of Minnesota Press.

Johnston, B. (2001). The power of the mundane. In J. Small & J. Onyx (eds), *Memory-work: A critique* (pp. 31–41). Sydney: UTS Working papers.

Karakayali, S. & Tsianos, V. (2005). Mapping the order of new migration. Undokumentierte Arbeit und die Autonomie der Migration. *Peripherie, 25*(97/98), 35–64.

Keane, H. (2001). Taxonomies of desire: Sex addiction and the ethics of intimacy. *International Journal of Critical Psychology*, *3*, 324–346.

Kippax, S. (2003). Sexual health interventions are unsuitable for experimental evaluation. In J. Stephenson, J. Imrie & C. Bonnell (eds), *Effective sexual health interventions: Issues in experimental evaluation* (pp. 17–34). Oxford: Oxford University Press.

Kippax, S. & Race, K. (2003). Sustaining safe practice: Twenty years on. *Social Science & Medicine*, *57*, 1–12.

Kleinman, A. (1988). *The illness narratives*. New York: Basic Books.

Kristeva, J. (1986). Women's time. In T. Moi (ed.), *The Kristeva reader* (pp. 187–213). Oxford: Basil Blackwell.

Larsen, L. T. (2003, September). *Biopolitical technologies of community in Danish health promotion*. Paper presented at the Vital politics: Health, medicine and bioeconomics into the twenty-first century conference in London, UK.

Lash, S. & Featherstone, M. (2001). Recognition and difference: Politics, identity, multiculture. *Theory, Culture & Society*, *18*(2–3), 1–20.

Lather, P. & Smithies, C. (1997). *Troubling the angels: Women living with HIV/ AIDS*. Boulder: Westview/HarperCollins.

Lazzarato, M. (2004a). From capital-labour to capital-life. *Emphemra: Theory & Politics of Organization*, *4*(3), 187–208.

Lazzarato, M. (2004b, May). *From biopower to biopolitics*. Seminar presented at the Centre for the Study of Invention of Social Processes, Goldsmiths College, London, UK.

Lefebvre, H. (1991). *Critique of everyday life. Vol. 1: Introduction*. London: Verso.

Lévi-Strauss, C. (1972). *The savage mind*. London: Weidenfield & Nicolson.

Luhmann, N. (1995). *Social systems*. Stanford, CA: Stanford University Press.

Macleod, C. (forthcoming). Radical plural feminisms and emancipatory practice in post-apartheid South Africa. *Theory & Psychology*.

Marvakis, A. & Papadopoulos, D. (2002). From universalism to cultural reductionism: Problematic conceptualizations of ontogenetic development in cultural psychology. In M. Hildebrand-Nilshon, C. W. Kim & D. Papadopoulos (eds), *Kultur (in) der Psychologie. Über das Abenteuer des Kulturbegriffes in der psychologischen Theoriebildung* (pp. 139–160). Heidelberg: Asanger.

Marx, K. (1970). *A contribution to the critique of political economy*. New York: International Publishers.

Massat, C. & Lundy, M. (1997). Empowering research participants. *Affilia*, *12*(1), 33–56.

Massumi, B. (2005). (ed.). *The politics of everyday fear*. Minneapolis, MN: University of Minnesota Press.

McDonald, K. (2004). Oneself as another: From social movement to experience movement. *Current Sociology*, *52*(4), 575–593.

McNay, L. (1994). *Foucault: A critical introduction*. Cambridge: Polity Press.

Mezzadra, S. (2001). *Diritto di fuga: Migrazioni, cittadinanza, globalizzazione*. Verona: Ombre Corte.

Michaels, E. (1990). *Unbecoming: An AIDS diary*. Rose Bay, NSW: Empress Publishing.

Middleton, D. & Brown, S. (2005). *The social psychology of experience: Studies in remembering and forgetting*. London: Sage.

Miller, P. & Rose, N. (1995). Production, identity and democracy. *Theory & Society*, *24*, 427–467.

Mos, L. (2005, June).*The human historical world: contributions to a renewal of psychology*. Paper presented at the International Society for Theoretical Psychology Conference, Cape Town, South Africa

Mos, L. (1996). On re-working theory in psychology. In C. W. Tolman, F. Cherry, R. V. Hezewijk & I. Lubek (eds), *Problems of theoretical psychology* (pp. 37–46). Toronto: Captus University Publications.

Murphie, A. (2005). Differential life, perception and the nervous elements: Whitehead, Bergson and Virno on the technics of living. *Culture Machine, 7*. Retrieved October 12, 2005, from http://culturemachine.tees.ac.uk/articles/murphie.htm

Murray, S. (2005). The rhetorics of life and multitude in Michael Foucault and Paulo Virno. In A. Kroker & M. Kroker (eds), *1000 Days of Theory*. Retrieved October 9, 2005, from http://ctheory.net/articles.aspx?id=479

National Centre in HIV Epidemiology and Clinical Research. (2004). *HIV/AIDS, viral hepatitis and sexually transmissible infections in Australia Annual Surveillance Report 2004*. Sydney, NSW/Canberra, ACT: University of New South Wales, National Centre in HIV Epidemiology and Clinical Research/ Australian Institute of Health and Welfare.

Nelson, E. & Herzog, W. (2005). *Grizzly Man*. [Motion picture]. USA: Lions Gate Films.

Newman, F. & Holzman, L. (2000). Against against-ism: Comment on Parker. *Theory & Psychology, 10*(2), 265–270.

Ong, A. (1999). *Flexible citizenship: The cultural logics of transnationality*. Durham, NC: Duke University Press.

Orgel, M. (2001, October). *Loitering with intent: Anarchists, anthropologists and other shady characters in a Spanish village*. Presentation at the Center for Cultural Studies Colloquium, University of California, Santa Cruz.

Osterkamp, U. (1999). On psychology, ideology and individuals' societal nature. *Theory & Psychology, 9*(3), 379–392.

Papadopoulos, D. (1999). *Lew S. Wygotski: Werk und Wirkung*. Frankfurt: Campus Verlag.

Papadopoulos, D. (2003). The ordinary superstition of subjectivity. Liberalism, development and technostructural violence. *Theory & Psychology, 13*, 73–93.

Papadopoulos, D. (2005). For a new materialist understanding of social science: Decomposing the fact-value debate. In A. Gulerce, A. Hofmeister, I. Staueble, G. Saunders & J. Kay (eds), *Contemporary theorizing in psychology: Global perspectives* (pp. 39–47). York: Captus Press Inc.

Papadopoulos, D. & Tsianos, V. (2006). How to do sovereignty without people? The subjectless condition of postliberal power. *Boundary 2, 34(1)*.

Parker, I. (1997). *Psychoanalytic culture: Psychoanalytic discourse in western society*. London: Sage.

Parker, I. (1999). Introduction: Marxism, ideology and psychology. *Theory & Psychology, 9*(3), 291–293.

Parker, I. (2000). Critical distance: Reply to Newman and Holzman. *Theory & Psychology, 10*(2), 271–276.

Parker, I., Papadopoulos, D. & Schraube, E. (2004). 'This world demands our attention.' Ian Parker in conversation with Dimitris Papadopoulos and Ernst Schraube. *Forum Qualitative Sozialforschung/Forum Qualitative Social Research, 5*(3).

Partridge, C. J. (1995). *Tristana: Buñuel's film and Galdós' novel: A case study in the relation between literature and film*. Lewiston, NY: Edwin Mellen Press.

Patton, C. (2000). Helping ourselves: Research after (the) enlightenment. *Health: An Interdisciplinary Journal for the Social Study of Health, Illness and Medicine, 4,* 267–287.

Patton, P. (2000). *Deluze and the political.* London: Routledge.

Pennycook, A. (2001). *Critical applied linguistics: A critical introduction.* Mahwah, NJ: L. Erlbaum.

Phillips, A. (1999). *Darwin's worms.* London: Faber.

Pickering, M. (1997). *History, experience and cultural studies.* London: Macmillan.

Pratt, M. L. (1992). *Imperial eyes: Travel writing and transculturation.* London: Routledge.

Prilleltensky, I. & Nelson, G. (2002). *Doing psychology critically: Making a difference in diverse settings.* London: Palgrave.

Prior, L. (1997). Following in Foucault's footsteps: Text and context in qualitative research. In D. Silverman (ed.), *Qualitative research: Theory, method and practice* (pp. 63–79). London: Sage.

Probyn, E. (1993). *Sexing the self: Gendered positions in cultural studies.* London: Routledge.

Rabinow, P. & Rose, N. (2003). Foucault today. In P. Rabinow & N. Rose (eds), *The essential Foucault: Selections from the essential works of Foucault, 1954–1984* (pp. vii–xxxv). New York: New Press.

Race, K. (2001). The undetectable crisis: Changing technologies of risk. *Sexualities, 4*(2), 167–189.

Race, K. (forthcoming). *Pleasure consuming medicine.* Durham, NC: Duke University Press.

Race, K., McInnes, D., Wakeford, E., Kleinert, V., McMurchie, M. & Kidd, M. (2001). *Adherence and communication: Reports from a study of HIV general practice* (Monograph 8). Sydney: University of New South Wales, National Centre in HIV Social Research.

Rancière, J. (1998). *Disagreement: Politics and philosophy* (J. Rose, Trans.). Minneapolis, MN: University of Minnesota Press.

Rancière, J. (2000). Dissenting words: A conversation with Jacques Rancière. *diacritics, 30,* 113–126.

Rancière, J. (2001). Ten theses on politics. *Theory & Event, 5*(3). Retrieved October 12, 2005, from http://muse.jhu.edu/journals/theory and event/

Riessman, C. (1993). *Narrative analysis.* London: Sage.

Rogoff, B. (2003). *The cultural nature of human development.* New York: Oxford University Press.

Rosaldo, R. (1993). *Culture & truth: The remaking of social analysis.* Boston: Beacon Press.

Rose, G. (1995). *Love's work.* London: Vintage.

Rose, G. (1996). *Mourning becomes the law.* Cambridge: Cambridge University Press.

Rose, N. (1985). *The psychological complex: Psychology, politics, and society in England, 1869–1939.* London: Routledge/Kegan Paul.

Rose, N. (1989). Individualizing psychology. In J. Shotter & K. Gergen (eds), *Texts of identity.* London: Sage.

Rose, N. (1992). The good society and the inner world: Psychoanalysis, politics and culture. *Sociology, 26*(3), 541–543.

Rose, N. (1996a). Identity, genealogy, history. In S. Hall & P. du Gay (eds), *Questions of cultural identity* (pp. 128–150). London: Routledge.

Rose, N. (1996b). *Inventing our selves: Psychology, power and personhood.* Cambridge: Cambridge University Press.

Rose, N. (2002, November). *From the psychological self to the somatic individual.* Paper presented at the University of Western Sydney Critical Psychology conference in Sydney, Australia.

Rosengarten, M. (forthcoming). *HIV: A traffic in information as flesh.* Washington: Washington University Press.

Rosengarten, M. (2004). Consumer activism in the pharmacology of HIV. *Body & Society, 10*(1), 91–107.

Rosengarten, M., Imrie, J., Flowers, P., Davis, M. & Hart, G. J. (2004). After the euphoria: HIV medical technologies from the perspective of London based clinicians. *Sociology of Health & Illness, 26*(5), 575–596.

Rosengarten, M., Race, K. & Kippax, S. (2000). 'Touch wood, everything will be okay': Gay men's understandings of clinical markers in sexual practice (Monograph 7). Sydney: University of New South Wales, National Centre in HIV Social Research.

Rubin, G. (1984). Thinking sex: Notes for a radical theory of the politics of sexuality. In C. Vance (ed.), *Pleasure and danger* (pp. 267–319). London: Routledge/ Kegan Paul.

Sandywell, B. (2004). The myth of everyday life: Toward a heterology of the ordinary. *Cultural Studies, 18*(2/3), 160–180.

Santos, B. (2001). Neustra America: Reinventing a subaltern paradigm of recognition and redistribution. *Theory, Culture & Society, 18*(2–3), 185–218.

Sassen, S. (1999). A new emergent hegemonic structure? *Political Power & Social Theory, 13*, 277–289.

Schor, N. (1995). *Bad objects: Essays popular and unpopular.* Durham, NC/ London: Duke University Press.

Schraube, E. (1998). *Auf den Spuren der Dinge: Psychologie in einer Welt der Technik.* Berlin: Argument Verlag.

Schraube, E. (2005). 'Torturing things until they confess'. Günther Anders's critique of technology. *Science as Culture, 14*(1), 77–85.

Scott, J. (1993). The evidence of experience. In H. Abelove, M. A. Barale & D. Halperin (eds), *The lesbian and gay studies reader* (pp. 397–415). New York/ London: Routledge. (Original work published 1991)

Sebald, W. G. (1997). *The emigrants.* (A. Bell, Trans.). London: Harvill Press. (Original work published 1993)

Sedgwick, E. (1992). Epidemics of the will. In J. Crary & S. Kwinter (eds), *Incorporations.* New York: Zone Books.

Seigworth, G. & Gardiner, M. (2004). Rethinking everyday life: And then nothing turns itself inside out. *Cultural Studies, 18*(2/3), 139–159.

Sennett, R. (1976). *The fall of public man.* Cambridge: Cambridge University Press.

Sennett, R. (1998). *The corrosion of character: The personal consequences of work in the new capitalism.* New York: W. W. Norton & Co.

Shotter, J. (1984). *Social accountability and selfhood.* Oxford: Basil Blackwell.

Shweder, R. A. (1991). *Thinking through cultures: Expeditions in cultural psychology.* Cambridge, MA: Harvard University Press.

Simmel, G. (1910–11). How is society possible? [Electronic version]. *American Journal of Sociology, 16*.

Simmel, G. (1950). The stranger. In *The sociology of Georg Simmel* (K. Wolff, Trans.), pp. 402–408. New York: Free Press.

Slack, J. D. (1996). The theory and method of articulation in cultural studies. In D. Morley & K.-H. Chen (eds), *Stuart Hall: Critical dialogues in cultural studies* (pp. 112–127). London: Routledge.

Smith, G. (2004). *Bugger me! Civilisation, perversion & power.* Unpublished PhD thesis, University of New South Wales, Australia.

Spivak, G. C. (1990). *The post-colonial critic: Interviews, strategies, dialogues.* New York: Routledge.

Spivak, G. C. (1999). *A critique of postcolonial reason: Toward a history of the vanishing present.* Cambridge, MA: Harvard University Press.

Spivak, G. C. & Rooney, E. (1994). In a word: Interview. In N. Schor & E. Weed (eds), *The essential difference* (pp. 151–184). Bloomington/Indianapolis: Indiana University Press.

Stephenson, N. & Kippax, S. (1999). Minding the gap: Subjectivity in research. In W. Maiers, B. Bayer, B. Duarte Esgalhado, R. Jorna & E. Schraube (eds), *Challenges to Theoretical psychology* (pp. 183–191). York: Captus Press Inc.

Stephenson, N., Kippax, S. & Crawford, J. (1996). You and I and she: Memorywork, moral conflict and the construction of self. In S. Wilkinson (ed.), *Feminist social psychologies* (pp. 182–200). Buckingham: Open University Press.

Stenner, P. (1998). Heidegger and the subject. Questioning concerning technology. *Theory & Psychology, 8*(1), 58–77.

StoryCorps. (2005). Retrieved May 4, 2005, from http://storycorps.net/about/

Taylor, C. (1971). Interpretation and the sciences of man. *The Review of Metaphysics, 25*(1), 3–51.

Taylor, C. (1989). *Sources of the self: The making of modern identity.* Cambridge, MA: Harvard University Press.

Thatcher, M. (1987, October). Douglas Keay's interview with Margaret Thatcher. *Woman's Own.*

Theunissen, M. (1991). *Negative Theologie der Zeit.* Frankfurt: Suhrkamp.

Thompson, E. P. (1968). *The making of the English working class.* Harmondsworth: Penguin.

Tolman, C. (1994). *Psychology, society & subjectivity: An introduction to German critical psychology.* London: Routledge.

Toulmin, S. (1985). *The inner life: The outer mind.* Worcester, MA: Clark University Press.

Tsing, A. (2000). The global situation. *Cultural Anthropology, 15*(3), 327–360.

Tsuchiya, A. (1990). *Images of the sign: Semiotic consciousness in the novels of Benito Pérez Galdós.* Columbia: University of Missouri Press.

UNAIDS. (2004). *AIDS epidemic update: 2004.* Geneva: UNAIDS.

Van de Ven, P., Murphy, D., Hull, P., Prestage, G., Batrouney, C. & Kippax, S. (2004). Risk management and harm reduction among gay men in Sydney. *Critical Public Health, 14,* 361–376.

Van de Ven, P., Rawstorne, P., Crawford, J. & Kippax, S. (2002). Increasing proportions of Australian gay and homosexually active men engage in unprotected anal intercourse with regular and casual partners, *AIDS Care, 14*(3), 335–341.

Van de Ven, P., Rawstorne, P., Treloar, C. & Richters, J. (eds). (2003) *HIV/AIDS, hepatitis C & related diseases in Australia: Annual report of behaviour.* Sydney: National Centre in HIV Social Research.

Vattimo, G. (1997). *Beyond interpretation: The meaning of hermeneutics for philosophy*. Stanford, CA: Stanford University Press.

Virno, P. (1996). Do you remember counterrevolution? In P. Virno & M. Hardt (eds), *Radical thought in Italy: A potential politics* (pp. 240–258). Minneapolis, MN: Minnesota University Press.

Virno, P. (1996). The ambivalence of disenchantment. In P. Virno & M. Hardt (eds), *Radical thought in Italy: A potential politics* (pp. 13–36). Minneapolis, MN: Minnesota University Press.

Virno, P. (2004). *The grammar of the multitude: For an analysis of contemporary forms of life*. Columbia, NY: Semiotext(e).

Vygotsky, L. S. (1934). Thinking and speech. In R. W. Rieber & A. C. Carton (eds), *The collected works of L. S. Vygotsky. Vol. 1: Problems of general psychology* (pp. 39–285). New York: Plenum.

Vygotsky, L. S. (1989). Concrete human psychology. *Soviet Psychology, 27*, 53–77.

Waldby, C. (1995). Feminism and method. In B. Cain & R. Pringle (eds), *Transitions: New Australian feminisms* (pp. 15–28). Sydney: Allen & Unwin.

Walkerdine, V. (1990). *Schoolgirl fictions*. London/New York: Verso.

Wallerstein, I. (1998). *Utopistics: Or historical choices of the twenty-first century*. New York: The New Press.

Warner, M. (2002). *Publics and counterpublics*. New York: Zone Books.

Watney, S. (1994). *Practices of freedom: Selected writings on HIV/AIDS*. London: Rivers Oram Press.

Weeks, J. (1995). *Invented moralities: Sexual values in the age of uncertainty*. Cambridge: Polity Press.

Weeks, J. (1998). The sexual citizen. *Theory, Culture & Society, 15*(3–4), 35–52.

Wetherell, M. & Edley, N. (1999). Negotiating hegemonic masculinity. *Feminism and Psychology, 9*, 335–356.

Wetherell, M. & Potter, P. (1992). *Mapping the language of racism: Discourse and the legitimation of exploitation*. New York: Columbia University Press.

Wilkinson, S. & Kitzinger, C. (1996). *Feminism and discourse*. London: Sage.

Williams, R. (1965). *The long revolution*. Harmondsworth: Penguin.

Williams, R. (1980). *Problems in materialisation and culture*, London: Verso.

Willig, C. (2000). A discourse-dynamic approach to the study of subjectivity in health psychology. *Theory & Psychology, 10*(4), 547–570.

Woolf, V. (1977). *To the lighthouse*. St Albans: Triad/Panther. (Original work published 1927)

Woolf, V. (1993). *A room of one's own*. London: Bloomsbury. (Original work published 1929)

Worth, H. (2004, May). *Am I my brother's keeper? Unsafe sex, individualism and responsibility*. Paper presented at the HIV/AIDS, Hepatitis C and Related Diseases (HHARD) Social Research conference, Sydney, Australia.

Index